CASE STUDIES IN
SUSTAINABILITY
MANAGEMENT

The oikos collection

VOLUME 3

Edited by Jordi Vives Gabriel

Routledge
Taylor & Francis Group

LONDON AND NEW YORK

First published 2014 by Greenleaf Publishing Limited

Published 2017 by Routledge
2 Park Square, Milton Park, Abingdon, Oxon OX14 4RN
711 Third Avenue, New York, NY 10017, USA

Routledge is an imprint of the Taylor & Francis Group, an informa business

Copyright © 2014 Taylor & Francis

Cover by LaliAbril.com

British Library Cataloguing in Publication Data:
  A catalogue record for this book is available from the British Library.

  ISBN-13: 978-1-78353-068-7 (hbk)
  ISBN-13: 978-1-78353-048-9 (pbk)

Contents

Acknowledgements

This book reaps the results from several years of successful entries to the oikos Case Writing Competition and an outstanding commitment of our jury members: Daniel Arenas, Frank-Martin Belz, Oana Branzei, Magali Delmas, Thomas Dyllick, Andrew J. Hoffman, P.D. Jose, Stephen Kobrin, Bala Krishnamoorthy, Michael Lenox, Renato Orsato, Esben R. Pedersen, Stefano Pogutz, Forest Reinhardt, Carlos Romero Uscanga, Michael V. Russo, Stefan Schaltegger, Christian Seelos, Paul Shrivastava, Claude Siegenthaler, Terence Tsai, Michael Yaziji, Friedrich M. Zimmermann. Thank you for providing the case authors with valuable guidance and insight as well as for raising the bar for quality year after year.

Thanks as well to John Stuart from Greenleaf for the opportunity to edit this book as well as his guidance and assistance through the entire process.

A big thank you also goes to the donors of the oikos Foundation: ABB, Accenture, AVINA Stiftung, Baer-Ammann, Helvetia, Kathrin Schweizer Stiftung, Knecht & Müller, State Secretariat for Education, Research and Innovation, Stiftung Mercator Schweiz, Swiss National Science Foundation, Swiss Post, UBS, United Nations Development Programme, University of St. Gallen, WWF and Zeix. Neither the oikos Cases Program nor any other oikos initiative would be possible without them.

Moreover, I am indebted to the restless and always energetic oikos management team (Lenka Parkanova, Adriana Troxler and Alex Barkawi) as well as Jost Hamschmidt and Liudmila Nazarkina, former teammates, for their ongoing support to the oikos Case Programme I lead. My work at the programme would also not be possible if I could not count on the support of colleagues from other institutions like Antoinette Mills (The Case Center), Jennifer Johnson (Aspen Institute/ caseplace.org), Sandra Vera (SEKN) and Beeta Ansari (Ashoka). Finally, I am grateful to the oikos Foundation for granting me the oikos PhD fellowship; without it I could not enjoy the highly intellectually stimulating, challenging and exciting experience of pursuing my PhD at the University of St. Gallen.

Contributors

Mr Brandon Arends
Portland State University, United States

Ms Andrea Erin Bass
University of Nebraska at Omaha,
United States

Mr Phil Berko
Portland State University, United States

Prof. Dr Darrell Brown
Portland State University, United States

Mr Robert J. Crawford
France

Mr Patrick Dedrick
Portland State University, United States

Ms Ximena García-Rada
Duke University, United States

Ms Brie Hilliard
Portland State University, United States

Prof. Dr John C. Ickis
INCAE Business School, Costa Rica

Mr Mark Langston
Portland State University, United States

Mr Shubo Philip Liu
China Europe International Business
School, China

Dr Rebecca J. Morris
University of Nebraska at Omaha,
United States

Prof. Dr Andrea M. Prado
INCAE Business School, Costa Rica

Mr Joshua Pfleeger
Portland State University,
United States

Mr Gregory Price
Portland State University, United States

Prof. Dr Madeleine Pullman
Portland State University, United States

Prof. Dr Debapratim Purkayastha
IBS Hyderabad, India

Dr Abhijit Roy
University of Scranton, United States

Dr Mousumi Roy
Independent Scholar, United States

Prof. Dr Murray Silverman
San Francisco State University,
United States

Prof. Dr Craig Smith
INSEAD, France

Mr Adapa Srinivasa Rao
IBS Hyderabad, India

Mr Greg Stokes
Portland State University, United States

Prof. Dr Ram Subramanian
Montclair State University,
United States

Prof. Dr Terence Tsai
China Europe International Business
School, China

Foreword
Case studies and experiential learning

Prof. Dr Thomas Dyllick

If business schools want to contribute effectively to the changes needed in addressing the global sustainability challenges they have to think very hard what it means to educate responsible managers and leaders for the transformation of business and the economy. We will need to prepare them for dealing with highly complex and normative issues, where critical, integrative and innovative thinking are demanded. On the methodological side, we will have to provide transformative learning experiences, based on a much higher degree of personal involvement in the learning process (Muff 2013; Muff et al. 2012; Sterling 2010).

The needed changes have to be seen in the context of the more fundamental criticisms concerning the effectiveness and relevance of management education in general, and MBA programs in particular. Serious doubts have been raised by many scholars about the business schools' ability to provide students with the skills needed to function at an executive level in modern organizations and to prepare them for the professional demands and challenges of globalized business in a pluralistic world. The reasons given for this include:

1. A focus on narrow functional knowledge instead of a broad issue centred approach embracing business and society as embedded in a plurality of contexts, in particular in culture, society, nature and history: there is little training in integrative thinking (Martin 2007).

2. A focus on disciplinary knowledge acquisition instead of development of an interdisciplinary and integrated perspective: business education remains fundamentally disciplinary based and rests in silos (Khurana 2007).

3. A missing focus on critical thinking, the capability to ask critical questions instead of giving answers to predefined questions, and on using multiple perspectives to understand difficult situations: as a consequence business graduates often are surprisingly naïve about organizations and their management (Datar et al. 2010).

4. A strong focus on analytical skills instead of soft skills, in particular social skills and personal skills: students learn analysis and thinking, but not action and reflection. They become knowledgeable about business, but remain uneducated in the art and craft of management (Mintzberg 2004).

5. A very selective focus on efficiency instead of the challenges of being really effective: business schools have shown to be very weak, in particular, with regards to supporting innovation and creativity.

6. A very narrow and dogmatic view of the world dominates management education: idealized markets have become the analytical framework to discuss all business issues, but also business and society issues. Firms are seen as groups of self-interested actors which are conceived primarily as vehicles for maximizing return to shareholders. How then will students learn about the plurality of values and logics in the worlds of science, public policy, the arts and other spheres of society (Colby et al. 2011)?

7. A missing and distorted focus on the importance of values and ethics in management: This reflects in a dominance of amoral theories taught to students, depicting managers as 'agents' of shareholders, dedicating their careers to the sole purpose of creating private wealth, for themselves and for shareholders as their 'principals', in effect stripping managers of any professional identity, self-respect, and personal responsibility (Goshal 2005; Khurana 2007).

8. A lack of attention for self-knowledge and the reflective exploration of meaning: rarely reflective spaces are offered and purposely used to develop a dialogue with oneself about how one intends to act as manager and leader and who one wishes to become. It is not sufficient to address values and ethics in a course, if the challenges are not connected with the students' own efforts to explore the meaning for them (Colby et al. 2011).

9. A lack of attention to learning to learn: in particular, self-directed and self-determined learning have continuously decreased. Instead of identifying personal development areas and pursuing specific development activities, students learn to become dependent on learning providers, who

identify what skills are most relevant for them and present them in an entertaining way.

10. A lack of attention to learning as opposed to teaching: how does faculty assure learning has happened? They are typically subject experts with little to no pedagogical training for assuring and measuring learning impact.

Case studies certainly were a major step forward away from the traditional lecture, solving some of the problems associated with lectures. But they have clear limitations also. Depending on the topic and context chosen by the author, they allow for an issue centred and integrative perspective, with different influences and perspectives taken into consideration. If the focus is not on case study analysis but on case study discussion and debate, they may lend themselves also to developing some soft skills, like public speaking, debating and communicating. Still, they will remain primarily a tool for analytical exercise. Case studies may encourage strategic scenario-thinking, but they may also create the illusion that students can effectively handle the situation they have encountered in their case studies. And case studies fall way short of serving as effective tools for personal involvement, personal reflection, personal growth and personal development. Developing personalities, not experts, however, may well be the crucial challenge for developing managers and leaders prepared to successfully address the global sustainability challenges.

Ever since the Carnegie and Ford foundation reports, business curricula have emphasized knowing at the expense of doing and being, with the latter focusing on values, attitudes and beliefs. As a result, Datar et al. (2010) have found not only a persistent knowing–doing gap among business graduates, but also a doing–being gap. For the most part students have to acquire knowledge, while there is little room and possibility for them to practice what they have learned. To be able to do effectively what they are supposed to do as managers and leaders, students must have learned the required practical skills and they must have practiced these skills. Mostly students are asked to practice distant substitutes for what faculty really wants them to know and be able to do. These substitutes are more likely to be selected based on academic tradition, limited understandings on the part of faculty of what the needs of practice really are and how they can be taught effectively, as well as ease of delivery (Colby et al. 2011).

Professional judgment must be guided by knowledge and technical skills. But it needs also be based on ethical sensitivity with regards to the public expectations and values related to the issues and decisions. Ethical sensitivity in action has to go well beyond creating ethical awareness of issues, it needs the chance to practice ('rehearse') for values-driven action in the context of practical management decisions (Gentile 2010). Only when students learn to move between the distanced, external stance of analytical thinking – the third person view – and the first and second person points of view, from which they have to act when solving real problems, will they have the chance to develop personal character and integrity. Such experience, however, is still extremely rare in management education (Colby et al. 2011; Shrivastava 2010).

To overcome the lack of integration between theory and practice, some business schools have complemented their learning approaches with forms of applied learning, placing learning directly into the field. And in order to better balance the different demands of knowing, doing, and being, business schools need to develop and use to a much larger extent pedagogies of engagement, which require students to enact their understanding and skills in extended, supervised practice (Colby et al. 2011). While case studies offer a higher degree of student engagement in learning than lectures do, this will not be enough to address the challenges at hand. We will have to move on to much higher levels of student engagement in learning, by using and developing new forms of experiential learning, thereby integrating the demands of knowing, doing and being. Case studies may still be used in such a context, but they probably have to look quite differently. They may have to describe and support a very different learning context for an engaged student learning, where faculty no longer serves as the knowledge expert, but much rather as facilitator of engaged learning processes driven primarily by the students themselves. We should be watching closely the development of higher-order learning tools and settings and the role case studies can and will have to play in them.

(The ideas developed here are based on the broader analysis in Dyllick (2014).)

Prof Dr Thomas Dyllick.
Chair of the Corporate Sustainability Track of the oikos
Case Writing Competition.
Member of the Board of Trustees, oikos.
Professor for Sustainability Management at the
University of St. Gallen, Switzerland.

Bibliography

Colby, A., Ehrlich, T., Sullivan, W.M., and Dolle, J.R. (2011), *Rethinking Undergraduate Business Education: Liberal Learning for the Profession.* San Francisco, Jossey-Bass.

Datar, S.M., Garvin, D.A., and Cullen, P.G. (2010), *Rethinking the MBA. Business Education at the Crossroads.* Boston, Harvard Business Press.

Dyllick, T. (2014), Responsible management education for a sustainable world: the challenge for business schools. *Journal of Management Development* (in press).

Gentile, M.C. (2010), *Giving Voice to Values.* New Haven, Yale University Press.

Ghoshal, S. (2005), Bad management theories are destroying good management practices. *Academy of Management Learning and Education,* 4(1), 75–91.

Khurana, R. (2007), *From Higher Aims to Hired Hands.* Princeton University Press, Princeton.

Martin, R. L. (2007), *The Opposable Mind: How Successful Leaders Win through Integrative Thinking.* Boston, Harvard Business School Press.

Mintzberg, H. (2004), *Managers not MBAs: A Hard Look at the Soft Practice of Managing and Management Development.* San Francisco, Berrett Koehler.

Muff, K. (2013), Developing globally responsible leaders in business schools. *Journal of Management Development*, 32(5), 487–507.

Muff, K., Dyllick, T., Drewall, M., North, J., Shrivastava, P., and Haertle, J. (2013), *Management Education for the World: A Vision for Business Schools Serving People and Planet.* Cheltenham, UK, Edward Elgar.

Shrivastava, P. (2010), Pedagogy of passion for sustainability. *Academy of Management Learning and Education*, 9(3), 443–455.

Sterling, S. (2010), Transformative learning and sustainability: sketching the conceptual ground. *Journal of Learning and Teaching in Higher Education*, 5, 17–33.

Introduction

Jordi Vives Gabriel

In 2013, the oikos Case Writing Competition celebrated its 10th edition. And indeed we celebrated. The programme has been one of the most successful initiatives incubated at oikos. Its reputation, the strong support it receives from business professors, and the fact that every year dozens of scholars from around the world submit their cases to the competition, are cases in point for this.

When the case competition was launched back in 2003 the context for management education for sustainability was certainly different than the one in which we live today. Teaching cases have always been one of the most preferred tools in business school classrooms. However, in 2003, the use of cases for discussing sustainability topics concerning business was still at an early stage. If one aimed at advancing the agenda for sustainability in business education, professors and lecturers had to be provided with high quality teaching materials. Dr Jost Hamschmidt, at that time managing director of the oikos Foundation, had the visionary idea to organize a competition to stimulate the production of excellent sustainability cases that could be used for teaching at business schools worldwide. The first call for cases had an overwhelming initial success. Twenty cases from leading American and European Schools including Babson College, Ivey School of Business, IMD Lausanne, McGill University, UNC Kenan-Flagler Business School, Stanford University and the University of St. Gallen were submitted. Kai Hockerts (today at Copenhagen Business School) won the first edition with his case 'Mobility Car Sharing – From Ecopreneurial Start up to Commercial Venture'.

Under the lead of Jost Hamschmidt and Liudmila Nazarkina the competition expanded its reach and gained the support of key partners in the field of both sustainability and management education; e.g. Ashoka, Greenleaf Publishing, WWF, the Case Center, as well as the Aspen Institute with its Caseplace.org internet portal. The competition also counted on the commitment from a terrific pool of reviewers who systematically evaluated submissions year after year and provided feedback to participants. Their support was critical in attaching a seal of quality to the winning cases.

Submissions to the competition grew significantly in numbers when a 'Social Entrepreneurship' track was added in 2009; followed, in 2013, by a new third track on 'Sustainable Finance'. The aim of the launch of the second and third track was the same as in 2003: to stimulate the creation of cases in sustainability related areas that so far lacked visibility in most management business courses. Education programs in management, entrepreneurship and finance equip students not only with tools and insights in theories and practice but also shape their perspectives and opinions on these fields. Making sustainability an integral pillar in this context is an essential step to catalyse global change towards a more sustainable economy. This book aims to help educators in pursuing this objective.

The works featured in this volume were selected from the winning cases in the Corporate Sustainability track of the oikos Case Writing Competition between 2010 and 2013. They are clustered in three different sections according to their focus topic and under the following titles: 'large corporations and corporate sustainabil-ity dilemmas', 'Managing stakeholder relations' and 'Sustainability as a source of differentiation strategies'. The teaching notes for these cases are available from the Greenleaf website, free of charge for teaching staff only. They can be requested at https://www.routledge.com/Case-Studies-in-Sustainability-Management-The-oikos-collection-Vol-3/Vives-Gabriel/p/book/9781783530489.

The adoption of a sustainability strategy is neither an easy nor a risk free move for any kind of corporation. It is argued that large enterprises can combine the financial capital, the human resources and the leverage on their supply chain to effectively implement and expand the reach of their social and environmental responsibilities. In contrast, big enterprises usually face the pressure of NGOs, gov-ernments and civil society; they operate in intricate webs of supply chain relations, most of them do so at a multinational level, and have to bear with complex internal organizational structures that not always enable agile decision-making processes. The selected cases in Part I are intended to help students to realize the level of com-plexity and difficulty in moving forward any type of sustainability initiative within large (multinational) organizations.

Part I starts with the Novo Nordisk case. Novo Nordisk, one of the leading glo-bal healthcare companies, produces diabetes medications and care equipment. It is widely recognized as a pioneer and champion of sustainability practices in both social and environmental dimensions. Novo Nordisk sells some of its insulin products at a subsidized price in some of the poorest countries in the world. How-ever, as the crisis hit Greece in 2010, it temporarily stopped the sale of its drugs in Greece when the government asked for a 25 percent reduction in the prices of all the medicines sold. Patients, the Greek government and NGOs accused Novo Nordisk of putting profits before its responsibility toward society. Students will face the challenge of striking the right balance between business and global health. The case will help them to understand the difficulties faced by even the best-in-class corporations when attempting to integrate sustainable development practices of a firm with its business strategy.

Walmart has often been the focus of intense criticism for its alleged lack of or poor sustainability standards. In contrast, the featured case shows the development and launch of Walmart's Love, Earth® – a sustainable jewelry product line with annual revenues of a billion dollars. Perhaps uniquely among corporate sustainability cases to date, it offers instructors a rich opportunity to explore a strategic sustainability move by a large multinational corporation from the perspective of both the firm and the NGO activists.

Large corporations also adopt sustainability strategies in a comprehensive way to move the entire company up to higher standards of social and environmental performance. The cases of PepsiCo and Florida Ice & Farm illustrate how the top management of these organizations deals with the complexity of moving forward a broad sustainability agenda within a corporation. The PepsiCo case puts students in the shoes of the company's CEO Indra Nooyi. Nooyi came under fire from key stakeholders such as shareholders and bottlers who contended that her focus on 'Performance with Purpose' had come at the cost of positioning of the company's products and had hurt sales. Ultimately, the case reflects on the challenge of aligning sound social and environmental goals with a profitable corporate strategy.

Florida Ice & Farm Co. (FIFCO) is Costa Rica's leading beverage company. The case involves the efforts of FIFCO to adopt a 'triple bottom line' for measuring its performance, not only in financial returns to its shareholders, but also from a social and environmental responsibility towards society. It describes the five-step process designed by the company under the leadership of its CEO to implement the 'triple-bottom-line' strategy. Additionally, the case focuses on three out of the twelve objectives set by the company management: becoming 'water neutral' in 2014; changing the culture of alcohol consumption in Costa Rica; and the 'choose to help' volunteer program implemented at the organization.

Finally, Part I concludes with the case of Holland America Line (HAL), a sustainability leader in the cruise line industry. This case contrasts with the previous ones featured for its concrete focus on a single decision rather than coping with the broad picture of the entire organization. Students will have to determine whether HAL should reconsider the idea of installing wind turbines on the decks of their ships in order to achieve a small reduction in fuel use through the generation of electricity. The case describes the workings of the committee in charge of the decision and asks the student to evaluate and consider the challenges and alternatives of taking such a specific decision intimately link to HAL's sustainability strategy.

Considering and responding to the demands of companies' stakeholders is essential for corporations to retain their so-called 'social license to operate'. Part II puts emphasis on how companies approach this issue, and how neglect of stakeholders can lead to dramatic consequences for businesses. Stakeholders can take different forms and exercise different degrees of power and pressure upon corporations. NGOs, local communities, governments or media are just a small representation of the variety of actors corporations have to engage with. They may also be a valuable source to better understand the landscape in which companies operate. And they play a central role in the cases highlighted in Part II.

The Hunghom Peninsula was a residential building complex initially intended to provide housing for middle-class residents at a discounted price. The complex was later sold to private property developers who planned to demolish and redevelop the area into a luxurious private estate. The project came under heavy criticism from the public in large part because the demolition process would produce extensive pollution to the environment. In the Hunghom case, students will have to assess the three options the company faced at that point: maintain the status quo ante, renovation and demolition. The case gives students a good chance to analyse stakeholders' needs and align them with profitability objectives and the company's social responsibilities.

The second case revolves around the Dharavi Redevelopment Plan, which attempts to improve the dweller living conditions of the densely populated Dharavi slum in Mumbai, India. The project contemplates a radical transformation of the area by rebuilding it as a whole. The case offers students the opportunity to reflect on the difficulties the project consultant faces in his attempt to align the diverse groups of interest needed to ensure the realization of the project; for instance, political leaders, civic organizations, builders and developers, the citizens of Mumbai and, foremost, the inhabitants of the Dharavi slum.

The closing case of Part II is centred on the sports garment company Lululemon. The company took its commitment to the environment one step too far and made environmental claims that could not support. Lululemon was accused of selling products that did not contain seaweed, as the product label claimed. A *New York Times* article ignited the controversy after receiving a tip from an anonymous investor planning to short Lululemon's stock. Together with ethical, marketing and supply chain components, the case also provides excellent triggers for a classroom discussion over the potential impact of certain stakeholders. An interesting case showcasing how stakeholders may not necessary be aligned with corporate interests and may harm a company's reputation, particularly when it does not live up to expectations the company has committed to.

The third and last part of this volume revolves around the use of sustainability as a differentiation strategy for corporations. The three selected cases belong to segments of the food industry where differentiation is a true challenge given the relative homogeneity of products they commercialize and the extremely competitive environment in which they operate. The cases of Burgerville and Chipotle – two quick service restaurant chains – and Portland Roasting Company – a specialty coffee roaster – reflect on approaches like the selective supply chain sourcing of raw materials or the adoption of certification schemes in order to achieve differentiation from competitors.

The Burgerville case discusses the conflicting sustainability attributes of deciding where and how to source chicken, a primary ingredient on Burgerville's restaurant menu. Burgerville is a company that has built a strong reputation with their sustainability efforts, which allow them to charge a premium in its products in a traditionally cost-based industry. The case serves as an excellent starting discussion point to tackle issues of counter-balancing potentially conflicting sustainability goals, the ability to maintain reputation, price premiums or influencing the supply chain beyond the reach of the company.

Portland Roasting Company (PRC) is a case similar to Burgerville in the sense that students are also dealing with a company with a robust sustainability reputation and with an emphasis on its challenges to differentiate its products through a social sustainability programme. However, the PRC case focuses on the visibility of the company's reputation and value proposition to its consumers and explores the pros and cons of using a certification scheme to enhance these two key aspects.

Finally, the Chipotle Mexican Grill (CMG), a restaurant chain in the quick serve segment as Burgerville, is the protagonist of our last featured case. CMG, whose chain's mission was 'Food with Integrity', positioned itself as a differentiator, using both food quality and a commitment to sustainability as factors that isolated the company from its competitors. However, the company was under pressure from his competitor Taco Bell and was hard pressed to both control input costs and find suppliers. At the same time, sales were not performing as expected and company's stock price was at the edge of a free fall. The case will bring students the opportunity to discuss how to achieve and sustain a company positioning through a sustainability differentiation strategy in a competitive market.

Part I
Large corporations and corporate sustainability dilemmas

CASE 1

Embedding sustainability at Novo Nordisk

The compassion vs competitiveness dilemma*

Debapratim Purkayastha and Adapa Srinivasa Rao

> How to strike the right balance between business and global health?
> Again, we were challenged by stakeholders... We set out to show that it
> is possible to be a profitable and a responsible business. We strength-
> ened our approach to sustainability, now revolving around the right to
> health and the need for improved diabetes care, actions to combat cli-
> mate change, ethical business behavior, human rights, and how we can
> connect the dots.[
>
> *Lise Kingo, Executive Vice President and Chief of Staffs,*
> *Novo Nordisk, in 2011*

ICMR
IBS Center for Management Research
www.icmrindia.org

The Danish pharmaceutical company, Novo Nordisk, was named as the 'most sustainable company in the world' by the business magazine *Corporate Knights*[1] for the year 2012. Another Novo group company, Novozymes A/S was also ranked fourth in the list of global 100 most sustainable corporations in the world (See Exhibit I for the top 20 companies in the list). Novo Nordisk received the recognition for a number of sustainability related initiatives that it had taken over the years since it had first faced a controversy regarding its business practices in the late 1960s. It started two important initiatives, viz. the Novo Nordisk Way of Management and the Triple Bottom Line philosophy to evolve as an organization with a key focus on sustainability.

Over the years, Novo Nordisk's business grew substantially and it emerged as a leader in the global insulin market. In the new millennium, Novo Nordisk's new sustainability strategy placed global health at the center of its sustainability initiatives. According to Novo Nordisk's vision statement, the company strove to find the right balance between compassion and competitiveness. From then on, Novo Nordisk started selling its products at a subsidized price in some of the poorest countries around the world. Despite all the efforts that it took to protect the interests of all its stakeholders, in 2010, Novo Nordisk was severely criticized by patients and NGOs when it stopped selling its drugs in Greece when the crisis-ridden government there ordered a 25 percent cut in the prices of all medicines sold in the country. Novo Nordisk was accused of putting profits above corporate social responsibility. Though the issue was settled later with the resumption of the sale of all its products in Greece, the episode badly dented the image of Novo Nordisk as a company with a focus on sustainability.

Faced with increased regulatory scrutiny and stakeholder activism, the challenge before the senior management of Novo Nordisk was how to tackle the issue and embed sustainability further in the company. According to them, as a global healthcare company focused on diabetes treatment, they had to often face the compassion vs competitiveness dilemma and the conflicting demands of multiple stakeholders. In their words: 'Even though our core business philosophy requires us to make a difference where we can, there are significant dilemmas involved for us as a company. What role should we assume in developing countries? How can we develop new sustainable business models? How will our investors respond to such business models? How do we avoid creating unhealthy dependencies between us and our project partners?'[ii]

---

1 Corporate Knights is a magazine focused on capitalism. The magazine focuses on how markets and companies can promote social and ecological sustainability. It is published four times a year in both the US and Canada.

Background note

Novo Nordisk, a global leader in insulin, was formed in 1989 through the merger of two Danish companies, Novo Industri A/S and Nordisk Gentofte A/S. Novo Nordisk's roots can be traced to Nordisk Insulinlaboratorium, which was founded in 1923 to produce insulin. Novo Nordisk pioneered many breakthroughs in diabetes treatment.

After the merger, Novo Nordisk A/S rolled out a lot of innovations like prefilled insulin syringes, oral treatment syringes, rapid acting insulin, etc. By the late 1990s, it started focusing more on international markets. In 2000, Novo Nordisk A/S was demerged into three separate companies—Novo Nordisk A/S (Novo Nordisk), Novozymes A/S, and Novo A/S. After the demerger of Novo Nordisk A/S, Novo A/S was made the holding company of the Novo Group and was wholly-owned by the Novo Nordisk Foundation. Majority shares in both Novo Nordisk and Novozymes A/S were transferred to Novo A/S. While Novo Nordisk continued to focus on pharmaceutical products and services, the enzymes business of Novo Nordisk A/S was transferred to Novozymes A/S. In the decade that followed the demerger, Novo Nordisk expanded its business across the globe and emerged as a leading pharmaceutical company in the area of diabetes care. By 2011, Novo Nordisk employed 32,000 people in 75 countries and marketed its products in 190 countries. For the financial year 2011, Novo Nordisk's revenue was Danish Kroner[2] (DKK) 66.35 billion (See Exhibit II for the income statement of Novo Nordisk from 2007 to 2011).[iii] It was placed 18th on the list of top pharmaceutical companies of the world by revenue.

History of sustainability at Novo Nordisk

In the late 1960s, Novo Nordisk faced severe stakeholder criticism for the first time in its history. During the 1960s, Novo Nordisk's predecessor, Novo, had started producing enzymes through new production processes of fermentation of microorganisms. These new processes used genetically engineered microorganisms and led to the evolution of a successful new product line of enzymes. These enzymes became important ingredients in many products, like detergents. Environmental organizations and activists alleged that the use of enzymes developed by Novo could cause skin allergies in people who came into contact with them. They also alleged that the dust generated during the production process of the enzymes could have serious effects on the health of Novo Nordisk's workers. An activist called Ralph Nader started a movement against the laundry industry in the US which created a stir both in the US and around the world. The sales of Novo fell dramatically between 1970

---

2   The Danish Kroner is the official currency of Denmark, Greenland, and the Faroe Islands. As of September 2012, one Danish Kroner was approximately equal to 0.1696 US$.

and 1971 due to the concerns raised by activists. Nearly 700 employees of Novo lost their jobs due to the crisis. Novo responded swiftly and developed dust-free enzymes which did not pose any risk to its consumers or employees. The sales of Novo's enzyme products rose soon and enzyme production became an important part of Novo's business in many countries like Denmark, the US, and Japan. This episode made Novo realize the importance of keeping the interests of all stakeholders in mind. Since then, Novo, and subsequently, Novo Nordisk, focused on producing products which did not affect the health of consumers and which were environmentally friendly.

Novo Nordisk took its first significant step toward sustainable development in 1989 when it conducted its first environmental management review. It took this significant step as an element of its proactive stakeholder strategy in the days when environmental reporting was not compulsory for companies like Novo Nordisk. From 1991, it started organizing visits of its laboratories and production facilities for representatives of NGOs as part of its stakeholder engagement strategy.[iv] In 1992, some people from Novo Nordisk attended the United Nations Conference on Environment and Development (UNCED) Earth Summit organized in Rio de Janeiro. The summit made Novo Nordisk realize the importance of environmental protection and led to its reinforcing its commitment to sustainable development. Commenting on the impact that the 1992 Earth Summit had on Novo Nordisk's commitment to sustainable development, Novo Nordisk's Executive Vice President and Chief Of Staffs, Lise Kingo (Kingo), said, 'We came back from Rio with a better understanding of how huge an agenda environmental protection was, how many stakeholders were involved, and that many other companies were taking an interest. It was a real eye-opener.'[v] In 1994, Novo Nordisk published its first environmental report. It became the first company in Denmark and one of the first in the world to publish an environmental report.[vi] The report contained details regarding resource consumption, emissions in its production processes, and the use of animals in its experiments. The environmental report was followed by Novo Nordisk's first social report in 1998. And since 1999, Novo Nordisk started publishing annual reports on sustainability which integrated its environmental, social, and economic concerns.

Novo Nordisk way of management

In 1996, Novo Nordisk introduced the 'Novo Nordisk Way of Management' (NNWM) to serve as an overall guidance system to reach its strategic goals. NNWM served as the value-based governance framework for the company. It described how people at Novo Nordisk put values into action and defined the principles to be followed by the company while doing business.[vii] NNWM offered a broad framework of guidelines to the employees and covered Novo Nordisk's activities beyond the products and manufacturing operations. The central part of the goal was to integrate and implement the various sustainable business practices of Novo Nordisk. NNWM consisted of three parts, viz. the vision, the charter, and global company policies (See Figure 1.1 for Novo Nordisk Way of Management and Exhibit III for its building blocks of sustainability).

Figure 1.1 **Novo Nordisk way of management**

Source: Novo Nordisk A/S: Sustainability Report 2000, www.novonordisk.com

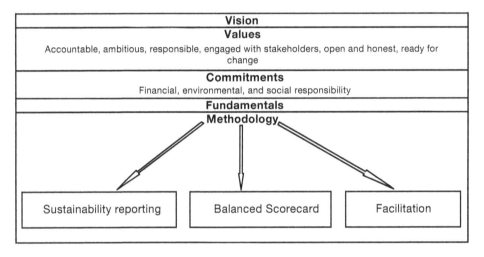

The vision of NNWM set the direction for Novo Nordisk. It expressed what goals Novo Nordisk was striving to achieve, how the company wanted to achieve its goals, and how the company was guided by its values to strike the right balance between its commercial interests and acting as a responsible business. The Charter explained the company's values, commitments, fundamentals, and follow-up methods. The values highlighted the company's commitment to the Triple Bottom Line and sustainable development. Fundamentals were a set of 11 management principles to ensure it stayed focused on its business objectives, customers, compliance, collaboration, and sharing of better practices, and quality mindset.[viii] Follow-up methods provided a systematic documentation of the performance of all material areas of Novo Nordisk. The global company policies set global standards for its managers and gave operational guidelines on 13 specific areas related to its business.

In addition to coming out with an innovative way of managing its activities through NNWM, Novo Nordisk took steps to ensure that the entire organization understood and followed it. It had developed a methodology consisting of three elements: facilitators, sustainability reporting, and balanced scorecard. The facilitators were a group of 16 senior professionals at Novo Nordisk's holding company Novo A/S. These facilitators traveled in pairs and visited all the business units and levels of the whole organization once every three years. They performed a well-planned and structured assessment of the implementation of NNWM within a project or unit. The main objective of the facilitation process was to develop agreed upon actions for improvement. The facilitation process consisted of three stages. The first was the pre-facilitation stage in which the scope of the facilitation process was identified. The second stage was the facilitation itself. In this stage, the facilitators met the unit and project members and arrived at an agreement regarding improvements to be made wherever non-compliance had been identified. In the third stage, the post-facilitation process was conducted in which the facilitator followed up on the progress and reports to the management team about the achievements and shortfalls, if any, from the facilitation process.

Sustainability reporting was used to ensure that sustainability became a part of Novo Nordisk's corporate culture. Novo Nordisk had come a long way in sustainability reporting since it first published its first environmental report in 1994. From 1999, it started publishing annual reports on sustainability which integrated its environmental, social, and economic concerns. The reports documented Novo Nordisk's ambitions, initiatives, goals, and results related to environmental and social responsibility. From the year 2004, information on sustainability was integrated with its financial results and published as part of its annual report.

In 1996, Novo Nordisk started using the balanced scorecard.[3] It was initially used as a finance initiative. Later, it began to be used to integrate the company's sustainability approach with all its business processes. One balanced scorecard was prepared for the organization as a whole and separate balanced scorecards were prepared at the executive VP, senior VP, and in some cases even at the sub-unit levels (e.g. a single factory). Novo Nordisk's balanced scorecard had a total of 24 objectives under four headings: customers and society, finance, business processes, and people and organization (See Exhibit IV for a sample Balanced Scorecard of Novo Nordisk).

Triple bottom line

In 1997, just one year after it introduced NNWM, Novo Nordisk started another important initiative to help it evolve as an organization practicing sustainable business practices. It introduced the Triple Bottom Line (TBL) philosophy to maximize value to all its stakeholders. The TBL philosophy focused on operating in a way that was financially, environmentally, and socially responsible (See Figure 1.2 for

---

3 Balanced scorecard is a strategic planning and management system used by both business and non-business organizations around the world. It was propounded by Robert Kaplan and David Norton. It adds non-financial measures to the traditional financial metrics to give managers a more balanced view of organizational performance.

Triple Bottom Line). The main objective behind the introduction of the TBL philosophy was to balance its short-term profitability with the long-term interests of the society. In this way, Novo Nordisk aimed at optimizing its business performance in all the societies in which it had its operations. It made the TBL philosophy its top strategic priority as it believed from the beginning that being socially responsible, environmentally sound, and economically viable made good business sense. Simply put, the TBL philosophy was the way Novo Nordisk chose to interpret its commitment toward sustainable development. Commenting on the importance of the TBL philosophy, Novo Nordisk's President and CEO, Lars Rebien Sorensen (Sorensen), said, 'The main foundation for Novo Nordisk is the triple bottom line because that is what's protecting our license to operate. That begs and obliges everybody in the company not only to see that we become a good business – that's the financial bottom line – but that we do so in a way that is socially and environmentally responsible.'[ix] Over time, Novo Nordisk embedded the TBL philosophy into the corporate governance structures, management tools, performance appraisal, and reward schemes of its employees.[x]

Figure 1.2 **Triple bottom line**

Source: Our Approach to Sustainability, www.novonordisk.com.

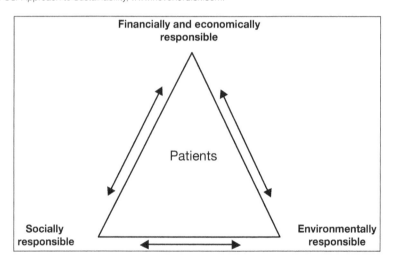

Novo Nordisk formulated its first environmental policy in the early 1980s and made a lot of progress in its environmental performance from then on.[xi] On the environmental front, Novo Nordisk committed itself to continuously improving its environmental performance. It aimed to achieve this by setting itself stiff targets and by merging environmental and bioethical considerations into its regular business activities. Novo Nordisk started to have an open dialogue with all its stakeholders regarding its commitment toward the conservation of the environment.

It also initiated annual reporting of its progress in environmental performance. It supported the United Nations Convention on Biological Diversity[4] to emphasize its focus on sustainability. On the social front too, Novo Nordisk started to set high objectives and to integrate social, human rights, and health and safety considerations into its daily business activities. Like environment reporting, Novo Nordisk annually reported on its social performance. It offered a patient-assistance program for those who did not have private health insurance and who did not get any medical assistance from their governments.[xii] Under the program, patients were required to apply to Novo Nordisk for medical assistance and medicines were supplied free of cost to applicants who qualified. Under the TBL philosophy, Novo Nordisk also committed itself to focusing on continuously improving its financial performance by reaching new milestones in growth and to creating value for its shareholders. It complied with international reporting standards of its financial statements.

In 2004, Novo Nordisk updated its Articles of Association and bylaws and included in the objectives the words 'the company seeks to conduct its business in a way that is financially, environmentally, and socially responsible'.[xiii]

Progress on sustainability

After the demerger of Novo Nordisk A/S, a new sustainability strategy focusing on the healthcare business of Novo Nordisk was developed. This new strategy marked the shift to Novo Nordisk's next stage of sustainability endeavors. According to the new strategy, Novo Nordisk would have global health at the heart of its sustainability initiatives.[xiv] Despite its focus on sustainability for such a long period of time, Novo Nordisk faced new criticism from activists and NGOs regarding its business practices after the demerger. In 2001, a consortium of 38 pharmaceutical companies along with Novo Nordisk filed a lawsuit against the South African government for violating their intellectual property rights, mostly in relation to the medicines used in the treatment of AIDS. The South African government sought to deliver generic versions of some AIDS medicines in South Africa by using a 1997 law called the Medicines and Related Substances Control Amendment Act (MRSCA).[xv] MRSCA allowed the South African government to procure the cheapest possible medicines for all purposes from both international and local suppliers. The law also gave the South African health ministry the right to override pharmaceutical patents whenever the government thought that public health was at stake. While the Agreement

---

4   United Nations Convention on Biological Diversity is an international legal treaty with the three main goals of conserving biological diversity, sustainable use of its components, and equal sharing of benefits arising from genetic resources. The treaty was opened for signature at the Earth Summit in Rio de Janeiro in June 1992 and came into force in December 1993.

on Trade Related Aspects of Intellectual Property Rights (TRIPS)[5] allowed countries to produce copies of patented medicines in cases of national emergencies like the AIDS epidemic, the consortium members felt that MRSCA gave the South African government the right to infringe the patent rights of any pharmaceutical product even if there were no national emergencies. Novo Nordisk and members of the consortium faced heavy criticism from activists and NGOs regarding the case. The consortium members were accused of giving more importance to profits than to the health of poor people living in the developing countries. The case also caused public concern in Denmark regarding the business practices of Novo Nordisk.

Novo Nordisk was quick to react to the criticism and it started a dialogue with the NGOs. It came out with a new policy to increase its presence in developing countries and to develop new medicines for combating diseases there. It adopted a new pricing policy under which it started supplying insulin to the 50 poorest countries designated by the United Nations at 20 percent of the average price in North America, Europe, and Japan. Through this new pricing policy called sustainable pricing, Novo Nordisk ensured that it did not earn any profits on its sales in poor countries. It also ensured that the research and development costs for Novo Nordisk's drugs sold in poor countries were borne by its consumers in the developed world. In effect, Novo Nordisk started cross subsidizing its products sold in developing countries. Commenting on the new pricing policy, Sorensen said, 'We advocate sustainable pricing. That means we will not levy a profit on these products sold to the developing world, but rather the costs of our research and development will be borne by the developed world. Of course, this hinges on a psychological contract – namely that developed countries are willing to subsidize developing countries.'[xvi] The case with the South African government was settled out of court with the consortium withdrawing the case and the South African government agreeing to honor its obligations under TRIPS. In 2001, Novo Nordisk established the World Diabetes Foundation with the objective of improving diabetes care in poor countries through education, capacity building, distribution, procurement of essential drugs, and monitoring of the care given.

The case filed against the South African government and the subsequent developments made Novo Nordisk think more about its role in increasing access to healthcare and essential medicines. It also highlighted the need to engage in continuous dialogue with its stakeholders and monitor their concerns. In 2001, Novo Nordisk started TBL. TBL reporting focused on the progress made by the company in its commitments toward the economy, society, and environment according to its TBL philosophy (See Exhibit V for the Novo Nordisk learning curve and Exhibit VI for its stakeholder maps over the years). Novo Nordisk became a signatory to the United

---

5 The Agreement on Trade Related Aspects of Intellectual Property Rights (TRIPS) is an international agreement related to intellectual property administered by the World Trade Organization (WTO).

Nations Global Compact,[6] a global platform for promoting good corporate principles and learning, in the year 2001. Over the years, Novo Nordisk changed the focus of its sustainability policy from the environment to health, safety, bioethics, and integrating issues related to social responsibility. In 2005, Novo Nordisk launched its 'Changing Diabetes' brand platform. The Changing Diabetes initiative aimed at bringing about a change in the lives of people suffering from diabetes through several other ways apart from treatment like science, humanitarian outreach, education, and public policy.[xvii] The ultimate goal of the Changing Diabetes program initiative was to defeat the diabetes pandemic.[xviii] Novo Nordisk took up ambitious challenges to tackle diabetes globally which was not an easy task considering that a huge percentage of the people afflicted were from developing countries and were less able to afford the treatment (See Exhibit VII for economic pyramid and access to diabetes care, and Exhibit VIII for Novo Nordisk's ambitions in improving access to diabetes care up to 2015).

Climate change

Manufacturing insulin was an energy intensive process. Therefore, another important area which Novo Nordisk focused on as part of its sustainable development initiatives was climate change. Novo Nordisk set long-term environmental targets in three areas, viz. CO_2 emissions from energy consumption, energy consumption, and water consumption. During 2003–2004, Novo Nordisk's environmental management practices at all its production facilities were certified according to the ISO 14001 standard[7]. After lot of preparation and assessment, Novo Nordisk signed an agreement with the World Wildlife Fund for Nature (WWF)[8] in 2006, which made it the 10th member of the Climate Savers Program. The Climate Savers Program required the participating organizations to commit themselves to cutting CO_2 emissions in their operations. Novo Nordisk followed the way of setting targets and implementing improvement measures to reduce its environmental footprint. It set a target of reducing its CO_2 emissions by 10 percent in absolute terms by 2014 when compared with the 2004 emission levels.

---

6 The United Nations Global Compact is a United Nations initiative to encourage businesses around the world to adopt policies which are sustainable and socially responsible and report on their implementation.
7 ISO14001 standard acts as a framework to assist organizations in developing their own environmental system. It belongs to the ISO 14000 family of standards which are related to environmental management.
8 World Wildlife Fund for Nature, headquartered in Gland, Switzerland, is an international NGO working in areas related to conservation, research, and restoration of the environment.

Along with the target to reduce CO_2 emissions, Novo Nordisk established a new climate strategy which required it to achieve the reduction in CO_2 emissions through improvements in productivity, savings in energy consumption, and shift to renewable sources. Manufacturing insulin was an energy intensive process and reducing CO_2 emissions required innovation. Novo Nordisk invested US$ 20 million to start a new global energy-efficiency campaign. The campaign required energy screenings to be conducted every three years at all its production sites and the appointment of energy stewards. The agreement with WWF required that Novo Nordisk could not rely on carbon offsets or buy power from existing renewable sources. Kingo said, 'It was a very ambitious target. We knew it would require innovation.'[xix] To achieve its target of CO_2 emissions, it pioneered a partnership model where Novo Nordisk entered into a partnership with Denmark's largest energy company, DONG Energy.[9] As per the partnership, the consultants of DONG Energy along with the employees of Novo Nordisk identified energy-reducing measures at its Danish production sites. After the energy-saving measures were identified and monetary savings achieved, Novo Nordisk pledged to utilize the resulting monetary savings to purchase green energy (electricity) produced through wind turbines from DONG Energy. Novo Nordisk helped DONG Energy to set up a wind farm from where it procured its required power. The green energy purchased from DONG Energy was used at its Danish production sites where 90 percent of its CO_2 emissions occurred. DONG Energy built a new offshore wind farm to supply green energy to Novo Nordisk's production facilities. By following this innovative approach, Novo Nordisk achieved its targeted reduction in CO_2 emissions by 2010, three years ahead of schedule (See Exhibit IX for Novo Nordisk's CO_2 emissions from 2007 to 2011). By 2011, its CO_2 emissions were down by 56 percent when compared with that in 2004.[xx] It also set a target of reducing its total energy consumption by 11 percent by 2011—to 2,425,000 GJ[10] when compared to the 2007 levels. Novo Nordisk reached its energy consumption target by 2009 itself and limited its total energy consumption to just 2,187,000 GJ by 2011[xxi] (See Exhibit X for Novo Nordisk's Energy Consumption from 2007 to 2011).

Commenting on the success of the partnership model, Per Valstorp, Senior Vice President of Novo Nordisk Product Supply division, said, 'This really was a very ambitious target. Had we not launched emission reduction programs, Novo Nordisk's emissions were projected to increase by approximately 67 percent during the period 2004–2014.'[xxii] Inspired by Novo Nordisk's success, many corporations around the world entered into similar partnerships to reduce their carbon emissions. Jon Hoff, senior Vice President at Novo Nordisk, who was involved in developing the partnership model said, 'We have demonstrated that there is a sensible, cost-neutral way to achieve reductions in CO_2 emissions. The fact that others have

---

9 DONG Energy, headquartered in Fredericia, Denmark, is the leading energy company in Denmark.

10 GJ refers to Gigajoule which is equal to one billion joules. Joule is a derived unit of energy, work or heat in the International System of Units.

been inspired means we have been able to have impact beyond what we could have done ourselves.'[xxiii]

In the year 2008, Novo Nordisk started a water management program to reduce the consumption of water in its operations. It put special emphasis on its production sites where there was a water shortage like Tianjin in China and Monte Claros in Brazil.[xxiv] Its water conservation efforts paid off and Novo Nordisk reduced its water consumption from 3,231,000 m^3[11] in 2007 to 2,136,000 m^3 in 2011 (See Exhibit XI for Novo Nordisk's Water Consumption from 2007 to 2011).

Greek price cut controversy

By the year 2005, Novo Nordisk had significantly grown its business around the world. In 2005, it emerged as the leader in the US insulin market for the first time since it had entered the market. By 2011, it got 40.1 percent of its sales from North America and 28.9 percent of its sales from Europe (See Exhibit XII for the sales of Novo Nordisk by geographic region for the year 2011). Novo Nordisk also emerged as the leading producer of insulin in the world with a market share of 50 percent.[xxv] Despite its growth and sustainable development, it again faced allegations regarding its business practices.

In the year 2010, Novo Nordisk stopped selling some of its insulin products in Greece. The decision to do so came after the government there decreed a 25 percent cut in the prices of all the medicines sold due to the debt crisis[12] that the country was facing. Novo Nordisk said that the price cut would result in a loss to its business. Commenting on the decision to stop selling its products in Greece, Mike Rulisthe, spokesperson of Novo Nordisk, said, 'A 25 percent price cut does not allow us to run a sustainable business in Greece, and this is what we have told the government.'[xxvi] Novo Nordisk further said that a price cut in Greece would lead to similar moves in other countries where the prices in Greece were taken as reference prices which would result in serious financial consequences for the company. At the time of their withdrawal from the market, nearly 50,000 people suffering from type 1 diabetes in Greece used Novo Nordisk's insulin products for their survival. Novo Nordisk was severely criticized by patients and NGOs for the withdrawal. Activists alleged that this decision ran contrary to the social responsibility that Novo Nordisk claimed in its annual reports. The Greek diabetes association called the withdrawal of Novo Nordisk's insulin products from Greece a 'brutal blackmail and a violation of corporate social responsibility'.[xxvii]

---

11 m^3 refers to SI derived unit of volume, cubic meter. 1 cubic meter is equal to 1,000 liters.

12 The Greek government-debt crisis was a financial crisis that the Greek government was facing since 2009 due to many factors like high government debt and rising fiscal deficit. The Greek government had implemented several austerity measures to deal with the crisis.

Novo Nordisk responded to the criticism saying that the Greece government owed it US$36 million in the form of unpaid bills and blamed the improper handling of the Greece economy by its government for the situation. The chairman of Novo Nordisk, Lars Sorensen, said that it was 'the irresponsible management of finances by the Greek government which puts both you and our company in this difficult position'.[xxviii] Novo Nordisk also said that it had stopped selling only its modern products like pen devices and patented insulin products in Greece. It said it continued to sell its other insulin product, Novollibiosynthetic human insulin.[xxix] It also continued to provide another of its cheaper insulin products, glucagen insulin, free of charge in Greece.[xxx] Novo Nordisk claimed that these products were sufficient for the survival of any person suffering from diabetes. Activists alleged that Novo Nordisk was trying to shift the responsibility on to the Greece government while focusing only on profits. The company had been steadily raising the price of its insulin products for six consecutive quarters across the world, which resulted in a higher profit margin for its insulin products, they said. Pavlos Panayotacos a Greek economist whose 10-year-old daughter suffered from diabetes, said in a letter to Novo Nordisk, 'As an economist I realize the importance of making a profit, but healthcare is more than just the bottom line. As you well may know, Greece is presently in dire economic and social straits, and you could not have acted in a more insensitive manner at a more inopportune time.'[xxxi]

Novo Nordisk resumed selling all its insulin products in Greece after the government agreed to raise the prices of its drugs there in July 2010.[xxxii] But, the prices were still 10 percent less than what they had been before the controversy erupted.

Looking ahead

Novo Nordisk got several recognitions for its progress in sustainable development. It was named as the most sustainable company in the world by the business magazine *Corporate Knights* for the year 2012. Commenting on the recognition, Kingo said, 'This is a wonderful recognition of our Triple Bottom Line approach and a clear indication that Novo Nordisk is poised for long-term business success. But most importantly, it is an encouragement to continue to find new ways of growing our business in a way that is profitable, responsible, and valuable for patients, employees, and society.'[xxxiii] Novo Nordisk was listed in the 2010/2011 Dow Jones Sustainability Indices (DJSI).[13,xxxiv] It was also awarded a gold class rating[14] by

---

13 Dow Jones Sustainability indexers are a group of indexes which evaluate the world's leading companies in their sustainability practices.

14 To qualify for the Gold Class distinction, a company's Dow Jones Sustainability Indexes score needs to be within the 5 percent of the respective sector leader's score.

Sustainability Asset Management (SAM)[15] in its Sustainability Yearbook 2011 in recognition of its integrated reporting, stakeholder engagement, and its consistent high sustainability performance.[xxxv]

Novo Nordisk continued its initiatives in sustainability. To inculcate a sense of responsibility among its employees toward all the stakeholders, it started training its employees in business ethics. By 2011, nearly 99 percent of the relevant employees had been trained in business ethics. Novo Nordisk also started to have diverse senior management teams to understand the needs of various sections of the society properly. By 2011, 62 percent of its senior management teams had members from diverse backgrounds. It set a target of having 100 percent of senior management teams from diverse backgrounds by the year 2014.

By the year 2011, Novo Nordisk was selling its insulin products at a subsidized price in 75 percent of the least developed countries (See Exhibit XIII for the percentage of poorest countries where Novo Nordisk sold its subsidized insulin). And, it had a long-term target of making its cheaper insulin products available in 100 percent of the least developed countries. However, despite the resumption of the sales of its products in Greece, the controversy regarding the Greek price cut was seen by many analysts as a big public relations disaster for Novo Nordisk. They said that the episode had dented its image as a champion of sustainable development. They contended that the problems faced by Novo Nordisk highlighted the increased regulatory scrutiny and stakeholder activism that companies around the world were facing in their operations. It also led some analysts to question the readiness of the company to face the new challenging environment. The question was, as a global healthcare company, how could Novo Nordisk strike the right balance between business and global health?

---

15 Sustainable Asset Management, headquartered in Zurich, Switzerland is an international investment company with exclusive focus on sustainability investments.

EXHIBIT I

Top twenty companies on the 2012 corporate knights global 100 most sustainable corporations in the world list

Company	Country	Industry
Novo Nordisk A/S	Denmark	Health care
NaturaCosmeticos S.A.	Brazil	Consumer staples
Statoil ASA	Norway	Energy
Novozymes A/S	Denmark	Materials
ASML Holding NV	Netherlands	Information technology
BG Group Plc.	United Kingdom	Energy
Vivendi S.A.	France	Telecommunication services
Umicore S.A./N.V.	Belgium	Materials
Norsk Hydro ASA	Norway	Materials
Atlas Copco AB	Sweden	Industrials
Sims Metal Management Ltd	Australia	Materials
Koninklijke Philips Electronics NV	Netherlands	Industrials
Teliasonera AB	Sweden	Telecommunication services
Westpac Banking Corp.	Australia	Financials
Life Technologies Corp.	US	Health care
Credit Agricole SA	France	Financials
Henkel AG & Co. KGaA	Germany	Consumer staples
Intel Corp.	US	Information technology
Neste Oil Oyj	Finland	Energy
Swisscom AG	Switzerland	Telecommunication services

Source: Tilde Herrera, Novo Nordisk Tops List of World's 100 Most Sustainable Firms, www.greenbiz.com, January 25, 2012.

EXHIBIT II
Income statement of Novo Nordisk from 2007 to 2011 (figures in DKK million)

	2011	2010	2009	2008	2007
Sales	66,346	60,776	51,078	45,553	41,831
Cost of goods sold	12,589	11,680	10,438	10,109	9,793
Gross profit	53,757	49,096	40,640	35,444	32,038
Sales and distribution costs	19,004	18,195	15,420	12,866	12,371
Research and development costs	9,628	9,602	7,864	7,856	8,538
hereof costs related to discontinuation of all pulmonary diabetes projects	–	–	–	(325)	(1,325)
Administrative expenses	3,245	3,065	2,764	2,635	2,508
Licence fees and other operating income, net	494	657	341	286	321
Operating profit	22,374	18,891	14,933	12,373	8,942
Share of profit/(loss) of associated companies, net of tax	(4)	1,070	(55)	(124)	1,233
Financial income	514	382	375	1,127	1,303
Financial expenses	959	2,057	1,265	681	507
Profit before income taxes	21,925	18,286	13,988	12,695	10,971
Income taxes	4,828	3,883	3,220	3,050	2,449
Net profit for the year	17,097	14,403	10,768	9,645	8,522

Source: Novo Nordisk Annual Report, 2011; Novo Nordisk Annual Report, 2009.

EXHIBIT III
Novo Nordisk's building blocks of sustainability

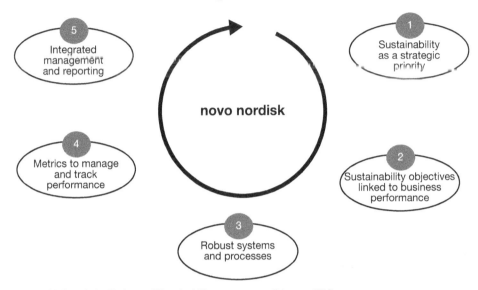

Source: 20 Years in the Business of Sustainability, www.novonordisk.com, 2012.

EXHIBIT IV
A sample balance scorecard of Novo Nordisk

Customers and society	Finance
Realize the full potential of strategic products Improve market share globally Ensure successful implementation of US and Japanese business plan Achieve superior customer satisfaction Improve social, environmental and bioethical performance	Growth in operating profit ROIC Operating margin Cash to earnings ratio
Business processes	**People and organization**
Discovery Speed quality and productivity Competitive development portfolio Ensure launch capabilities with GP segment Improve quality management focus in all business processes Timely and efficient execution of investment portfolio Ensure effective use of IT supporting the business strategies	Customer relations Winning culture Attract and retain the best Development of people Social responsibility

Source: F. Zingales and K. Hockerts, 'Balanced Scorecard and Sustainability: Examples from Literature and
    Practice,' CMER Working Paper Series.

EXHIBIT V
The Novo Nordisk learning curve

Source: 20 Years in the Business of Sustainability, www.novonordisk.com, 2012.

EXHIBIT VI
Novo Nordisk stakeholder maps over the years

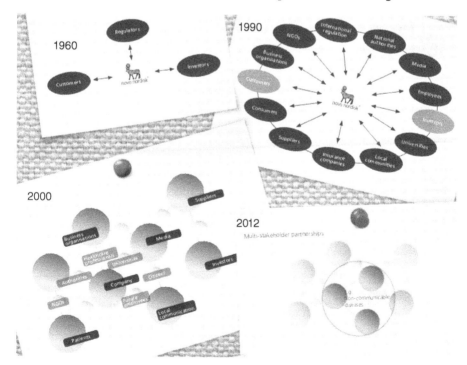

Source: 20 Years in the Business of Sustainability, www.novonordisk.com, 2012.

EXHIBIT VII
Economic pyramid and access to diabetes care

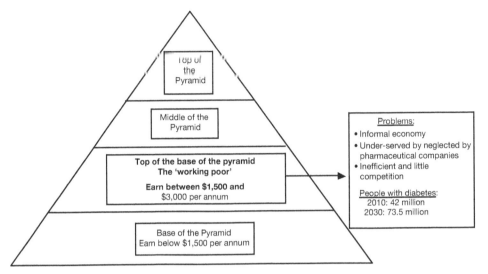

Source: Access to Health: Our Approach, www.novonordisk.com.

EXHIBIT VIII
Novo Nordisk's ambitions in improving access to diabetes care up to 2015

Ambition	Focus area	Approach
Availability of treatment: Develop quality-assured diabetes treatment for all	Make insulin available to people with diabetes globally	Ensure continued supply of human insulin to low- and middle-income countries for at least another 10 years
		Support research to document consequences and implications of diabetes
		Share discoveries and knowledge that could have application in infectious-disease areas
	Address distribution challenges at the base of pyramid (BOP)	Explore business models for people living with diabetes in the BOP segment
	Facilitate technology transfer	Work with public and private institutions in low- and middle-income countries to enhance healthcare provision to the benefit of all patients

Ambition	Focus area	Approach
Accessibility of healthcare: Work with partners to make diabetes care more accessible for those in need	Support strengthening of healthcare systems	Contribute to the training of healthcare professionals
	Improve accessibility to insulin in remote areas	Reach out to people with diabetes in remote areas
	Improve access to diabetes care for women and children	Establish partnerships for the improved delivery of care to children with diabetes in low- and middle-income countries
		Establish partnership-based interventions as part of a long-term commitment to the improvement of health of women and the next generation
Affordability of treatment: Work to improve affordability of treatment for patients, particularly in resource-poor settings	Improve funding for diabetes healthcare	Continue our annual endowment to the World Diabetes Foundation
	Improve affordability of insulin	Continue our differential pricing policy and provide insulin to the governments in least developed countries at maximum 20 US cents per patient per day
		Work in partnership with governments and other organizations to increase the number of patients we reach in low- and middle-income countries
Quality for patients: Quality assurance in diabetes treatment for patients	Conduct responsible and ethical clinical trials	Support and ensure full transparency of clinical-trial activities and results
		Ensure that all persons enrolled in Novo Nordisk-sponsored research are protected by the same rights, high ethical standards and regulations, regardless of geography
	Work for safe medicines	Maintain one global quality standard
		Work against counterfeiting
		Work with ministries of health and distributors to establish effective supply chains for delivery of insulin
	Empower people with diabetes to achieve better health and quality of life	Continue research into the understanding of patient needs, including the psychosocial barriers against adhering to treatment regimens
		Continue engaging with stakeholders, with a view to identifying areas for improvement in the management of diabetes
		Support healthcare professionals to deliver better quality healthcare, building on principles of patient involvement and ongoing support

Source: Access to Health: Our Approach, www.novonordisk.com.

EXHIBIT IX
CO_2 emissions from energy consumption (1,000 tons)

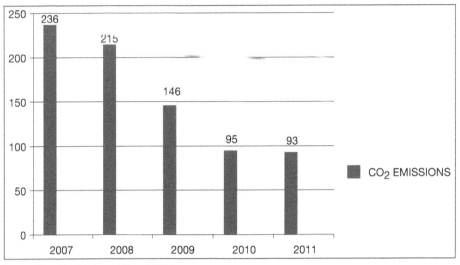

Source: Novo Nordisk Annual Report, 2011.

EXHIBIT X
Energy consumption from 2007 to 2011 (1,000 GJ)

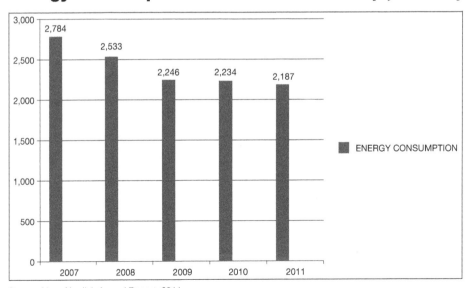

Source: Novo Nordisk Annual Report, 2011.

EXHIBIT XI
Water consumption (1,000 m³)

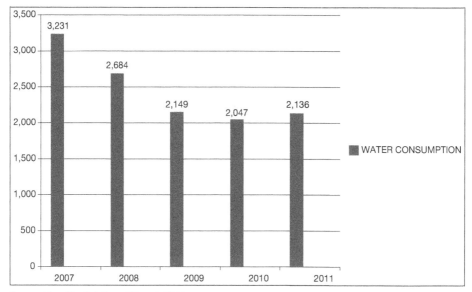

Source: Novo Nordisk Annual Report, 2011.

EXHIBIT XII
Sales of Novo Nordisk by geographic region for the year 2011 (in percentage)

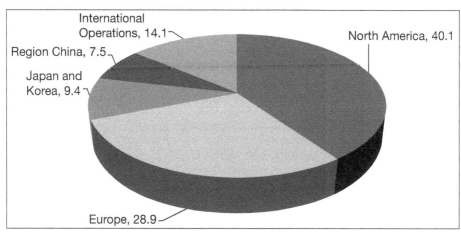

Source: Novo Nordisk Annual Report, 2011.

EXHIBIT XIII
Percentage of poorest countries where Novo Nordisk sold subsidised insulin

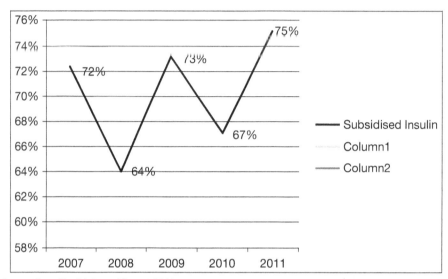

Source: Novo Nordisk Annual Report, 2011.

Notes

i   20 years in the business of sustainability, www.novonordisk.com, 2012.
ii   Novo Nordisk, Access to health: our approach, www.novonordisk.com, September 2011.
iii   Novo Nordisk Annual Report, 2011.
iv   20 years in the business of sustainability, www.novonordisk.com, 2012.
v   Ibid.
vi   Milestones in Novo Nordisk's history, www.novonordisk.com.
vii   Novo Nordisk way of management, www.novonordisk.com.
viii   Ibid.
ix   Marc Gunther, Novo Nordisk, www.corporateknights.com.
x   Triple bottom line, www.annualreport2008.novonordisk.com.
xi   Case study collection: Novo Nordisk's approach, www.partnersinprojectgreen.com.
xii   Our triple bottom line, www.novonordisk-us.com.
xiii   Susanne Stormer, Story: How Novo Nordisk's Corporate DNA – 'to act responsibly' – Drives Innovation, www.managementexchange.com, April 30, 2012.
xiv   20 years in the business of sustainability, www.novonordisk.com, 2012.
xv   Novo Nordisk TBL Report 2001, www.tbl2001.novonordisk.com.
xvi   Annual Review 2001, www.novonordisk.com.
xvii   Changing Diabetes, www.novonordisk.co.in.

xviii   About Changing Diabetes, www.novonordisk.com.

xix   Marc Gunther, Novo Nordisk, www.corporateknights.com.

xx   Novo Nordisk sustainability report: CO_2 down 2 percent, waste up 61 percent, www .environmentalleader.com, February 13, 2012.

xxi   Limiting our footprint, www.annualreport2010.novonordisk.com.

xxii   20 years in the business of sustainability, www.novonordisk.com, 2012.

xxiii   Ibid.

xxiv   Limiting our footprint, www.annualreport2010.novonordisk.com.

xxv   Novo-Nordisk: diabetes and dollars, www.money.msn.com, April 5, 2012.

xxvi   Novo Nordisk rejects Greek drug price cut, www.reuters.com, May 31, 2010.

xxvii   Malcolm Brabant, Insulin giant pulls medicine from Greece over price cut, www.bbc .co.uk/news/10189367, May 29, 2010.

xxviii   Ibid.

xxix   The business of diabetes: is Novo Nordisk's Pullback from Greece Really a Greek Tragedy?, www.blog.sstrumello.com, June 2, 2010.

xxx   Ed Silverman, Novo Nordisk pulls insulin from Greece over money, www.pharmalot .com, May 29, 2010.

xxxi   Ibid.

xxxii   Ed Silverman, Novo Nordisk to supply Greece with diabetes drug, www.pharmalot .com, June 15, 2010.

xxxiii   Novo Nordisk tops global list of 100 most sustainable companies, www.novonordisk .com/sustainability/news.

xxxiv   Novo Nordisk in the lead of the Dow Jones Sustainability Index, www.novonordisk .com.

xxxv   Jessi Copeland, ReportAlert.Info: Novo Nordisk (CPH:NOVO.B) publishes 2010 Annual Report,' www.businessfightspoverty.org, February 21, 2012.

CASE 2

Walmart: Love, Earth®*

Craig Smith and Robert J. Crawford

A

In late 2004, Assheton Carter was contemplating what projects he should take on. Carter was an activist at Conservation International (CI) in mining safety, working conditions, the environment, and the rights of community and indigenous peoples. From his CI unit, the Center for Environmental Leadership in Business (CELB), he was seeking to find a high-profile, high impact project that would both accomplish something concrete and set a precedent – of transparency in extractive industries, of activist methods, and of cooperative interaction between non-governmental organizations (NGOs) and multi-national corporations (MNCs). His desk was littered with documents from current projects, including the overall strategy for CI as well as engagements with Disney and the oil and natural gas industries.

One of his potential projects included Walmart's jewellery business. Walmart, he knew, was the world's largest jewellery retailer, with annual sales of US$2.75 billion, which represented nearly 2% of total world sales. Change Walmart's approach to sustainability, he reasoned, and MNCs throughout the world would take notice. However, after nearly two years of attempting to engage with the company, he had

* This case was written by Robert J. Crawford under the supervision of N. Craig Smith, the INSEAD Chaired Professor of Ethics and Social Responsibility. It is intended to be used as a basis for class discussion rather than to illustrate either effective or ineffective handling of an administrative situation. Copyright © 2012 INSEAD.

recognized that Walmart personnel changed so fast that he seemed to have to re-educate a new set of managers in the same issues every few months. Not only did that add up to a major commitment of his time, but he felt increasingly frustrated with the lack of momentum.

Then his phone rang. Dee Breazeale, Vice President for jewellery at the Walmart affiliate Sam's Club, was on the line. 'Can you fill me in', she asked, 'on sources of rubies and the challenges with buying rubies from Burma?' He had met Breazeale earlier that year at Walmart headquarters in Bentonville, Arkansas, in a CI delegation that was negotiating the modalities of an advisory arrangement with the company. Her honesty and willingness to learn had deeply impressed him, though little had happened in the months that followed. Nonetheless, he knew that, once convinced, she had the power to act – immediately.

Within a week, she decided to purchase all of her unit's rubies from suppliers in Brazil rather than Burma; this represented a major shift in the jewellery market, with global implications. It was at that moment that Carter decided to work more intensively with the company. 'Dee was not what I was used to when dealing with corporate execs,' he recalled. 'No pretence, no "silver tongue", just "I've got an issue, I don't like being associated with dirty business, and I want your help to put it right." To me, that was wonderful. I could work with that.'

Carter had many ideas on how he might proceed. Executives like Breazeale in Walmart, he observed, were beginning to take a straightforward approach to issues of corporate responsibility and sustainability: 'Figure out what the problem is; find people who want to help solve it.' Those who preferred to denounce Walmart from the sidelines, it was clear, would not be invited. This was, he believed, an opportunity to impact not just the jewellery market, but to establish a new approach to sustainability for global businesses. While the 'conflict diamonds' campaign earlier in the decade had been relatively successful, he wanted to do something different by creating a project that would largely rely on MNCs to change and monitor their behaviour – in a way that made *business sense* to them – rather than depend on enforcement by governments and international organizations in accordance with international treaties.

One of the most promising ideas might be the creation of a 'green' line of jewellery – free of 'dirty gold' and 'conflict diamonds', with sustainable operations and careful attention paid to working conditions along the entire supply chain. Once they established the proper standards for mining companies, and indeed the entire supply chain, the system would have to be transparent and verifiable. No one had ever done this for the mining industry. So it was with these ideas in mind that a few days later Carter picked up the phone to call some NGO colleagues.

Background

Sam Walton founded Walmart in 1962, to bring big-city discounting to his corner of the rural American South. His idea was to offer the same range of merchandise found in nearby stores, but at about 20% lower prices every day rather than by short-term sales promotions. While this would lower his profit margins, he calculated that Walmart could triple gross sales. Furthermore, as the company grew Walton instilled a relentless drive in managers to lower costs by going directly to manufacturers, as well as by constantly increasing worker productivity.[1] As computer technologies became available, Walmart also developed a distribution network of state-of-the-art precision, enabling the company to predict consumer tastes but also to deliver goods where and when they were desired.[2]

Walton's formula was a phenomenal success. By 2004, Walmart had become the world's largest corporation and non-governmental employer. Net sales in fiscal 2009 exceeded US$400 billion, serving 200 million customers each week in over 8,400 stores worldwide; operating income reached US$24 billion.[3] Walmart accounted for approximately 10% of all retail sales in the US.[4]

Combined with its sheer size, Walmart's technological capabilities enabled the company to exert an unprecedented degree of control over not only its employees, but also its business partners (independent manufacturers, suppliers, and distributors).[5] A centralized management style placed high expectations on local managers, who routinely worked 60-hour weeks. While managers faced brutally demanding targets for cost containment and profitability, they were given an extraordinarily free hand with which to achieve them, the so-called 'tight/loose' management practice. As long as they acted within their mandate and with support from their superiors, this freedom empowered Walmart managers to pursue their own ideas with energy and creativity so long as they respected certain limits. Walmart's centralization represented a fundamental shift of market power to the retailer and away from manufacturers, in effect creating a near-monopsony – it could impose its will on partners to set prices, to package goods to fit Walmart requirements, and even to adopt management and accounting practices in accordance with Walmart requirements.[6]

---

1 See Robert Slater, The Walmart triumph: inside the world's #1 company, *Portfolio*, 2003, p. 30–34.

2 See James Hoopes, 'Growth through knowledge' in *Walmart: The Face of Twentieth Century Capitalism*, Nelson Lichtenstein (ed.), The New Press (2006), p. 91, and Misha Petrovic and Gary G. Hamilton, Making global markets, in Lichtenstein, ibid., p. 133.

3 Walmart Annual Report 2010, www.walmartstores.com/sites/annualreport/2010/financial_highlights.aspx.

4 Charles Fishman, *The Walmart Effect: How the World's Most Powerful Company Really Works – and How It's Transforming the American Economy*, Penguin Press, 2006, p. 103.

5 See Nelson Lichtenstein (ed.), *Walmart: The Face of Twentieth Century Capitalism*, The New Press, p. 11.

6 Petrovic and Hamilton, op. cit., p. 130.

The critics

Walmart's power and behaviour galvanized an army of critics and activists, who condemned its practices and began to mount grassroots protest campaigns, boycotts, and media attacks in an effort to tarnish the brand.[7] First, critics argued, Walmart had to somehow ameliorate its impact on the communities that it entered. Not only did they believe that Walmart destroyed local 'mom and pop' stores that could not compete on price, but it also generated the second-hand effects of increased traffic, reduced demand for other local businesses, such as competing shops and newspapers that lost advertising revenues, and imposed additional infrastructure costs that generated new tax burdens.[8]

Second, Walmart's labour practices, they demanded, had to improve. Employees must be allowed to unionize, earn better wages, obtain affordable health insurance benefits, and enjoy more humane treatment.[9] As it stood, many critics charged, the tight/loose management style forced managers to resort to degrading and even illegal practices in the relentless pursuit of 'improvements' in employee performance, allegedly in the form of unpaid over-time, the effective elimination of rest or meal breaks, and the exploitation of overseas sweatshop labour.[10]

Third, they charged, Walmart had to provide a more equitable and environmentally friendly management of its supply chain, from the treatment of 'sweatshop workers' in China by supply partners to its means of transportation. To meet these goals, many observers believed, Walmart would have to change its business model: the company would have to pay more for the goods and services it bought, which would diminish its razor-thin profit margins and necessitate higher prices. This would violate the principle behind Walmart's 'everyday low prices' formula.[11]

Walmart responds

For its first few decades of explosive growth, Walmart had ignored the critics as a matter of company policy. The company had virtually no lobbying presence in

---

7 See Maria Halkias, Walmart's urban push, *The Dallas Morning News*, November 1, 2005.
8 See Bill Quinn, *How Walmart is Destroying America (and the World) and What You Can Do About It*, Ten Speed Press, 2005, pp. 1–26.
9 According to Fishman, op. cit., pp. 240–1, in Tennessee 10,261 children of Walmart employees were enrolled in state health care for the poor; in Georgia, 9,617 Walmart associates were provided healthcare by state-aided programmes for the poor. Wake-Up Walmart claimed that one in seven US Walmart employees had no healthcare coverage and that a substantial number earned below the poverty line. See: www.wakeupwalmart.com/facts/#healthcare.
10 Ellen Israel Rosen, How to squeeze more out of a penny, in Lichtenstein, op. cit., pp. 245–246.
11 See Liza Featherstone, Walmart's P.R. war, Salon.com, August 2, 2005.

Washington, DC, and devoted little attention to its image.[12] That changed in 2004. Faced with mounting criticism and a momentarily declining stock price, then-Chief Executive Lee Scott decided that Walmart should become a more responsible company, to jump ahead of the curve in a move assailed by some as a blatant public relations counter-offensive.[13]

The first big success of Scott's new strategy was the company's relief efforts in 2005 on behalf of the victims of Hurricane Katrina in Louisiana and Mississippi. Scott, who claimed that the Katrina episode led to a personal 'epiphany', promised that this was only the beginning of the company's transformation.[14] Articulating a vision in cooperation with CI and other external groups, Scott promised that the company would become a leader in sustainability, reducing greenhouse gases produced by Walmart stores by 20% over the next seven years, enhancing the efficiency of its truck fleet, which was the largest in the US, and innumerable similar measures. Moreover, Scott emphasized, Walmart was taking steps to improve the treatment of its workers: health-care coverage would be provided to Walmart associates for as low as $25 per month. To further publicize these efforts, Scott even called on the US Congress to raise the minimum wage.[15]

Walmart began to take concrete steps to implement Scott's vision, which he disseminated within the company in a series of 'aspirational goals' that were realistic and transmitted a message of change – both internally and externally. With the help of consultants, Scott encouraged Walmart employees to undertake 'Personal Sustainability Projects', which were designed to educate them through voluntary activities, hopefully inspiring them to pursue their own sustainability initiatives. Later, employees elected 'sustainability captains' to communicate their goals and explain their activities to others in the company, eventually growing to include just under one third of all Walmart employees. In addition, Walmart began a number of initiatives to increase the transparency of the company's practices, including:

- a company-wide effort to identify and openly acknowledge 'environmental blind spots';

- a series of reports on its progress toward the aspirational goals;

- the opening of the company to constructive outside stakeholders.

---

12 Bethany Moreton, To Serve God and Walmart: The Making of Christian Free Enterprise, Harvard University Press, 2009, pp. 1–5.

13 Michael Barbaro, A new weapon for Walmart: a war room, The New York Times, November 1, 2005. From 2000 to 2005, Walmart's share price dropped approximately 20%; at that time, Walmart appeared to have reached the saturation point of its rural expansion strategy, necessitating a move into urban markets, where it faced a more effective political opposition.

14 See Robert Berner, 'Can Walmart wear a white hat?' BusinessWeek, October 3, 2005.

15 As cited in Pia Sarkar, Walmart's world view: giant retailer says it's ready to tackle hot-button issues, San Francisco Chronicle, 26 October, 2005.

Such transparency would, Scott stated, encourage employees to think in new ways, spark an influx of new ideas for improvement, and finally, uncover business opportunities that Walmart had not considered. It was not, in his view, merely greenwashing, as critics continued to charge.[16]

By early 2006, with the aid of CI under a consultancy arrangement, a group of Walmart executives were designating 'actionable priorities' they could pursue. Combining Walmart's sales data with environmental impact factors as articulated by the Union of Concerned Scientists, a science-based nonprofit advocacy group, they focused in on 14 areas, which were called 'Sustainable Value Networks'. (See Exhibit 1) In each of the 14 areas, Walmart assigned an Executive Vice President as sponsor along with a 'network captain', who was usually a Senior Vice President. Dee Breazeale was designated a network captain for jewellery. Like the others, she was mandated to contact academics, NGOs, suppliers, and other stakeholders to join discussions on sustainability measures that Walmart might undertake.[17] At this early stage, their actions were voluntary, according to Carter: 'Dee was acting on her own sense of responsibility, there was no obligation' for her or any other participants.

A native of Arkansas, Dee Breazeale went to a local university. At one time, she had worked as a backup singer to a Country Western band. She had been at Walmart for nearly two decades. After graduating with an MBA, she took an entry-level job as a merchandise assistant at Walmart on an hourly wage. Quickly recognizing her commitment to the company and high potential, her bosses recommended Breazeale for the management fast-track programme. She rotated through every area in the company, from real-estate, human resources, and marketing to information systems and operations. Later, Breazeale ran a district of stores in northern California, served three years in Germany with the international division, and returned to Arkansas as Vice President in the jewellery division. At Walmart, she recalled, 'I was allowed great autonomy to pursue my vision... You set a goal, get the signoff, and then you have the freedom to do it just about any way you want... If it didn't work, they [upper-level managers] let you try something different but just don't make the same mistake twice!'

During the internal discussions on sustainability in 2005, which led to the creation of Walmart's Sustainable Value Networks (SVN), Breazeale had become interested in contributing to the effort and participating in the jewellery SVN. 'I loved to take on more,' she explained. With the support of her boss, she also committed herself to interface with and represent the LGBT (Lesbian, Gay, Bisexual and Transgender) community in Walmart, which began to attract some critical attention in the local 'family' press. 'The typical role of the retailer was to buy product from the suppliers at the best price,' she recalled. 'I found the concept of digging into every

16 Adam Werback, *Strategy for Sustainability: A Business Manifesto*, Harvard Business Press, 2009, pp. 35–36; 92–118; 132–135; 157–158.
17 See Erica L. Plambeck, The Greening of Walmart's Supply Chain, *Supply Chain Management Review*, 1 July, 2007.

aspect of getting jewellery to market – transparently – a daunting task, but a very positive goal.'

The success of an SVN depended in large measure on the energy that their captains devoted to them. Nonetheless, the Walmart employees involved in them still had to accomplish their full-time jobs. Some critics worried that network captains and participating employees lacked the time either to devote themselves to these tasks or indeed to engage their minds in areas they had never had time to contemplate. With few exceptions, there were no new full-time staff hired to run the networks. Some of them, such as the packaging network, had 500 members or more; others, such as Breazeale's jewellery SVN, consisted of only 15 or so. Often, even Walmart's determined outside critics were invited to participate.[18]

Earthworks and the NGOs

When Stephen D'Esposito joined the NGO Earthworks in 1997, the 'extractive sector' – the mining of gold, diamonds, and other minerals – was viewed by activists as fragmented and unfocused, in spite of documented environmental degradation, ongoing health issues in mining communities, and innumerable instances where corporations had failed to correct or even examine their conduct. 'The premise,' he recalled, 'was that, due to the remoteness of mining sites, our leverage was severely limited.' As VP for Policy and later President and CEO, D'Esposito believed that a new approach, based on the entire life cycle of the products involved, would create opportunities to promote Earthworks' agenda in clean water, community health, and corporate social accountability. 'I wanted to work on the mining companies,' he explained, 'but also involve the refineries, the jewellers, and even the retailers at the end of the life-cycle chain.'

As a visible industry that was deeply concerned with branding, he believed that the jewellery sector offered the best opportunity to create influence throughout the overall sector. Indeed, gold mining was one of the dirtiest industries in existence. Not only was it getting more difficult to extract as deposits dwindled – to produce the gold for a single finger ring generated approximately 20 tons of waste, much of it toxic, including cyanide – and its slag was responsible for the pollution of waterways, vast areas were deforested, and it often displaced communities nearby.[19]

Over the previous decade, D'Esposito had helped to transform Greenpeace from a collection of local activist groups carrying out their own initiatives into an integrated, global advocacy and campaign organization. Through its provocative actions, Greenpeace could draw attention to the conduct of corporations or

---

18 Ylan Q. Mui, 'At Walmart, 'green' has various shades', *Washington Post*, November 16, 2007.

19 See Earthworks, 'Tarnished Gold? Assessing the jewellery industry's progress on ethical sourcing of metals,' March 2010.

governments that it deemed harmful to the environment. It was the quintessential 'protest NGO' that ran campaigns of opposition. Nonetheless, D'Esposito felt that a positive message–some species to protect, some specific environment to preserve– was key to his fundraising efforts. 'We preferred to build campaigns around saving an animal or a beautiful place, not just attack companies,' he explained. 'It is an over-simplification to say that NGOs must appear in opposition to MNCs to raise money,' he argued. 'That is repeated way too often.'

For Earthworks, D'Esposito resolved to combine protest actions with a more constructive engagement. The times, he observed, were changing: not only were efforts from within the extractive sector underway to create formal deliberative structures regarding sustainability, but in January 2000 a major mining accident in Baia Mare, Romania, had captured world media attention and led to demands for action.[20] There was also the example of 'conflict diamonds'. In the late 1990s, a grassroots campaign sought to restrict the exportation of diamonds as a means to finance civil wars in several countries, such as Sierra Leone and the Democratic Republic of Congo. In a few years, the conflict diamonds campaign led directly to the establishment of the Kimberly Process Certification Scheme, whereby the governments of diamond producing and importing countries would exchange only sealed packages of diamonds; traffickers in conflict diamonds would face criminal prosecution; and exporting countries violating its terms could be expelled from the scheme, in effect blocking their trade revenues. Backed by public opinion, the Kimberly Process was the result of a collaboration between the United Nations, governments, NGOs, and diamond producers. Not only did it succeed in curtailing trade in conflict diamonds, but it aided in the stabilization and development of fragile countries.[21]

Some MNCs in the extractive sector, D'Esposito was coming to believe, appeared ready to act as more responsible corporate citizens and even to take concrete steps. 'I found some companies were doing their own analyses,' he said. 'They had seen the writing on the wall' about sustainability and increasing consumer involvement, particularly in the luxury industry. For example, the mining company Rio Tinto was spearheading the Global Mining Initiative, which initiated a dialogue with stakeholders. To D'Esposito, this suggested that a more inclusive approach was becoming possible, relying on a network of groups – local activists, governments at various levels, and media, but also for-profit corporations – to pursue Earthworks' goals in negotiations with MNCs. 'We would start with pressure,' he said, 'but then try to collaborate if the [target] corporation should demonstrate some willingness to work with us.' It was a stick and carrot approach.

One key collaborator was Keith Slack, a campaign activist with Oxfam America. According to D'Esposito, 'He had the best early ideas. Earthworks needed him because we had weaknesses, we were small with limited reach… and lacked a well-known brand' among NGOs. As such, Earthworks was able to combine its

---

20 See UNEP/OCHA Report on the Cyanide Spill at Baia Mare, Romania.
21 See blooddiamonds.org/the-kimberly-process.

substantive expertise in the industry with Oxfam's ability to mobilize international protests against specific corporations or sectors via its regional and global activist networks. Raising awareness about the mining accident in Baia Mare, Romania, had been one of their early successes.

D'Esposito and Slack began to work with civil society leaders worldwide to establish a set of 'Golden Rules' for responsible mining that would form the basis of both a public advocacy campaign and segue into an engagement with mining companies and others in the supply chain. This included an in-depth analysis of best practices–a 'Framework for Responsible Mining' – that was co-sponsored by Tiffany & Co. By 2002, in addition to other initiatives, the efforts of D'Esposito, Slack, and other NGOs culminated in the No Dirty Gold campaign, which employed protest action as a means to leverage the industry to open negotiations.

By early 2004, No Dirty Gold had introduced the Golden Rules pledge (see Exhibit 2), to which signatories would commit themselves on a voluntary basis, in effect refusing to buy gold from suppliers that failed to respect human rights and its environmental criteria for mining. By signing, retailers acknowledged that they felt 'morally obligated' to address these issues. It was an unmistakable acknowledgment that gold suppliers were susceptible to pressure from consumer groups, setting a precedent for that sector of the mining industry.[22] The eventual goal was to create a multi-stakeholder system (of retailers, mining companies, manufacturers, and NGOs), similar to those that existed for wood products and diamonds, to independently verify compliance with the Golden Rules.[23] No Dirty Gold, they believed, would open the way to further dialogue with leaders from civil society organizations and industrial groups.

By late 2005, 17 of the world's most important retailers had signed on – most at the luxury end, including Tiffany & Co. and Cartier. But Walmart, Sears, and Target had not. 'That was when we initiated our "leaders and laggards" strategy,' D'Esposito said, according to which additional public pressure would be brought to bear. Walmart, he knew, might be attempting to change, but its managers so far had failed to respond to letters from the campaign.

In February 2006, Earthworks and Oxfam named Walmart a No Dirty Gold 'laggard' in a full page ad in the New York Times. After extensive discussions with Assheton Carter, Dee Breazeale extended an invitation on his recommendation to D'Esposito, Slack, and a few others to meet.

22 See John Tepper Marlin, 'The 'No Dirty Gold' campaign: what economists can learn from and contribute to corporate campaigns,' The Economics of Peace and Security Journal, Vol. 1, No. 2 (2006), pp. 57–60.

23 See www.nodirtygold.org/fact_sheet.cfm.

The Vancouver dialogue

CI was a NGO with a history of dialogue and negotiation with MNCs as a stake-holder; CI did not engage in protest campaigns against corporations from the out-side but chose instead to work with them closely and discreetly. CI's association with Walmart had begun in 2002, when biologist Peter Seligman, co-founder and CEO of CI, began to cultivate a friendship with Sam Walton's eldest son, Robert Walton, a member of the company's board. In 2004, this led to a consulting arrangement with CI, which was engaged to investigate opportunities and make recommendations for sustainability initiatives at the company.[24]

Assheton Carter had been attempting unsuccessfully to engage Walmart since 2003. He was tired of the lack of response and had felt tempted to move on to other projects. Nonetheless, he hoped, the consulting arrangement might open up the company. The moment, in his view, was unusually propitious. 'There was a shift in the concept of CSR [corporate social responsibility],' he said. It was moving, he believed, from a kind of elitist concern – 'of carping NGOs' – to a more democratic movement involving direct pressure from consumer activists in new areas, such as conflict diamonds, rare hardwoods, and sea resources. One method, he contin-ued, was to attack the brand of large MNCs in an effort to get them to direct their managers and business partners to act in a more ethical manner. Then his CI unit, the Center for Environmental Leadership in Business (CELB), could bring innova-tive approaches for sustainability to corporations. According to Carter, CI was not directly paid for its advice, but instead received donations in a general conserva-tion fund. 'Campaign NGOs play a vital role,' he explained, 'but are only part of a bigger process.'

Even more important, according to Carter, was a shift in focus: 'We are not just looking at environmental impacts like the "carbon footprint",' he said, 'but also at the core business itself. That is the way to establish *strategic* sustainability.' In other words, he saw it as his mission to move CSR into the heart of a company's business model from the peripheral, somewhat esoteric concerns that NGOs had long pur-sued. 'If you don't understand the business model,' he explained, 'you are not going to get anywhere. It's the starting point for real dialogue.' Otherwise, he cautioned, public relations concerns tended to dominate the results for MNCs, with simple actions tacked on after the business decisions had already been made. 'We want to open their eyes to sustainability. CELB's goal is transformational,' that is, to embed CSR and sustainability into everyday decision-making as a matter of course. This could only occur, he argued, when it was a component of the business model and hence part of the company's incentive systems that rewarded managers for per-formance. To do so, Carter explained, 'We would offer advice that was relevant to

24 Marc Gunther, 'The Green Machine,' Fortune, July 31, 2006.

their business concerns, but that also fit our mandate regarding sustainability... We were business consultants, but with our own agenda.'

From the first months of 2004, Carter had patiently attempted to establish a professional relationship with Breazeale. 'I began to educate Dee on the issues,' he recalled. 'It was very hard. She rarely had any time – every time we talked she was multi-tasking on something else. I wanted to know that she was taking what I had to say seriously, that she was committed. Sometimes weeks or months would go by with no response, but she always came back to me.' Carter was attempting to engage her in a number of processes:

- To gain her trust as an advisor.

- To provide basic information and context on the issues, in particular those beyond the normal purview of her job.

- To explain what she could expect from the various NGOs.

- To bring Walmart into formal, constructive dialogues with other stakeholders.

- To gain access to other sustainability leaders within Walmart.

- To keep concrete goals and missions at the forefront of the company's concerns.

- To formulate and help to implement company strategies.

In spite of the frustration, Carter had persisted. Eventually, this resulted in Breazeale's decisive action on his advice about rubies from Burma. Carter concluded: 'Dee wanted to engage with NGOs who were challenging Walmart...I facilitated conversations and kept things going.' They discussed many issues, including the idea of creating a line of jewellery that had traceable source materials.

In June 2006, Carter organized a meeting in Vancouver, Canada, which included mining companies, Tiffany & Co., Walmart, various NGOs, and many others. It was the culmination of a long effort to bring the stakeholders together. At the meeting, he introduced D'Esposito and Slack to Breazeale and her team. It was, he explained, a mixture of information and putting the companies on notice that there was a concerned activist community ready to take action. The suggestions from NGOs included signing onto the 'Golden Rules' standards for responsible mining and better controlling the use of recycled gold. They were suggesting putting the buying power of Walmart behind direct sourcing from specific mines as a way to create a dedicated chain-of-custody, that is, establish tighter control over the behaviour and policies of all segments in the supply chain.

For their part, most of the mining companies wanted to get the NGOs off their backs and saw that a line of traceable products might go some way to accomplish that. In addition, because Walmart and Tiffany & Co. – the end-users of mining products – were pushing the mining companies to work with NGOs, some recognized the advantages in doing so. Interestingly, according to Carter, the retailers learned that the mining companies Rio Tinto and Newmont were far more verti-cally integrated than they had thought.

D'Esposito and Slack took on the development of mining standards through IRMA, the Initiative for Responsible Mining Assurance, a multi-stakeholder effort that included mining companies, trade organizations, NGOs, retailers, and individ-ual consultants. Walmart indicated that, should IRMA come up with 'good stand-ards', it would incorporate them into its sustainability requirements. Nonetheless, it would be an extremely ambitious multi-stakeholder effort.

The Vancouver meeting was exciting for Breazeale. 'I wasn't plugged in at all to the NGOs and activist groups surrounding mining. I needed to educate myself to tear apart every step of the process and determine what path to take,' Breazeale recalled, 'so we [within Walmart] began to put our heads together and engage lead-ing mines and manufacturers to work together for a common goal.' Her chief collab-orator was Assheton Carter, who had become intimately involved with all aspects in the formulation of her sustainability initiatives at Walmart, including not just the provision of information, but also writing, editing, and commenting on documents for both public and confidential, in-company purposes, and sometimes even the implementation of its sustainability strategy. But Walmart did not pay him. While CI received funds from Walmart, as Oxfam and other NGOs did from many corpo-rations, Carter emphasized, his unit did not. 'My job never depended directly on Walmart funding,' he said.

Working together

After the Vancouver meeting, Breazeale and Carter invited D'Esposito and Keith Slack of Oxfam to the Bentonville, Arkansas, headquarters to continue the dia-logue. They began to brainstorm about what might be done concretely, perhaps even in the creation of sustainable product lines. 'It was the most intense half-day meeting – really good,' D'Esposito recalled, 'because it was all operational people leading it... We told them what we are doing, they asked me what they should do, where they might get traction.'

However, the IRMA effort turned into a time-consuming and frustrating episode that advanced at a glacial pace. A big issue was that Breazeale – and the Walmart col-leagues to whom she was delegating tasks – sometimes lacked the mental space to come up with ideas in new areas beyond their regular jobs. Unlike some other SVNs, they were not given any additional resources to fulfil their sustainability mission. For their part, the NGOs found the commitment onerous as well. According to Keith Slack, 'It required a real investment of time. NGOs don't have the bandwidth or resources to do this... We had to educate them and continually follow up on things, like reviewing the countless draft documents for the standards that we were trying to negotiate.'

Slack was disappointed in the mining standards that were emerging from Walmart. He also felt increasingly worried that the involvement of Oxfam might somehow co-opt the organization. 'We did not,' he emphasized, 'wish to see Oxfam's participation as an endorsement of the results. We wanted to talk and contribute, but that was as far as it went.' He did not want to be paid as a consultant, in his view, 'because that would have led to a loss of independence.' CI, he believed, 'could no longer publicly be critical when it is necessary.' Regarding the results, like many participants and observers, Slack was disappointed that representatives of the local communities were not sufficiently consulted as they went forward. 'Even though we had a constructive dialogue that allowed export input, it wasn't inclusive enough,' he explained. 'No one could speak on behalf of the miners or the people living nearby.'   Furthermore, Slack was concerned about the disposal of waste generated in the mining process (or 'tailings') as well as the regulation of mining in environmentally protected areas. Beyond that, he remained suspicious about Walmart's motives. 'The most important issue,' he concluded, 'was the treatment of Walmart labourers [employees]. I began to wonder if the whole sustainability effort was a way to deflect attention from that.'

According to Carter, 'Keith was unwilling to compromise on these issues, even when we [at CI] felt that we were making significant progress.' In Carter's opinion, the outcome had much more positive potential. 'We spent a lot of time trying to push the players to think,' he recalled. 'We didn't want them to take something off the shelf. We wanted to create something together, to be part of a process. Walmart saw itself as only a retailer, but we were arguing that there were immense scale-up possibilities, that the company could have a major impact by changing the way that it did things. They were listening.' For many months, Carter was also striving to convince mining companies – which were reluctant to deal with retailers because they were unaccustomed to collaborating with that segment of the supply chain – into a traceable jewellery deal. Nonetheless, he was confident that Breazeale could make things happen with Walmart's market clout.

By the end of the summer, Breazeale and Carter were championing the creation of a line of jewellery, later named 'Love, Earth®', all inputs of which would be able to be traced to sustainable sources and practices. Carter took on the role of doing much of the legwork for the project; beyond sustainability issues, this included input into the formulation of the business case, its sales goals, and the documents to present their ideas within the company. In particular, with a long-term commitment by vertically integrated suppliers, Carter and Breazeale advanced the arguments that a traceable line would carry a number of business advantages: (1) the creation of an exclusive jewellery line differentiated by its pioneering sustainability and unique design; (2) a less complex (or 'truncated') supply line, based on closer relations with suppliers, that should reduce prices of input materials; as well as (3) assure a more secure supply line; and (4) provide a guarantee of product quality for the duration of the arrangement.

In October 2006, the initiative suffered a number of serious setbacks. The IRMA negotiations on standards for an industry-wide certification system had apparently stalled. Carter reluctantly concluded that voluntary criteria only for Walmart, such as those in No Dirty Gold, would have to do for the time being. This would generate controversy among NGOs, some of which wanted to continue to push for a comprehensive voluntary agreement rather than a one-off commitment from Walmart. For other NGOs, not even a comprehensive voluntary agreement would be enough: they wanted governments to impose stricter regulations on the mining companies. Soon thereafter, Keith Slack exited the process, convinced that he could accomplish more from the outside. Perhaps worst of all, Dee Breazeale left Walmart to open her own consulting business, which threatened to derail the entire process. If her attention had appeared sporadic, at least she had known how to get things done from within the Walmart culture.

Love, Earth®

After some initial scepticism, Breazeale's successor, Pam Mortensen, became interested in the traceable jewellery project, though she needed to get up to speed on the issues. In Carter's view, they were starting over once again 'from square 1'. It was, he reasoned, just part of the cost of doing business with Walmart. As soon became evident, Mortensen brought her own inspiration and energy to the process. In Carter's opinion, Walmart was prepared to invest in a real business initiative with sustainability at the heart of its business model. On Mortensen's recommendation, Walmart finally signed the Golden Rules pledge in early 2007, and was taken off the Earthworks/Oxfam 'laggard' list.

By April, 2007, a concrete business plan emerged for a line of traceable jewellery, from mining to delivery for sale. The jewellery line would be designed and manufactured for Walmart, carrying an exclusive brand name. It would meet Walmart's sustainability goals, yet would not charge consumers any kind of green premium. Instead, the jewellery line would be affordable in accordance with Walmart's 'everyday low prices', ranging approximately from less than US$ 40 to no more than $150, which was not appreciably different from the other jewellery lines that Walmart currently sold. Finally, as a measure of success, traceable jewellery should account for 10% of all Walmart sales in both gold and diamond jewellery by 2010, which based on public figures would add up to approximately US$ 60 million and US$ 50 million respectively. 'Pam was a brilliant champion for the idea,' Carter said. The plan was finalized and approved in early 2008, though some pieces still had yet to fall into place, not least of which was assuring traceability.

For his part, Carter continued in his role as an advisor, coaching Mortensen on how to interact with NGOs, but also helping her to implement the project. 'We continued to run it together,' Carter explained, in a relationship based on trust and mutual respect rather than obligation. Soon, Carter was writing documents on behalf of Mortensen and Walmart, from internal memos to press releases and web materials. Carter also maintained relations with NGOs and the mining companies. Regarding Slack's departure, he understood that Oxfam as an organization no longer felt the outcomes likely to emerge from the traceable jewellery line would be sufficient to warrant its continued participation. In other words, Oxfam found that too many compromises had been made. According to Carter, 'Campaign NGOs face a real dilemma. Their opposition to MNC practices is their legitimate strategy to raise awareness about irresponsible business and is how they build their support base. They are comfortable and effective being unequivocal opponents, but they aren't sure how to constructively engage corporations and, at the same time, satisfy their supporters.'

Moreover, in his view, Slack and many other NGOs lacked the technical exper-tise in the extractive sectors that CI and Earthworks had developed. CI, for exam-ple, specifically sought to engage scientists and academics in their work. In Great Britain, Carter had earned a PhD in business strategy and sustainability in the international mining sector; he was able to write a business plan that would be profitable and do the right thing in accordance with his vision.

Without agreed-upon voluntary standards, Carter decided that separately nego-tiated criteria, a 'mini-certification scheme', was a viable option that also had the potential to revitalize other efforts. (See Exhibit 3 for Walmart Mining Criteria.) Carter based them largely on the Golden Rules pledge. To verify compliance, third-party inspectors were supposed to be allowed into the supply chain. Unfortunately, no matter what commitments they established, Carter acknowledged that some critics would denounce these as greenwashing from both Walmart and the mining companies.

There were also technical challenges to overcome. The principal problem with traceability was the complexity of inputs: any product could have hundreds of entry points along the supply chain. When it came to gold, the challenge was to differen-tiate sources when the refining process typically destroyed the possibility of tracing its origins: the output from multiple mines and even recycled gold were melted and mixed together into an indistinguishable molten mass. Furthermore, the labour practices of subcontractors in both processing and manufacturing jewellery would come under scrutiny and hence had to be controlled. Finally, Walmart's implemen-tation and oversight would also receive vigorous attention from activists. Would it be acceptable if any of these inputs were 'ethically tainted', that is, came from ques-tionable sources that employed unsustainable mining practices, paid the miners too little, or even used methods of transportation damaging to the environment? It appeared that there were few straightforward answers to these challenges. Any claim that Walmart made was guaranteed to receive minute critical scrutiny.

The mining companies Rio Tinto and Newmont agreed to join the effort as long-term partners. Newmont was highly vertically integrated: it had its own mines and refineries. This meant that Newmont could arrange to refine all the gold that it mined, making virtually all inputs traceable, from mining to manufacturing. Rio Tinto, it turned out, could accomplish a similar arrangement for both gold and diamonds. Both companies would use only their own mines (gold from the US, diamonds from Australia), which guaranteed their responsibility and control over all raw material inputs. To offer transparency to consumers – the opportunity to follow the overall process for sustainability – Carter found a software engineer, Tim

Wilson, who had created a wiki for collaborative input at each stage in the supply process. Carter introduced Wilson to Mortensen, who was leading the effort within Walmart for Love, Earth®. With her support, Walmart signed them on to the project immediately. Finally, the jewellery manufacturer Aurafin, which was owned by the philanthropist Warren Buffett, was brought on board.

Though Mortensen soon moved on to another job, her successor Gail Campbell oversaw the final stages of development of the Love, Earth® line of jewellery. By going online, a consumer could input the batch number of their purchase and instantly learn where and how it was mined, where it was refined, and who manufactured it, including details of the conditions they worked in. (See Exhibit 4, Love, Earth® Press Release; Exhibit 5, Process Comparison; Exhibit 6, Online Trace It; Exhibit 7 Example of Walmart Love, Earth® products and Trace It Batch Query Box.) Launched in July 2008, the process and product line were touted as a precedent-setting breakthrough, receiving wide coverage in the popular press.

EXHIBIT 1
Sustainable Value Network goals

Background. The Sustainable Value Networks were launched during the Business Sustainability milestone meeting on November 9th, 2005. Since that time, most of the Sustainable Value Networks have had a Network kickoff meeting with suppliers, supplier's suppliers, non-governmental organizations (NGOs), government organizations, academics and other external thought-leaders.

Network Deliverables. All Networks have completed the following deliverables:

- Identified 6 quick wins

- Identified at least one innovation project

- Developed an understanding of the systemic barriers to achieving 'big game change' (reaching full sustainability) and identified the critical success factors for overcoming those barriers

- Developed a draft product scorecard or metrics

Progress. In general, momentum and excitement continues to build and most networks have framed exciting projects that deliver business value and environmental performance. In addition to material economic and environmental benefits, common business benefits include:

- Expanding the internal network of working relationships – associates are working across organizations and functions to solve issues;

- Developing an external network of stakeholders, relationships and capabilities related to listening, internalizing and acting on new information and perspectives; and,

- Increased employee engagement and job satisfaction.

Opportunities. The common challenges that many networks are experiencing are:

- Resource issues – time commitments associated with learning our way into a new way of working;

- Ability to maintain ongoing productive relationships with external stakeholders outside of Network meetings;

- Getting suppliers out of an incremental mindset and truly innovating; and

- Gap between current global procurement function and a strategic, global sourcing function, designed to address sustainability issues and build capabilities in the extended supply chain.

In addition, we see opportunities to accelerate progress and results through competency building on key skills, including systems thinking, strategic planning and fact-based decision making.

For details on each network's deliverables, go to the intranet site, www.walmart-plus.com, and select the network you want in the upper right corner of the page. At the bottom of each network page is a downloadable .pdf file with the detailed report for that network.

Source: CELB.

Walmart Sustainable Value Networks

Greenhouse Gas

Sustainable Building

Alternative Fuels

Logistics

Waste

Packaging

Wood and Paper

Agriculture and Seafood

Textiles

Jewellery

Electronics

Chemical Intensive Products

Source: walmartstores.com/sustainability/7672.aspx.

EXHIBIT 2
Golden Rules Pledge

The Golden Rules

The Golden Rules are a set of criteria for more responsible mining. These criteria are based on broadly accepted international human rights laws and basic principles of sustainable development.

The No Dirty Gold campaign developed the Golden Rules based on extensive reviews of documents and research prepared by the mining industry, civil society organizations, scientific researchers and technical experts, international bodies such as the UN, the World Bank's Extractive Industries Review, and other multi-stakeholder processes.

The No Dirty Gold campaign calls on mining companies to meet the following basic standards in their operations:

- Respect basic human rights as outlined in international conventions and laws.

- Obtain the free, prior, and informed consent (FPIC) of affected communities.

- Respect workers' rights and labor standards, including safe working conditions.

- Ensure that operations are not located in areas of armed or militarized conflict.

- Ensure that projects do not force communities off their lands.

- Refrain from dumping mine waste into oceans, rivers, lakes, or streams.

- Ensure that projects are not located in protected areas, fragile ecosystems, or other areas of high conservation or ecological value.

- Ensure that projects do not contaminate water, soil, or air with sulfuric acid drainage or other toxic chemicals.

- Cover all costs of closing down and cleaning up mine sites.

- Fully disclose information about social and environmental effects of projects.

- Allow independent verification of the above.

Source: Earthworks and Oxfam, No Dirty Gold Brochure; www.nodirtygold.org/goldenrules.cfm.

EXHIBIT 3
The Walmart Voluntary Criteria

Walmart JSVN vision and principles for sustainable sourcing of jewellery

The vision of the JSVN is to provide Walmart and Sam's Club customers with affordable, quality products that aim to have a net positive effect on the environment and human health. We plan to achieve this vision by striving to ensure the application of the following principles in our supply chain throughout the life-cycle of our products:

1. Incorporation of lifecycle analysis into business decisions planning and management plans and to recover material value wherever possible

2. Continual improvement of health and safety performance

3. Efficient production and minimization of waste and pollution

4. Safe disposal and management of waste and hazardous materials

5. Protection of ecological functioning, ecosystem services and important bio-diversity and respect legally designated protected areas

6. Respect for the rights of individuals, indigenous peoples and communities

7. Respect for employee rights regarding safe working conditions and terms of employment

8. Contribution to the sustainable development of communities affected by operations

9. Transparency of sources and assurance of sustainability performance

10. Compliance with applicable laws, regulations and treaties at international, national, state and local level

Long Term Goal: 100% of gold, silver and diamonds used in the jewellery sold in Walmart will be sourced from mines and produced by manufacturers that meet Walmart's sustainability standards and criteria. We also want to incorporate recycled materials used in the jewellery by working with mines, refineries and manufacturers.

Target: By 2010 achieve 10% traceability of all diamonds, gold and silver in jewellery sold in Walmart from mines, refineries and manufacturers meeting Walmart's sustainability standards and criteria.

Long Term Goal – Packaging: All jewellery poly-bags to be bio-degradable and convert all pallets and all boxes to recyclable materials.

How the Walmart sustainability criteria are developed

To help us develop the Walmart criteria for responsible mining we reviewed many existing commitments and continuing initiatives on sustainable mining, including the International Council of Mining and Metal's (ICMM) Sustainable Development Framework, the Initiative for Responsible Mining Assurance's (IRMA) emerging standards for mine site assurance, the 10 Gold Rules put forward by the No Dirty Gold Campaign, the standards championed in the Framework for Responsible Mining, and the International Financial Organization's (IFC) environmental and social performance standards. While we have made all final decisions as to these criteria, over many months, we engaged and sought input from a wide spectrum of experts, some of which included Rio Tinto Ltd., Newmont Mining Corporation, Conservation International, Earthworks, World Wildlife Fund, and Oxfam America. We sought input from these organizations because of their perspective and energy they bring to advancing the sustainable development agenda. In line with their institutional policies, we understand that the valuable participation of these organizations does not imply their endorsement of the Love, Earth® product line or sourcing criteria.

Walmart's initial environmental and social sourcing criteria for mining and metals in jewellery

Company Criteria: Mines supplying precious metals and gemstones for jewellery sold in Walmart and Sam's Club stores are operated by companies that:

1. Are committed to incorporate the *principles of sustainable development* and the respect for human rights into policies and operating practices pursuant to the International Council on Mining and Metals Sustainable Development Framework or an equivalent standard;

2. Are signatories to and in compliance with the *Voluntary Principles on Security and Human Rights*;

3. Are signatory to the *Global Compact*;

4. Are committed to supporting the *Extractive Industries Transparency Initiative* practices;

5. Are signatory to the *World Economic Forum's Partnering Against Corruption* Initiative;

6. Seek to reduce *Greenhouse Gas Emissions* and report their emissions annually using a credible reporting protocol (for example The World Resources Institute and World Business Council on Sustainable Development Greenhouse Gas Protocol or the Carbon Disclosure Project);

7. Annually publish an externally assured *environmental and social performance report* using the Global Reporting Initiative guidelines and sector supplement, and AA1000 Assurance Framework, or equivalent process.

8. Adhere to *Kimberley Process* certification scheme and the World Diamond Council system of warranties where appropriate;

Mine Criteria: Mines supplying precious metals and gemstones for jewellery sold in Walmart and Sam's Club stores will:

9. Have in place policies and practices that uphold fundamental human rights and respect cultures, customs and values in dealings with employees including:[i]

    a. Elimination of forced, compulsory or child labor;

    b. Fair remuneration of employees that is in compliance with the local and national laws and consistent with the prevailing local standards in the countries of operation;

    c. Policies and practices designed to eliminate harassment and unfair discrimination;

    d. The freedom of association and the effective recognition of the right to collective bargaining;

   e. Maintain reasonable employee work hours in compliance with local standards and applicable laws;

   f. Provision of appropriate cultural and human rights training and guidance for all relevant staff, including security personnel;

When operating in zones of *armed conflict*, through initial due diligence and, thereafter, by careful monitoring of risk and in consultation with local communities and other stakeholders as appropriate, should seek to ensure that, through their actions or inaction, they are not benefiting from, supporting, contributing to, nor tacitly permitting human rights abuses or atrocities, either directly or indirectly.

Conduct public consultation and disclosure to achieve the *widest possible acceptance and support of communities* directly affected by project activities throughout the project's lifecycle from earliest exploration activities, prior to commencement of mining, during mine operations and through to closure;

Engage with communities directly affected by the project *on an ongoing basis and* in an inclusive and culturally appropriate manner, ensuring that their rights are respected and their interests and development aspirations are considered in major mining decisions and community-related programs; and implement and utilize compensation and a grievance and mediation mechanism where and when appropriate;

Seek to avoid or at least minimize involuntary resettlement of communities for new operations and expansion of existing operations and where this is unavoidable compensate fully, appropriately and fairly for adverse effects on individuals and communities with the objective of improving or at least to restore the livelihoods, standards of living, and living conditions of displaced people;

Complete an *environmental and social impact assessment*, including an analysis of mine closure, that follows credible and recognized guidelines for impact assessment (for example the US National Environmental Policy Act (NEPA) and International Association for Impact Assessment (IAIA));

Utilize a recognized *environmental management system* that explicitly states the company's environmental policy and objectives and includes management plans, as is appropriate, for acid rock drainage, water, cyanide, mercury, waste management, overburden, tailings, and releases (for example, the International Standards Organization 14001 standard);

Prepare an *appropriate closure and reclamation plan* for the operation that includes a financial guarantee, sureties or provisions, to meet costs of closure and reclamation;

Certification under the *International Cyanide Management Code (ICMI)* Verification Protocol, where cyanide is used;

Implementation of emerging MACT (Maximum Achievable Control Technology) where by-product *mercury* is produced, pursuant to the Nevada Administrative Code, for point source air emissions;

Adopt *tailings management* practices that maintain terrestrial, marine and river ecosystem functioning and services at the landscape scale;

Not operate in *World Heritage Sites* and sites of *critically important biodiversity,*[ii] including *Alliance for Zero Extinction* sites and *protected areas categorized as 1 and 3 under The World Conservation Union (IUCN)* system of Protected Area Management Categories;[iii]

Adopt practices that contribute to the long-term conservation of species and the integrity of biotic communities, ecosystem processes and services;

Compensate within a landscape context for any significant residual adverse impacts on biodiversity, and the direct users of biodiversity, after appropriate avoidance, minimization and reclamation (rehabilitation) measures have been taken;

Develop and maintain an Emergency Response Plan, in collaboration with local communities and relevant agencies, pursuant to guidance provided by Awareness and Preparedness for Emergencies at the Local Level (APELL);

Comply with, at a minimum, applicable host country *laws and regulations.*

---

i Criteria 8 and 9 have been in part guided by Walmart's Stores Inc., Standards for Suppliers, The International Finance Corporation (IFC), Performance Standard 2: Labor and Working Conditions; the International Council of Mining and Metals, Sustainable Development Principle 3; the UN Global Compact; and, a number of international conventions negotiated through the International Labour Organization (ILO) and the United Nations (UN) including:

ILO Convention 87 on Freedom of Association and Protection of the Right to Organize
ILO Convention 98 on the Right to Organize and Collective Bargaining
ILO Convention 29 on Forced Labor
ILO Convention 105 on the Abolition of Forced Labor
ILO Convention 138 on Minimum Age (of Employment)
ILO Convention 182 on the Worst Forms of Child Labor
ILO Convention 100 on Equal Remuneration
ILO Convention 111 on Discrimination (Employment and Occupation)

ii Sites with habitat required for the survival of critically endangered or endangered species; 4 areas having special significance for endemic or restricted-range species; sites that are critical for the survival of migratory species; areas supporting globally significant concentrations or numbers of individuals of congregatory species; areas with unique assemblages of species or which are associated with key evolutionary processes or provide key ecosystem services; and areas having biodiversity of significant social, economic or cultural importance to local communities.

iii There may be unique situations where the development of a mine can benefit or enhance the conservation and protection of valuable ecosystems. If it can be demonstrated that material benefit from mining will occur – a 'net-positive' outcome - development in these areas may be considered.

Source: CELB.

EXHIBIT 4
Love, Earth® press release

Walmart adds a new facet to its fine jewellery lines: traceability

Retailer partners with Conservation International to launch Love, Earth® jewellery and new sustainable criteria

Bentonville, Ark. and Arlington, Va. – July 15, 2008 – Walmart Stores, Inc. (NYSE: WMT) today launched Love, Earth® jewellery , its first completely traceable fine jewellery line available exclusively at Walmart stores, Sam's Club locations and on Walmart.com and Samsclub.com.

Marking a shift in how affordably-priced fine jewellery is produced and sold, the new line is the result of collaboration between Walmart, Conservation International (CI) and Walmart's supply chain partners. It will give customers the ability to trace the path of their Love, Earth® jewellery from mine to store by simply going online.

Love, Earth® is the retailer's first step toward having all of the gold, silver and diamonds used in the jewellery sold in its Walmart stores and Sam's Club locations come from mines and manufacturers that meet Walmart's sustainability standards and criteria. The criteria address both environmental, human rights and community issues. By 2010, the retailer aims for at least 10 percent of its jewellery offerings to achieve these standards.

'Walmart recognizes that our customers care about the quality of their jewellery and its potential impact on the world,' said Pam Mortensen, vice president and divisional merchandise manager for Walmart. 'With Love, Earth®, customers are getting an affordable and beautiful piece of jewellery that also helps sustain resources and strengthen communities.'

Consumers can visit www.loveearthinfo.com to see where their Love, Earth® jewellery was mined and manufactured, and learn about suppliers' environmental and social programs. The site also offers information about the standards used to select suppliers and ensure the entire process is more sustainable.

'With its considerable influence, market reach and commitment to sustainability, Walmart has brought together like-minded suppliers, mining companies and conservation partners to work together to build a traceable jewellery supply chain at an impressive scale,' said Dr Assheton Stewart Carter, Senior Director of Business Policies and Practices at Conservation International.

'We hope others in the jewellery industry will follow this leadership example and thus enable consumers to make simple choices that benefit the environment and mining communities when shopping for jewellery.'

To create Love, Earth®, Walmart selected partners in the mining and jewellery manufacturing industries that already demonstrated environmental and social leadership, including Rio Tinto, an Anglo-Australian mining company; Newmont Mining Corporation, a global gold producer headquartered in Denver, Colorado; and Aurafin, a Florida-based jewellery manufacturer. During the next phase of the partnership, the retailer plans to expand the number of approved mining and man-ufacturing suppliers and introduce diamonds in the Love, Earth® line.

The Walmart Love, Earth® collection is made from 10 karat gold and sterling sil-ver; the Sam's Club collection from 14 karat gold and sterling silver. Each collection includes fashion pendants, hoop earrings, bangles and fashion beads. Created with gold and silver, the Love, Earth collection is designed to symbolize the Earth's ele-ments and based on the precepts of recycle, reduce, and respect.

Want to trace a piece of Love, Earth® jewellery from mine to market?

Go to www.loveearthinfo.com, find the 'Trace it from Mine to Market' box and enter: SMPM88.

Source: Walmart and CI.

EXHIBIT 5
Process comparison

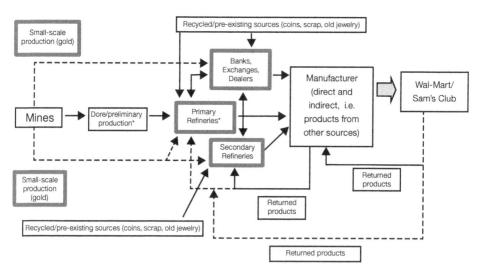

Current Gold jewelry Supply Chain

*Dore production and primary refineries are often part of large-scale industrial mining operations.

Boxes in grey show links that produce ores/metals that are most difficult to trace.

'Love, Earth®' Actual Chain of Custody

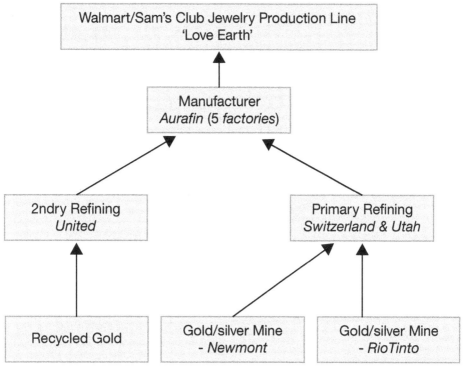

Source: CELB.

EXHIBIT 6
Online Trace It

Product History

Walmart Stores Inc Retailer - USA Love Earth Jewellery [147713]

Aurafin Jewellery Design and Manufacture - USA Tagged Love. Earth® Item| 147856 |

Exportadores Bolivianos S.R.L Jewellery Manufacturer - Bolivia 06 Castings[4 batches]

Arin Jewellery Manufacturer - Peru 05 Rope[2 batches]

Aurafin Jewellery Design and Manufacture - USA Gold bars[144775]

Kennecott Utah Copper Mining and Refining - -- Gold bars[144667]

Exportadores Bolivianos S.R.L Jewellery Manufacturer - Bolivia 07 Rope[146493]

Aurafin Jewellery Design and Manufacture - USA Gold bars[2 batches]

Kennecott Utah Copper Mining and Refining - -- Gold bars[2 batches]

Aurafin Jewellery Design and Manufacture - USA Silver bars[2 batches] | Gold bars[140543]

Kennecott Utah Copper Mining and Refining - -- Silver bars[2 batches] | Gold bars[139353]

Spiral Heart Pendant

The Love, Earth® sterling silver and 10K spiral heart pendant. This pendant represents the spiral of positive effect that each of us has on the Earth.
Each piece in the Love, Earth® family is created with materials from responsible sources and can be traced to its origin.

Batch Details

Batch No: 785ZT0019/080527

Source: www.loveearthinfo.com

EXHIBIT 7
Love, Earth® – Walmart Collection

B

D'Esposito remained distinctly uneasy about the name Love, Earth®, which he felt oversold the reality of the programme. 'It was fair to say that the operators were committing themselves to act responsibly at their sites and this was positive, but the brand name was too aggressive,' he believed. The multi-stakeholder process, the criteria, and the supply chain tracking system were very important advances,' he said, 'but we wanted to be very clear that Earthworks was not in the business of endorsing products.' D'Esposito felt that this struck the right balance of support and encouragement, while signalling that more needed to be done. For the time being, Earthworks took a public position supporting the underlying programme as an important step by Walmart.

However, this was a controversial decision both in the NGO community and even within Earthworks. Many felt that the programme did not go far enough – particularly the sustainability criteria. Others felt uncomfortable expressing any kind of support for Walmart. Moreover, when the programme was announced, a number of community groups near the participating mine sites expressed concerns that the participating mining companies, in their view, had failed to adequately address issues they had raised. Earthworks understood their concerns and had attempted to set up meetings to resolve them, both during the project's development and afterwards.

In spite of all this, D'Esposito felt that it was important to publicly acknowledge the progress that this represented, i.e. in both the chain of custody and the criteria. He also took the view that Earthworks, which had remained at the negotiating table through the entire process, had gotten enough – not everything it wanted, but more than had ever been achieved to date in the mining industry and with a retailer, Walmart.

It was at that moment, in October 2008, that D'Esposito left Earthworks to become president of Resolve, an organization designed to facilitate collaboration and forge partnerships between NGOs, corporations, and other civil society stakeholders. He had spent 10 years there. In April, 2010 Carter left CI to take a position as Senior Vice President for Global Engagement and Strategy at Pact, where he pursued sustainability projects as a contract consultant with developmental agencies and mining, oil, and gas companies.

Perhaps the most controversial issue was the implementation of Love, Earth®. At the beginning of 2011, Jean Friedman-Rudowsky, a freelance writer in Bolivia, produced a scathing assessment of Love, Earth®. Among many critical observations, she concluded that:

- Aurafin operated sweatshops in Bolivia, paying wages 10% below the legal minimum wage and engaging in brutal suppression of workers' rights, including firings in retaliation for worker protests;

- Rio Tinto and Newmont continued to rely on extraction methods that were extremely deleterious to the environment;

- Walmart had failed to allow independent, third-party inspectors to verify compliance. Many entries on the website appeared to have been done for purely public relations purposes.[25]

Friedman-Rudowsky's article set off a flurry of denunciations by activists opposed to Walmart, most of them repeating her findings adding corroborating or additional information to make their case. One blogger claimed to have discovered that a senior manager for Walmart sustainability communications, Kory Lundberg, said that independent auditors had been 'unable to substantiate the allegations' in the Friedman-Rudowsky article, only to admit later that the auditor was a Walmart employee and not independent.[26]

An important sign was the increasingly critical assessment of Love, Earth® from Earthworks, which sent a letter to S. Robson Walton, chairman of the board and son of the founder. The letter called on the company to live up to its promises to adhere to the Golden Rules. 'From mine to manufacturer,' the letter stated, 'Love, Earth®'s supply chain is riddled with environmental and human rights problems that are not compatible with an eco-friendly label.'[27]

For his part, Carter remained a strong supporter of the effort. Not only had Walmart hugely surpassed its goal of making 10% of its jewellery sales completely traceable, he argued, but it had set an example for other corporations in the sector. According to Carter, Love, Earth® accounted for 30% of Walmart's jewellery sales. 'It's the strongest programme of its kind in existence,' he said, 'and Walmart set the bar. Many companies are saying, "If Walmart can do it, why can't we?"' The traceability approach – engaging a vertically integrated mining group to control all inputs – was said to be spreading to other areas in Walmart, such as products containing tin and other 'conflict minerals'. 'These groups look to Love, Earth® to shape their strategies,' Carter claimed. Outside groups, such as the Responsible Jewellery Council and Cartier, were also said to have been inspired by Walmart's experiment.

---

25 See 'Walmart's 'Love, Earth®' Jewelry Line Doesn't Live Up to Green Promises," Miami New Times, 6 January, 2011.
26 www.treehugger.com/files/2011/01/real-picture-behind-walmarts-love-earth-jewelry-line.php
27 www.earthworksaction.org/publications.cfm?pubID=488

Both he and D'Esposito believed that many of Friedman-Rudowsky's criticisms of the programme were 'the same old accusations' that were routinely trotted out by activist opposition groups – charges that remained disputed and for the most part added nothing new. However, Carter acknowledged that Walmart had perhaps 'taken its eye off the ball' regarding independent verification. The company was, he said, re-evaluating its position in order to formulate a response to Friedman-Rudowsky's allegations.

CASE 3

Sustainable development at PepsiCo*

Debapratim Purkayastha and Adapa Srinivasa Rao

> Great companies are built to succeed today, tomorrow, and well into the
> future. Our commitment to balancing excellent operating performance
> with sustainable business practices is a big reason PepsiCo has become
> one of the world's top performing food and beverage companies.[i]
>
> *Indra Nooyi, Chairman and CEO of PepsiCo,*
> *in September 2011*

Since mid-2011, PepsiCo's Chairman and CEO, Indra Nooyi (Nooyi), had been facing some difficult questions. During the first five years of her tenure at the helm of
the consumer packaged goods major, Nooyi had been credited with transforming
PepsiCo by spearheading the company's sustainable development journey with
her 'Performance with Purpose' strategy. But since mid-2011, she had been facing
criticism that this had come at the cost of marketing and positioning of PepsiCo's
products to boost sales.

Faced with environmental and social criticism, PepsiCo started an ambitious new
sustainable development program called 'Performance with Purpose' in 2009. The

ICMR
IBS Center for Management Research
www.icmrindia.org

five-year mission was based on the philosophy that that the organization should not only keep focus on financial performance but also on its responsibilities. The new program listed 47 commitments that PepsiCo had toward society and these came under four broad areas: performance, human sustainability, environmental sustainability, and talent sustainability. The first commitment was to its shareholders to give good returns for their investments while the others were to its other stakeholders. PepsiCo took several steps to fulfill its commitments. It increased the content of fruits, vegetables, nuts, grains, and low-fat dairy in its global product portfolio. It achieved a positive water balance in India where it had been involved in controversies regarding the use of groundwater for its operations. It introduced several affordable and nutritious products for the underprivileged sections of society and reduced the use of electricity and fuel for its operations. It also undertook several steps to increase the diversity of its workforce around the world. For the year 2011, PepsiCo was named the top food and beverage company in the DJSI Food and Beverage Super sector and was included in the Dow Jones Sustainability Indexes[1].[ii] PepsiCo was the only company based in the US to earn the top ranking in the 19 super sectors assessed for the year 2011. This was the third consecutive year that the company had been named the leader in the beverage sector. The top ranking achieved by PepsiCo was the result of its focus on sustainable development practices around the world, according to some analysts.

However, with PepsiCo's flagship cola brand Pepsi being relegated to the #3 position in the US market behind arch-rival The Coca Cola Company's[2] (Coca Cola) Coke and Diet Coke, key stakeholders such as shareholders and bottlers had begun to question Nooyi's focus. They contended that her philosophy had also led her to back 'Pepsi Refresh' and social-responsibility positioning of the same kind, and that this had cost the company in terms of the sales of the products themselves. In addition to this, they felt that the company's revamped food product lines had produced mixed results. Moreover, despite all the measures taken under the new sustainable development program, PepsiCo still continued to face criticism from certain quarters regarding the social and environmental impact of its business practices.

Company background

The origins of Pepsi date back to the late 19th century when a young pharmacist Caleb Bradham (Bradham) started selling a refreshing drink called 'Brad's Drink' in his pharmacy. The drink was later renamed Pepsi-Cola after the digestive enzyme

---

1 Dow Jones Sustainability indexers are a group of indexes which evaluate the world's leading companies in their sustainability practices.

2 The Coca Cola Company, headquartered in Atlanta, Georgia, US, is a maker of non-alcoholic drinks. It is best known for its flagship product Coke. Its revenue and profit for the fiscal year 2010 were US$ 35.12 billion and US$ 11.81 billion respectively.

pepsin[3] used in the recipe. The sales of Pepsi soon started to increase. This convinced Bradham to form a company called the Pepsi-Cola Company. Bradham got an official patent for the drink in 1903 and then started to sell it in bottles. The business showed spectacular growth and Bradham sold 7,968 gallons of the drink in the year 1903. He later started to award franchises to grow his business and the Pepsi-Cola Company's franchisees spread to 24 states of the US. The strong franchise system developed by Bradham was one of the main reasons for Pepsi's initial success. The sales of Pepsi also reached 100,000 gallons by 1910. The outbreak of World War I, however, affected the company's business due to fluctuations in the price of sugar. It was bankrupt by the year 1923. Bradham sold the Pepsi-Cola trademark to Craven Holdings Corporation and resumed his pharmacy business. Pepsi Cola Company was declared bankrupt for a second time in the year 1931 as the Great Depression[4] affected its sales.

Pepsi's fortunes changed when its assets were purchased by a successful candy manufacturer Charles G. Guth (Guth). Guth had been thinking of selling his own soft drink at his stores after Coca Cola declined to give him a discount on its drinks. He reformulated the Pepsi formula and started to sell it in 12-ounce bottles at a cheaper price than its competitors. Under Guth's leadership, Pepsi grew to be a national brand once again. The Pepsi-Cola Company started to expand into international markets like the Soviet Union, Latin America, and Canada. After the end of World War II, Pepsi-Cola Company's international headquarters were moved to Manhattan and it continued to expand further into international markets. In 1964, it introduced some other successful soft drinks to its product portfolio like 'Diet Pepsi' and 'Mountain Dew'.[iii]

Pepsi-Cola Company and Frito-Lay, the world's largest maker of snack chips in the world, were merged in the year 1965 to form PepsiCo Inc. (PepsiCo). PepsiCo soon started to diversify into the restaurant business to generate faster growth for the company. It purchased Pizza Hut in 1977, Taco Bell in 1978, and Kentucky Fried Chicken in 1986. With these takeovers, PepsiCo emerged as the world leader in the restaurant business. PepsiCo's operations were split in 1986 with the beverage operations being combined under PepsiCo Worldwide Beverages and snack food operations under PepsiCo Worldwide Foods. In 1986, PepsiCo purchased 7-Up International, the third largest franchise soft drink outside the US.

By 1990, PepsiCo's revenues had reached US$17.80 billion and it was ranked in the top 25 of the Fortune 500[5] companies. Its revenues further increased to US$30.42 billion by the year 1995 and it became the world's third largest employer. But, the company's performance had deteriorated by the year 1996, both in the domestic and international markets due to intense competition from Coca-Cola. For the year

3 Pepsin is an enzyme released by the cells in the stomach. It degrades the food proteins into peptides.
4 The Great Depression was a worldwide economic depression that started in 1929 and lasted till the late 1930s.
5 Fortune 500 is the list of top 500 US companies published by the *Fortune* magazine.

1996, the beverages division of PepsiCo posted an operating profit of just US$582 million. Many analysts felt that the main reason for PepsiCo's decline in performance was its diversification into the restaurant business. Many other restaurant chains were also not willing to offer PepsiCo's products in their outlets as it owned a restaurant business which directly competed with them. So PepsiCo decided to restructure its business and spin off its restaurant business as an independent publicly traded company called Tricon Global Restaurants, Inc. The spin-off was completed in October 1997. Tricon was later renamed Yum! Brands Inc. in the year 2002. PepsiCo decided to focus on its packaged foods business to effectively compete with Coca Cola. It also acquired Tropicana, the world's biggest producer of branded juices, in July 1998. Other steps taken by PepsiCo included hiving-off of its bottling operations into a separate new company called Pepsi Bottling Group (PBG). The restructuring efforts paid off and its operating profits rose from US$2.58 billion for the year 1998 to US$3.23billion in 2000. In the year 2000, PepsiCo acquired Quaker Oats, a food conglomerate. The acquisition was aimed at offering healthier alternatives to its consumers. The new acquisition was aimed at capturing a new trend among the consumers who were abandoning carbonated drinks in favor of bottled waters, herbal teas, and juice drinks.

Controversies surrounding PepsiCo

Despite its spectacular turnaround, PepsiCo started facing criticism regarding the effect of its operations on the environment. In the early and mid-2000s, it faced controversies regarding the usage of water for its bottling operations which reportedly caused water shortages in some parts of India and the US. In India, PepsiCo faced controversies regarding its usage of water as water shortages were getting acute in the country due to the rapid increase in population. PepsiCo was accused of diverting water, which could be used for drinking purposes, for making its beverage products. Critics said PepsiCo's excessive reliance on groundwater for making its products had resulted in a shortage of drinking water in the areas in which it operated. Activists from 13 Indian states launched a campaign against companies such as PepsiCo for exploitation and pollution of groundwater. Commenting on the business practices of beverage companies, a prominent social activist said, 'Coke and Pepsi are engaged in a water war against India. Their bottling plants are stealing millions of liters of water, denying local communities their fundamental right to water.'[iv]

In 2003, the village council of Pudussery, a village in the south Indian state of Kerala, revoked the water-use license of a bottling plant of PepsiCo, alleging that its operations in the area had resulted in water shortage in the village.[v] But Pepsi denied that its operations had led to depleting water resources in the areas. However, it accepted that it depended on groundwater for its bottling operations.[vi] PepsiCo along with Coca Cola faced the wrath of judiciary when the High Court of India's southern state Kerala criticized them and commented that, '(ground) water belongs to people, not to Coke and Pepsi...'[vii] PepsiCo faced similar allegations over its usage of groundwater in some areas of the US where it had its bottling operations.

PepsiCo also faced criticism from activist groups regarding the effect of its products on the health of its consumers. In 2006, PepsiCo faced a huge controversy in India when the Center for Science and Environment (CSE), a public interest research and advocacy organization based in India, alleged that the level of pesticides in its soft drinks exceeded the safety standards prescribed by the regulatory bodies. PepsiCo refuted the allegations saying that the pesticide residuals found in its beverage products were within the limits prescribed by the concerned regulatory body. It said that it followed the same quality standards in India that it followed across the globe. Commenting on the controversy, Nooyi said, 'For somebody to think that Pepsi would jeopardize its brand – its global brand – by doing something stupid in one country is crazy.'[viii]

PepsiCo questioned the CSE report and the data gathering techniques employed by the organization. The Government of India stood by PepsiCo. But Kerala temporarily banned the sales of beverage products made by PepsiCo.[ix] Several other Indian states too banned the sale of PepsiCo's products in government-run schools and colleges.[x] The High Court of Kerala later lifted the ban, which was subsequently upheld by India's Supreme Court subsequently.[xi] The sales of PepsiCo's products came down drastically. Analysts said that more than the sales, it was the reputation of PepsiCo and the other beverage companies that had taken a beating due to the controversy.

Another controversy that PepsiCo was involved in was with regard to the contents of its snack and beverage products, which critics said, led to an increase in health problems like obesity and diabetes. Critics said that PepsiCo was not focusing on making healthy low calorie products but was expanding its product base in the high calorie segments. PepsiCo also faced the wrath of activist groups with regard to the effect its products were having on the health of children. Activist groups accused PepsiCo of marketing products with high calorie contents to children, leading to health risks at a younger age. Some research directed at junk food found that repetitive advertisements targeted at children could influence their purchasing decisions towards high calorie junk food.[xii]

Some other controversies faced by PepsiCo were the impact that the contents used in manufacturing and packaging its products were having on the environment. Its beverage products were packed in plastic bottles and tin cans, which environmental activists alleged, could cause environmental pollution. Other companies in the beverages and snacks sector, such as CocaCola, also faced similar controversies. In 2003, Coca-Cola was accused of dumping the waste generated in its bottling plants as fertilizer on farmers. In a study conducted by the BBC's Radio 4, it was found that Coca Cola had supplied wastes from its bottling plant in Kerala to farmers as fertilizer. These contained dangerous toxic metals like cadmium and lead.[xiii] When cadmium entered the human body, it slowly accumulated in the kidneys and caused kidney failure. Lead could cause mental retardation and anemia. The study was conducted by the BBC on the basis of complaints received from local people about groundwater levels becoming depleted due to Coca Cola's operations in that area.

Sustainable development practices of PepsiCo

PepsiCo has overtaken its archrival Coca Cola in 2005 and has grown to nearly twice the size of the latter. For the year 2010, Coca Cola's revenues stood at US$35.12 billion while that of PepsiCo stood at US$57.84 billion (Refer to Exhibit I for the consolidated income statement of PepsiCo from 2006–10). PepsiCo's tremendous growth was possible because of a shift in its focus from the beverages business and the mergers and acquisitions it has undertaken in the 1990s and later. After overtaking Coca Cola in terms of revenues, PepsiCo decided to focus on corporate sustainability to differentiate itself from Coca Cola. The growth in its business led to more controversies regarding its operations.

In the face of growing criticism, PepsiCo started to focus more on sustainable development practices worldwide. It started a new sustainable development program in 2009. The program was started with a five-year mission 'Performance with Purpose' under the leadership of Nooyi, who took charge as CEO in 2006 (Refer to Exhibit II for the performance with purpose mission of PepsiCo). The India-born Nooyi was a graduate from Madras Christian College in chemistry, physics, and mathematics, and a management graduate from the Indian Institute of Management, Calcutta. She also had a Master's in Public and Private Management from Yale. After stints with companies such as ABB,[6] Johnson and Johnson,[7] and management consulting firm Boston Consulting Group, she joined PepsiCo as chief strategist in 1994. She served as the Senior Vice-President of Strategic Planning and Development and Chief Financial Officer of PepsiCo before becoming CEO.

The 'Performance with Purpose' mission was based upon the belief that the financial performance of the organization must go hand-in-hand with its responsibilities toward society and the environment. The declaration by PepsiCo called the 'The Promise of PepsiCo' had 47 commitments, which would guide the organization for the following decade.[xiv] (Refer to Exhibit III for PepsiCo's Goals and Commitments) The 'Performance with Purpose' mission constituted both promises made to its shareholders for providing good financial returns and promises to society and the environment.[xv] In its promise to shareholders viz. 'Performance', PepsiCo vowed to deliver superior and sustainable financial performance to maximize their wealth. PepsiCo's responsibilities toward society and the environment

6 ABB is a multinational headquartered in Zurich, with operations in power and automation technology.
7 Johnson and Johnson is a global American pharmaceutical, medical devices, and consumer packaged goods manufacturer.

were broadly categorized into three areas viz. human sustainability, environmental sustainability, and talent sustainability. Human sustainability referred to the efforts made by PepsiCo to meet the different nutritional needs of the people. Environmental sustainability focused on protecting the environment and reducing PepsiCo's reliance on natural resources and conserving them for future generations. It also focused on mitigating the impact of its operations on the environment. Talent sustainability focused on developing its employees by developing the skills required to meet its growth needs and for making PepsiCo an attractive target for the world's best brains.

Commenting on PepsiCo's initiatives in sustainable development, Nooyi said, 'The talents and skills of our global workforce, coupled with our operational capabilities, provide PepsiCo with a unique opportunity to have a positive impact on society. The goal of our sustainable development journey is to operate as a force for bringing greater good to the world.'[xvi]

The new sustainable development program initiated at PepsiCo was part of an overall realization among many business organizations regarding the strategies to deal with a future where resources were limited. Commenting on the realization among business organizations, Jonathan Kaplan, senior policy specialist at Natural Resources Defense Council[8], said, 'Food manufacturers, in general, are closer to recognizing that we're headed toward a future with finite resources, where water, grain, and other inputs are less available and more expensive. Companies that figure out how to become part of the solution will have an advantage.'[xvii]

Performance

As per the Performance promise to its shareholders, PepsiCo made a lot of commitments regarding the performance of PepsiCo. The Performance promise included growing its international revenues at a rate which was double the global GDP growth rate. PepsiCo promised to achieve this through a series of measures. It promised to increase its market share of the beverage and snack products in the top 20 markets. It also promised to improve the brand equity scores for PepsiCo's brands in the top 10 markets. Other measures included expanding the division operating margins, increasing cash flow in proportion to the growth in the net income growth, delivering the best possible returns in the industry to its share holders, and following high standards of corporate governance.

Human sustainability

PepsiCo's human sustainability initiatives focused on helping people live healthy lives by offering them a healthy portfolio of products which were also enjoyable. As per the commitments given by the company with regard to its products, PepsiCo promised to increase the content of fruits, vegetables, nuts, grains, and low-fat dairy

---

8 Natural Resources Defense Council, headquartered in New York, USA, is an international environmental advocacy group.

in its global product portfolio. It also promised to reduce the amount of sodium, saturated fat, and added sugar in its products by 25, 15, and 25 percent respectively. As per its commitments regarding its marketing practices under human sustainability, PepsiCo also promised to display calorie count and key nutrients on its product labels, restrict selling some of its products to children under the age of 12, and eliminate the sale of products which were primarily made of sugar in all schools around the globe by 2012. PepsiCo said it would invest more in businesses and research and development activities to produce more nutritious products which were affordable for the low-income communities around the globe. PepsiCo also proposed to promote healthier communities by enhancing the diet and physical activity programs.[xviii]

Environmental sustainability

Under its environmental sustainability initiatives, PepsiCo promised to be a good citizen of the world committed to protecting the natural resources by proper use of land, energy, and packaging in its operations. PepsiCo committed itself to increasing its water-use efficiency by 20 percent by 2015. In view of the protests that PepsiCo was facing in countries like India regarding its water use practices, it promised to strive for a positive water balance in its operations in areas water was scarce. PepsiCo promised to provide access to safe water to 3 million people living in developing countries by 2015.[xix] It also promised to use more recycled material in its packaging operations which would reduce environmental damage. PepsiCo committed itself to countering climate change by improving electricity use efficiency by 20 percent by 2015, reducing the fuel used by 25 percent by 2015, reducing the greenhouse gas (GHG) emissions from its operations, and applying agricultural practices which had been proven sustainable, in its farmed land.

Talent sustainability

PepsiCo's talent sustainability initiatives were focused on one of its most important stakeholder communities – its employees. PepsiCo promised to invest in the development of its associates to improve the skills necessary to drive the company's growth as well as improving employment opportunities in the communities it served. PepsiCo aimed at increasing diversity in its workforce by recruiting people from diverse ethnic backgrounds. It said that it would be able to properly understand the needs and demands of the local people by giving better representation to the people where it had operations. It also planned to improve the engagement with its employees when compared with other big Fortune 500 companies.[xx] PepsiCo committed itself to supporting education programs in poor countries through charitable contributions globally. Focusing on the welfare of its employees, PepsiCo committed itself to improving workplace safety by decreasing lost-time injury rates[9] and increasing health and safety metrics.

---

9 Lost-time injury rates refer to an occurrence which results in fatality, permanent disability, or time lost from work due to injury or disablement.

PepsiCo's progress in sustainable development

PepsiCo made good progress on its promises regarding sustainable development, according to some analysts. At PepsiCo, the 'Performance with Purpose' agenda came from top down. Nooyi became a prominent advocate of its sustainable development practices. She believed in the organization's responsibility toward society and in giving back. This belief in conscious capitalism made her a leader in implementing the sustainable development programs at PepsiCo. Another person who was prominent in the implementation of the new sustainable development program was David Walker (Walker). Walker was a 25 year veteran of PepsiCo and was serving as the director of environmental sustainability. He managed several programs at PepsiCo and was responsible for PepsiCo's programs on responsibility toward the environment.

Sticking to its commitment, PepsiCo made rapid progress in its financial performance. In 2009, when the world economy was still recovering from the great economic recession of 2008, PepsiCo increased its global revenues at a Compounded Annual Growth Rate (CAGR) of 13.6 percent for the three preceding years. This was well ahead of its target of growing at double the global GDP growth. In 2010, PepsiCo's revenues outside the US grew at a rate of 30 percent, which constituted 45 percent of its total revenues. Its businesses in India and Brazil grew at 2.5 and 3.5 times their real GDP growth rates.[xxi] PepsiCo increased its market share in its top 20 markets by introducing new products like 'Pepsi Max' – a zero-calorie beverage – and extending its portfolio into sub-segments. PepsiCo also focused on increasing its brand equity for its brands in the top 10 markets through some consumer engagement programs, which were very successful. Some of these programs allowed the consumers to give their opinions on the new flavors introduced by the brands.

PepsiCo acquired some of its bottlers in North America and Europe, which helped it to reduce its overall division operating margins in 2010. Its cash flow for the three years ended 2010 increased more than its growth of net income and it increased its annual dividend in 2010 by 7 percent from US$1.80 to US$1.92. This was the 38th consecutive year for which PepsiCo increased its revenues.

PepsiCo made great strides in increasing the content of fruits, vegetables, nuts, grains, and low-fat dairy in its global product portfolio (Refer to Table 3.1 for food portfolio of PepsiCo). Its Quaker division's contribution of whole grains to the American diet was 500 million pounds for the year 2010. As part of its human sustainability initiatives, PepsiCo formed the Global Nutrition Group to increase the 'Good for You' foods and beverages in its product portfolio. PepsiCo's 'Good for You' product portfolio delivered revenue of US$10 billion for the year 2010 and it had plans to increase it to US$30 billion by 2020. In December 2010, PepsiCo acquired 66 percent of Wimm–Bill–Dann Foods, Russia's leading branded food-and-beverage company, for US$3.8 billion to bolster its nutrition portfolio. This increased the company's annual global revenues from nutritious and functional foods from approximately US$10 billion to nearly US$13 billion.[xxii] PepsiCo continued its efforts to reduce the amount of sodium, saturated fat, and added sugar in its products as per the targets that it had set. It continued to invest in developing different salt crystal shapes that would help deliver good taste using less sodium. Though it was tough to develop products which had less sugar, PepsiCo entered into partnerships with other organizations for developing an all-natural sweetener which would eventually replace sugar.

Table 3.1 **Food portfolio of PepsiCo Inc.**

Source: www.PEP.com/Download/PEP_Annual_Report_2010_Full_Annual_Report.pdf.

Fun for You	These products are a part of PepsiCo's core food and beverages business. They include Pepsi Cola, Mirinda, Doritos, Lays, Cheetos, Mountain Dew, 7Up, and Red Rock Deli Potato Chips.
Better for You	These products are foods and beverages that have levels of total fat, saturated fat, sodium, and sugar that are in line with global dietary intake recommendations. They include Lay's Baked Potato Crisps, Pepsi Max, Diet Mug Root Beer, Diet Sierra Mist, H₂OH!, Diet Pepsi, and Propel Zero water.
Good for You	These products offer positive nutrition through inclusion of whole grain fruits, vegetables, low-fat dairy, nuts, and seeds, or significant amounts of important nutrients, while moderating total fat, saturated fat, sodium, and added sugar. They also address the performance needs of athletes. They include Quaker Instant Oatmeal, G Series, Tropicana, Nut Harvest, and Naked juice.

* Data as of 2011.

PepsiCo implemented front-of-pack labeling for its products in many countries which displayed calorie and basic nutritional information. The company developed strict science-based criteria, which would ensure that only its most nutritious products met the standards for advertising to children under 12. PepsiCo achieved 100 percent compliance for advertising standards to children in the US and 98.5 percent compliance for the same in countries such as India, China, Mexico, and some countries of the European Union. To keep its promise of providing low cost nutritious food to the underprivileged sections of society, PepsiCo launched several initiatives. In India, it launched affordable snacks and biscuits to tackle iron-deficiency anemia. PepsiCo decided to expand PepsiCo Foundation[10] to increase contributions and help people with high disparities in health achieve improved health and nutrition through sustainable programs. PepsiCo increased its contribution from US$4.2 million in 2006 to US$4.7 million in 2010 to achieve improved health and nutrition by launching effective and sustainable programs.

---

10 PepsiCo Foundation was the philanthropic arm of PepsiCo. It was responsible for providing charitable contributions to eligible nonprofit organizations.

The PepsiCo Foundation also developed partnerships with non-governmental and charitable organizations like Save the Children[11] and the World Food Program[12] to increase its contributions toward promoting healthier societies. In the year 2010, it created a new arm to facilitate innovation in the area of nutrition and increase its nutrition businesses called 'Global Nutrition Group'.[xxiii] It would have its own CEO and would be responsible for delivering breakthrough innovation in the areas of fruits and vegetables, grains, dairy, and functional nutrition. PepsiCo's Chief Scientific Officer Mehmood Khan, who was a key person in its implementation of sustainable development program, was named CEO of the new group. Commenting on the creation of the new 'Global Nutrition Group', Nooyi said, 'The creation of this Global Nutrition Group is part of our long-term strategy to grow our nutrition businesses from about US$10 billion in revenues today to US$30 billion by 2020.'[xiv]

On the environmental front, in view of the criticism it faced in water use, PepsiCo reduced the water-use intensity by 19.5 percent by the third quarter of 2010 and nearly achieved its target of improving its water-use efficiency by 20 percent per unit of production by 2015. It achieved a positive water balance in its Indian operations by 2009. PepsiCo also started to have watersheds in China, Mexico, Europe, India, and the US to replenish the water used for its operations. The PepsiCo Foundation had invested US$15 million for water projects since 2005 and expected to provide safe drinking water to 1 million people by the end of 2011 and to 3 million people by 2015.[xxv] PepsiCo launched a new initiative called the Dream Machine recycling initiative to increase the beverage-container recycling rate from 38 percent in 2009 to 50 percent by 2018. It planned to enter into partnerships with organizations to establish recycling systems and encourage consumers to recycle. In March 2011, PepsiCo introduced a new beverage bottle that was fully recyclable and made of plant-based materials.[xxvi] With an eye on warding off further controversies, the company made sure that the new material used to make beverage bottles did not compete with food crops.

PepsiCo increased its electricity-use efficiency by 9 percent and fuel-use efficiency by 12 percent by the third quarter of 2010 compared to the 2006 baseline. To reduce the GHG emissions from its operations, it invested in electric-powered delivery trucks which emitted 75 percent less greenhouse gases. PepsiCo launched the 'Global Sustainable Agriculture Policy' in the year 2009 to encourage everybody to protect and nourish land and communities. PepsiCo launched an important initiative in 2010 with some British farmers to reduce carbon emissions and water use by 50 percent over five years. It developed a new precision farming technology in

---

11 Save the Children founded in London, UK, is a non-governmental organization that enforces children's rights and provides relief and support to children in developing countries.

12 The World Food Program, headquartered in Rome, Italy, is a branch of the United Nations and provides food aid around the world.

partnership with Cambridge University[13] called 'i-crop' to produce more output utilizing less water. In India, PepsiCo started teaching sustainable agricultural practices to farmers and helped them to form themselves into cooperatives. To promote environmental education, PepsiCo's 'Green Volunteer Organization' inspired associates around the world to voluntarily raise awareness regarding eco-friendly practices both at work and at home.

In 2011, PepsiCo announced that it was planning to launch global ethical-farming standards to promote sustainable agriculture. The initiative was aimed at putting an economic value on the impact that its supply chains were having on the environment and society.[xvii] The initiative would focus on resource management, farm productivity, preservation of soil fertility, and social impacts like effects on farming communities, human rights, and compliance with local laws where it was operating. Dan Bena, PepsiCo's director of sustainable development, said apart from helping PepsiCo in improving its supply chain management, the new initiative aimed at helping other businesses to measure and monitor the impact their supply chains were having on the environment. In 2011, PepsiCo signed a memorandum of understanding with China's Ministry of Agriculture to promote sustainable farming. The new partnership with the government of China was part of PepsiCo's focus on investing in sustainable agriculture projects.[xviii]

To improve diversity and inclusion (D&I) in the organization, PepsiCo took steps to include D&I as a part of its culture. It took care that its D&I activities were supported at every level of the organization. In 2009, 80 percent of its employees responded in a survey that their managers supported their involvement in D&I activities which was a 14 percent increase from 2004. PepsiCo implemented its D&I strategy top-down with 33 percent of its board of directors being women and 33 percent being people of color in the year 2010 (Refer to Exhibit IV for diversity and inclusion statistics of PepsiCo for the year 2010).[xxix] To encourage its employees to lead healthier lifestyles, PepsiCo offered on-site health and wellness services in many countries around the world such as China, India, Mexico, South Africa, the UK, and the US. It gave paramount importance to the health and safety of its workers. It created a new 'Global Operations Organization' in 2011 to increase the health and safety in its global operations to leverage the best safety practices across all its sectors. In the year 2020, the PepsiCo Foundation contributed a total of US$7.6 million as grants to promote education. The Foundation also provided educational scholarships to the children of PepsiCo's associates.

To increase the transparency, PepsiCo commissioned Bureau Veritas[14] to provide independent verification of the data it provided to its various stakeholders and in its corporate sustainability report.

---

13 Cambridge University is a public research university located in Cambridge, UK. It was established in 13th century and is one of the top rated universities in the world.

14 Bureau Veritas, headquartered in Paris, France was an organization which provided conformity assessment, certification and consulting services to industry, government, and individuals.

Looking ahead

PepsiCo's focus and the progress it had made on sustainable development had yielded good results, according to analysts. Despite its shift of focus from beverage business to other businesses, more than 50 percent of its revenues for the year 2010 came from its beverage business both in the US and outside the US (Refer to Exhibit V for PepsiCo's Revenue Mix). More than 70 percent of its revenues came from the Americas signifying the importance of home market for PepsiCo despite its global expansion. However, in recognition of the progress it had made on sustainable development, PepsiCo was named the top food and beverage company in the DJSI Food and Beverage Super sector and included in the Dow Jones Sustainability Indexes for the year 2011.[xxx] It was the only company based in the US to earn the top ranking in the 19 super sectors assessed. This was the third consecutive year that PepsiCo had been named leader in the beverage sector. However, PepsiCo's successes on sustainable development did not steer it completely away from controversy. Some environmental activist groups continued to criticize its practices. Activist groups remained critical of the trash generated from the plastic bottles and tin cans used to pack PepsiCo's beverage products.

While Nooyi was praised for her leadership and 'Performance with a Purpose' strategy, she also came in for some strong criticism. Critics dismissed her 'Performance with Purpose' strategy as a marketing ploy that happened to be in vogue. They pointed out that the company was still best known for making soda and potato chips.[xxxi] Nooyi was also vehemently criticized for her infamous comment in a Fox Business show: 'Doritos is not bad for you ... Doritos is nothing but corn mashed up, fried a little bit with just very little oil, and then flavored in the most delectable way.'[xxxii] Her strategy was also criticized as there were reports that developing markets were not seeing a change in dietary habits. For instance, PepsiCo was banking on a successful launch of Pepsi Max in the summer of 2010 to extend its market share in India. However, the launch was not successful. Experts believed that many people in the developing world were not buying into the healthy food habits concept being propagated by PepsiCo. Sales of 100 percent juices continued to lag behind sugary ones by a wide margin while pizza chains like Dominos continued to beat sales targets.[xxxiii] Moreover, some of PepsiCo's new forays were not doing too well: its Flat Earth chips[15] had disappointed at the market and had to be discontinued because of slow sales.[xxxiv] Critics accused the products of having a taste-barrier and even went to the extent of saying that some of them had a really awful taste.[xxxv] Meanwhile, Quaker Oats had had little success in attracting attention to oatmeal, which was tagged as a 'Best for You' food by PepsiCo.

---

15 Flat Earth Chips were snacks that had half a serving of fruits or vegetables per ounce.

The company was criticized for diverting funds from expensive Super Bowl[16] commercials to the 'Pepsi Refresh' challenge.[17] Critics pointed out that PepsiCo had returned to TV advertising in June 2011 after three years of focus on social media and crowd sourcing through corporate philanthropy based on programs like Pepsi Refresh. Critics said that Coca Cola had emerged stronger during Nooyi's tenure as the CEO at PepsiCo, with increasing sales and a much lower costs structure. According to a report in 2011, Coke had held on to the #1 slot in sales and unseated Pepsi from the #2 spot as well with Diet Coke in the US (Refer to Exhibit VI for the top 10 carbonated beverage brands in the US). Globally, while PepsiCo was being affected by increased commodity costs and the uncertain economic conditions and had to cut its earnings growth to single digit levels in 2011, Coca Cola had reported increasing sales volumes. Nooyi was accused of ignoring marketing and positioning of products while placing too much of an emphasis on 'Performance with Purpose'. A shareholder had earlier remarked, 'I think it is hard to give Indra much better than a C-plus as a CEO, given the fact that PEP shares had fallen by 7 percent by 2009, compared to a 28 percent surge for Coke during the same period, from the time she took over.'[xxxvi] (Refer to Exhibit VII for the chart of PepsiCo's share price from 2006 to 2011 (October))

Nooyi rubbished criticism that she had not paid attention to PepsiCo's leading brands and argued that emphasis on corporate citizenship and healthy foods did not come at the cost of driving sales.[xxxvii] However, there was considerable pressure on Nooyi from shareholders to improve the market share of PepsiCo's flagship brands and her every move was being closely watched.[xxxviii]

---

16 Super Bowl is the annual championship for the National Football League in the US. It is one of the most highly watched sporting events in the US. Due to high viewership, the commercial airtime during its broadcast is the most expensive of the year and companies develop their most expensive advertisements for this broadcast.

17 The Pepsi Refresh Challenge aimed at finding innovative not-for-profit organizations.

EXHIBIT I
Consolidated income statement of PepsiCo from 2006–10 (In US$ Millions)

	2010	2009	2008	2007	2006
Net Revenue	57,838	43,232	43,251	35,137	39,474
Cost of sales	26,575	20,099	20,351	18,038	15,762
Selling, general and administrative expenses	22,814	15,026	15,877	14,208	12,774
Amortization of intangible assets	117	63	64	58	162
Operating Profit	8,332	8,044	6,959	7,170	6,439
Bottling equity income	735	365	374	560	616
Interest expense	(903)	(397)	(329)	(224)	(239)
Interest income	68	67	41	125	173
Income before income taxes	8,232	8,079	7,045	7,631	6,989
Income taxes	1,894	2,100	1,879	1,973	1,347
Net income	6,320	5,946	5,142	5,658	5,642

Source: "PepsiCo: 2010 Annual Report," www.pepsico.com.

EXHIBIT II
Performance with purpose

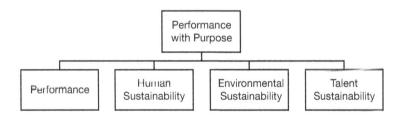

Human Sustainability	Ensuring that products ranging from treats to health foods allow customers to make balanced, sensible choices.
Environmental Sustainability	Ensuring that the company replenishes the planet and leaves the world a much better place than it was before.
Talent Sustainability	Ensuring that the employees of PepsiCo also have a life while they earn their living with the company.

Source: PepsiCo: 2010 Annual Report, www.pepsico.com; www.leadership.bcg.com/americas/nooyi.aspx.

EXHIBIT III
Goals and commitments of PepsiCo

Performance

Top Line	Grow international revenues at two times real global GDP growth rate.
	Grow savory snack and liquid refreshment beverage market share in the top 20 markets.
	Sustain or improve brand equity scores for PepsiCo's US$ 19 billion brands in top 10 markets.
	Rank among the top two suppliers in customer (retail partner) surveys where third-party measures exist.
Bottom Line	Continue to expand division operating margins.
	Increase cash flow in proportion to net income growth over three-year.
	Deliver total shareholder returns in the top quartile of our industry group.
Corporate Governance	Utilize a robust corporate Governance structure to consistently score in the top quartile of corporate Governance metrics.
	Ensure our PepsiCo value commitment to deliver sustained growth through empowered people acting with responsibility and building trust.

Human sustainability

Products	Provide more food and beverage choices made with wholesome ingredients that contribute to healthier eating and drinking .
	Increase the amount of whole grains, fruits, vegetables, nuts, seeds and low-fat dairy in our global product portfolio.
	Reduce the average amount of sodium per serving in key global food brands by 25 percent.
	Reduce the average amount of saturated fat per serving in key global food brands by 15 percent.
	Reduce the average amount of added sugar per serving in key global beverage brands by 25 percent.
Market Place	Encourage people to make informed choices and live healthier.
	Display calorie count and key nutrients on our food and beverage packaging by 2012.
	Advertise to children under 12 only products that meet our global science-based nutrition standards.
	Eliminate the direct sale of full-sugar soft drinks in primary and secondary schools around the globe by 2012.
	Increase the range of foods and beverages that offer solutions for managing calories, like portion sizes.

Community

Actively work with global and local partners to help address global nutrition challenges.

Invest in our business and research and development to expand our offerings of more affordable, nutritionally relevant products for underserved and lower-income communities.

Expand PepsiCo Foundation and PepsiCo corporate contribution initiatives to promote healthier communities, including enhancing diet and physical activity programs.

Integrate our policies and actions on human health, agriculture and the environment to make sure that they support each other.

Environmental sustainability

Water

Respect the human right to water through world-class efficiency in our operations, preserving water resources and enabling access to safe water.

Improve our water use efficiency by 20 percent per unit of production by 2015.

Strive for positive water balance in our operations in water-distressed areas.

Provide access to safe water to three million people in developing countries by the end of 2015.

Land and Packaging

Rethink the way we grow, source, create, package and deliver our products to minimize our impact on land.

Continue to lead the industry by incorporating at least 10 percent recycled polyethylene terephthalate (rPEt) in our primary soft drink containers in the US., and broadly expand the use of rPEt across key international markets.

Create partnerships that promote the increase of US beverage container recycling rates to 50 percent by 2018.

Reduce packaging weight by 350 million pounds—avoiding the creation of one billion pounds of landfill waste by 2012.

Work to eliminate all solid waste to landfills from our production facilities.

Climate Change

Reduce the carbon footprint of our operations.

Improve our electricity use efficiency by 20 percent per unit of production by 2015.

Reduce our fuel use intensity by 25 percent per unit of production by 2015.

Commit to a goal of reducing greenhouse gas (GHG) intensity for US operations by 25 percent through our partnership with the US Environmental Protection agency climate leaders program

Commit to an absolute reduction in GHG emissions across global operations.

Community

Respect and responsibly use natural resources in our businesses and in the local communities we serve.

Apply proven sustainable agricultural practices on our farmed land.

Provide funding, technical support and training to local farmers.

Promote environmental education and best practices among our associates and business partners.

Integrate our policies and actions on human health, agriculture and the environment to make sure that they support each other.

Talent sustainability	
Culture	Enable our people to thrive by providing a supportive and empowering workplace.
	Ensure high levels of associate engagement and satisfaction as compared with other Fortune 500 companies.
	Foster diversity and inclusion by developing a workforce that reflects local communities.
	Encourage our associates to lead healthier lives by offering workplace wellness programs globally.
	Ensure a safe workplace by continuing to reduce lost time injury rates, while striving to improve other occupational health and safety metrics through best practices.
	Support ethical and legal compliance through annual training in our code of conduct, which outlines PepsiCo's unwavering commitment to its human rights policy, including treating every associate with dignity and respect.
Career	Provide opportunities that strengthen our associates' skills and capabilities to drive sustainable growth.
	Become universally recognized through top rankings as one of the best companies in the world for leadership development.
	Create a work environment in which associates know that their skills, talents and interests can fully develop.
	Conduct training for associates from the frontline to senior management, to ensure that associates have the knowledge and skills required to achieve performance goals.
Community	Contribute to better living standards in the communities we serve.
	Create local jobs by expanding operations in developing countries.
	Support education through PepsiCo Foundation grants.
	Support associate volunteerism and community involvement through company-sponsored programs and initiatives.
	Match eligible associate charitable contributions globally, dollar for dollar, through the PepsiCo Foundation.

Source: "PepsiCo Corporate Citizenship Report 2009," www.pepsico.com.

EXHIBIT IV
2010 inclusion statistics at PepsiCo

	Total	Women	Percentage of women	People of color	Percentage of people of color
Board of directors	12	4	33	4	33
Senior executives	13	2	15	3	23
Executives	2,970	915	31	600	20
All managers	17,790	5,690	32	4,690	26
All associates	100,415	19,530	19	29,360	29

Source: "PepsiCo: 2010 Annual Report," www.pepsico.com.

EXHIBIT V
PepsiCo's mix of net revenue

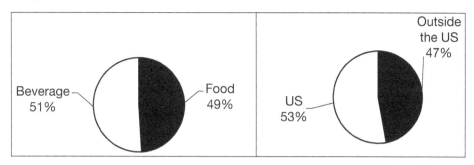

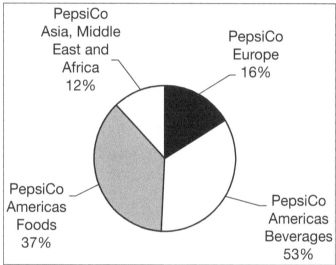

Source: "PepsiCo: 2010 Annual Report," www.pepsico.com.

EXHIBIT VI
Top 10 carbonated beverage brands in the US

Brand	Year of introduction	Owned by the company
Coca Cola	1886	Coca Cola
Diet Coke	1983	Coca Cola
Pepsi Cola	1898	PepsiCo
Mountain Dew	1948	PepsiCo
Dr Pepper	1885	Dr Pepper Snapple Group
Sprite	1961	Coca Cola
Diet Pepsi	1964	PepsiCo
Diet Mountain Dew	1988	PepsiCo
Diet Dr Pepper	1963	Dr Pepper Snapple Group
Fanta	1941	Coca Cola

Source: Peter Hartlaub, "Sweet! America's Top 10 Brands of Soda," www.msnbc.msn.com.

EXHIBIT VII
Chart of PepsiCo's Share Price (2006–2011)

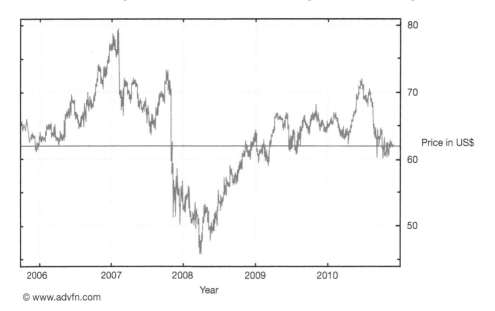

© www.advfn.com

Source: www.in.advfn.com/p.php?pid=qkchart&symbol=NY^PEP.

Endnotes

i "PepsiCo Named Top Food and Beverage Company in 2011 Dow Jones Sustainability Index," www.csrwire.com, September 9, 2011.

ii Ibid.

iii "The Pepsi-Cola Story," www.pepsi.com.

iv "India: Coke, Pepsi Attacked over Ground Water Issue," www.thehindu.com, September 18, 2004.

v "Controversy over Coke and Pepsi Water Usage," www.beverageonline.com, May 21, 2003.

vi "India: Controversy over Coke and Pepsi Water Usage," www.just-drinks.com, May 21, 2003.

vii "India: Coke, Pepsi Attacked over Ground Water Issue," www.thehindu.com, September 18, 2004.

viii Diane Brady, "Pepsi: Repairing a Poisoned Reputation in India," www.businessweek .com, May 31, 2007.

ix Sanjay Majumder, "Indian State Bans Pepsi and Coke," www.news.bbc.co.uk, August 9, 2006.

x "More Indian States Ban Coke, Pepsi Products," www.msnbc.msn.com, August 11, 2006.

xi "Kerala Court Lifts Cola Ban: Coke, Pepsi Relieved," www.siliconindia.com, September 22, 2006.

xii Rhonda Jolly, "Marketing Obesity? Junk Food, Advertising and Kids," www.aph.gov .au/library/pubs/rp/2010-11/11rp09.htm, January 12, 2011.

xiii "Coca-Cola's Toxic India Fertiliser," www.news.bbc.co.uk, July 25, 2003.

xiv "PepsiCo Corporate Citizenship Report 2009," www.pepsico.com.

xv "PepsiCo: 2010 Annual Report," www.pepsico.com.

xvi "PepsiCo Releases Sustainable Development Report," www.bevnet.com, January 6, 2009.

xvii Adam Aston, "Meet the Change Makers: The New Pepsi Challenge," www.onearth .org, September 20, 2011.

xviii "Performance with Purpose: The Promise of PepsiCo," www.pepsico.com.

xix "Performance with Purpose: The Promise of PepsiCo," www.pepsico.com.

xx "PepsiCo Corporate Citizenship Report 2009," www.pepsico.com.

xxi "PepsiCo: 2010 Annual Report," www.pepsico.com.

xxii "PepsiCo to Acquire 66 percent of Russia's Wimm-Bill-Dann Dairy and Juice Company for $3.8 Billion," www.pepsico.com, December 2, 2010.

xiii "PepsiCo Creates a Global Nutrition Group to Facilitate Innovation," www.ift.org, October 11, 2010.

xiv Ibid.

xv "Water Stewardship," www.pepsico.com.

xvi Adam Aston, "Meet the Change Makers: The New Pepsi Challenge," www.onearth .org, September 20, 2011.

xvii Jessica Shankleman, "PepsiCo to Launch Global Ethical-Farming Standards," www .businessgreen.com, August 25, 2011.

xviii "PepsiCo to Partner with China's Ministry of Agriculture to Promote Sustainable Farming," www.dailymarkets.com, September 19, 2011.

xix "PepsiCo: 2010 Annual Report," www.pepsico.com.

xxx   "PepsiCo Named Top Food and Beverage Company in 2011 Dow Jones Sustainability Index," www.csrwire.com, September 9, 2011.

xxxi   "Indra Nooyi: Keeping Cool in Hot Water," www.businessweek.com, June 11, 2007.

xxxii   "Quotes in the News," www.newsweek.com/2011/02/08/quotes-in-the-news.html

xxxiii   Gus Lubin, "Pepsi Learns the Hard Way that Indians Don't Like Diet Soda," www.wikinvest.com, July 11, 2011.

xxxiv   "Feedin Mama," www.feedinmama.blogspot.com/2008/11/sad-sad-news.html

xxxv   "Flat Earth Baked Veggie Crisps Wild Berry Patch," www.taquitoo.not/chips/FlatEarthVeggieCrispsWildBerry

xxxvi   "Indra Nooyi Faces Flak for Falling PEP Shares," www.zeenews.india.com, December 30, 2009.

xxxvii   Dale Buss, "Stakes Rising for PEP's Nooyi," www.brandchannel.com, June 29, 2011.

xxxviii   Ibid.

CASE 4

Florida Ice & Farm

Sustainability champion from an emerging economy

Andrea M. Prado, John C. Ickis, and Ximena García-Rada

Ramón Mendiola, CEO of Florida Ice & Farm Company (FIFCO), was seated in the front row of the packed auditorium where the 'Annual Meeting of the New Champions' was taking place. He could not overcome his surprise at finding himself in Dalian, China, participating in this world event. It was September 2011, and Mendiola had been invited to the meeting – organized by the World Economic Forum in conjunction with the Boston Consulting Group – to receive an award. FIFCO, Costa Rica's largest beverage group, was chosen as one of 'Sixteen New Sustainability Champions'.

In a rigorous contest, the company was selected from among 1,000 organizations in emerging countries. Participating firms were using innovative practices to achieve not only economic results, but also social and environmental improvements in the communities in which they operated. Selection criteria included sustainability, innovation, and scalability. It was FIFCO's 'triple bottom line' strategy, initiated by Mendiola three years earlier that placed the firm among the winners. The company's development and use of a sustainability 'balanced scorecard' to implement the strategy played a key role in its selection.

While satisfied with the results achieved over the past three years, Mendiola was already looking ahead to new challenges. Many of the company's suppliers and customers had not yet adopted sustainability practices. Should FIFCO work with its business partners to extend these practices to other participants in the company's value chain?

Company background

Four brothers of Jamaican descent founded FIFCO in 1908 as an ice plant and tropical farm in Limón, Costa Rica. The company acquired a brewery and, with capital from local investors, soon came to dominate the national beer industry. Considered a great employer for its generous benefits and working conditions, FIFCO became a source of pride for Costa Ricans. Employees described the company culture as 'brotherly and democratic', with everyone sharing Costa Rican values of solidarity and egalitarianism (Appendix A presents a briefing on Costa Rica).

The company enjoyed a leadership position throughout the past century, with the only locally produced beer brands in the Costa Rican market. However, the early 2000s saw the entry of global giants in the surrounding Central American countries. The world's largest brewery, Anheuser-Busch InBev (ABI), a Brazilian–Belgian consortium, was challenging established local brands in Guatemala and Nicaragua with aggressive prices, but with limited success. In El Salvador, Honduras, and Panama, the national breweries were acquired by South African Breweries, which had merged with the Miller Breweries of the US to become the world's second-largest producer.

In 2003, FIFCO's Board of Directors announced the sale of 25% of the company shares to Heineken N.V. of the Netherlands and the retirement of FIFCO's long-time general manager. He was replaced by Mendiola, a young Costa Rican executive with an MBA from Northwestern University's Kellogg School of Management. Mendiola was formerly Regional Vice President of Kraft for Central America and the Caribbean. He was an avid tennis player, with an energetic and competitive personality.

After spending his first week on delivery trucks, Mendiola concluded that the company needed a better sense of its priorities. His first act was to replace the company's functional organization with four strategic business units: beer, non-alcoholic beverages, sales and distribution, and finance and corporate services. He then proceeded to hire managers whose profiles matched the new decentralized structure.

At Mendiola's suggestion, FIFCO's Board of Directors hired the international consulting firm McKinsey & Co. to validate the new structure. The scope of the consultancy was later broadened, at Mendiola's urging, to include a search for efficiencies 'at every link in the value chain'. McKinsey initially identified savings opportunities of US$6 million (of total costs of $116 million), but working with FIFCO's management team, the consulting firm uncovered additional savings of $16 million, including a workforce reduction from 2,480 to 2,025.

Mendiola invited former colleagues from multinationals in Mexico to share their experiences with the latest technological advances that industry leaders were pioneering worldwide. 'This was a wake-up call,' he recalled. 'We realized how far behind we were, so we began an in-depth diagnosis of our organization to find areas needing improvement.' In September 2003, a strategic planning workshop was organized to discuss the results of the diagnosis. The company's 60 managers committed themselves to the long-term vision of becoming the most important beverage company in Central America in terms of both volume and profitability, while maintaining corporate values of innovation, responsibility, passion, recognition, and teamwork.

FIFCO dedicated fiscal year 2003–04 (ending September 30) to reorganization. The company turned a small operating profit but showed a loss in economic value added (EVA) when the cost of capital employed was subtracted (Exhibits 1 and 2 show income statements and balance sheets for 2003–11). Mendiola promptly announced that for the first time in the company's recent history, there would be no year-end bonus. 'Not a cent, for any of us,' he said. 'We wanted to send a clear message.'

In September 2004, the company organized a strategic-planning retreat at which it set ambitious cost-cutting goals for the next two-year period. All 60 managers participating in the retreat made a firm commitment to the budget. Actions included the installation of SAP, an enterprise resource planning tool and a change in the compensation system for sales employees varying from 30 to 70%. 'There was strong resistance to this change,' recalled Mendiola. 'So we told salespeople that they could keep the 30% system during a trial period, but we also showed them what they would have earned under the 70% variable system during that same period. Within two months they were all convinced that the change was to their benefit.'

In September 2006, FIFCO held a second strategic-planning retreat. Having met cost-reduction goals, Mendiola challenged the management team by setting a goal of doubling sales revenues and profits in two years. This came as a surprise since it had previously taken the company seven years to double sales. This ambitious goal was achieved partly through acquisitions such as Kern's in Guatemala and the Pepsi bottling company in Costa Rica. The former was a food and beverage company with a strong presence throughout Central America. The company purchased the latter from South African Breweries, along with Reserva Conchal, a real estate project that included a beach hotel and resort on the Pacific coast. Much of the company's growth during this two-year period was generated internally, through organic growth of the beer and non-alcoholic businesses. Exhibit 3 shows the company's business units and major brands, including an investment division.

The triple bottom line

By August 2008, FIFCO had achieved its goal of doubling sales and profits, and Mendiola began to search for a new goal. Not satisfied with generating economic value, he began to consider the company's social and environmental impact. Influenced by John Elkington's book, *Cannibals with Forks: The Triple Bottom Line of 21st Century Business*, he incorporated a triple- bottom-line strategy in FIFCO's business model. This strategy would require the integration of the firm's environmental and social performance with the company's financial results. In Elkington's view, the wealth generated by business could not come at the sacrifice of the planet or the abuse of its inhabitants. Companies accepting this view recognized that the triple bottom line had important implications for strategic resource allocation. If an investment did not meet one of the three criteria – economic, environmental, and social – it would not be approved.

Gisela Sánchez, a young Costa Rican woman with an MBA in strategy and marketing from Kellogg Graduate School of Management at Northwestern University, was hired as FIFCO's Director of Corporate Affairs. Before joining FIFCO, Sánchez worked as a consultant for governments, NGOs, and companies in the areas of competitiveness and corporate social responsibility. She also worked at the AVINA Foundation, supporting the development of social entrepreneurs in Latin America, and as a researcher and project coordinator for the Latin American Center for Competitiveness and Sustainable Development at INCAE Business School in Costa Rica.

As Director of Corporate Affairs, Sánchez reported directly to Mendiola, was a member of FIFCO's Executive Committee, and supervised the Environmental Management area. She was also responsible for managing FIFCO's social investments and coordinating the firm's relationships with its many stakeholders, and she was given responsibility for leading FIFCO's triple-bottom-line strategy. Working closely with Mendiola, she developed a five-step process to implement the strategy:

Step 1: Consultations and dialogue with stakeholders. The purpose was to understand public perceptions and expectations regarding FIFCO's social and environmental footprints. Interviews and focus groups were conducted among four stakeholder groups: business partners (including suppliers and employees); clients and consumers; civil-society groups; and government and regulatory agencies. While some stakeholders had concerns about the company's environmental impact, they all identified the social impact of irresponsible alcohol consumption as the major footprint.

Step 2: Strategic planning. In September 2008, FIFCO's 90 top managers participated in the third strategic-planning retreat, held at the newly acquired resort on the Pacific coast. At this event, Mendiola laid down the challenge of the triple bottom line, supported by data from consultations with stakeholders. The mood was one of optimism. The company had just completed the most successful year in its 100-year history, and despite rumblings in the US financial markets, the future of Costa Rica seemed bright.

FIFCO managers took up the challenge of the triple bottom line, spending one day working on each of the three dimensions. The retreat ended with the participants' commitment to communicate the strategy to the other 2,200 members of the organization in what Mendiola called 'the evangelization'. Rolando Carvajal, Director of the Beverages Division, explained, 'We are not imposing this, but rather looking for ways to get people enjoying, innovating, and supporting the design of the program, before defining any performance indicators.'

A new mission statement also came out of this strategic-planning meeting. FIFCO was to become the industry leader in beverages and canned foods in the Central American region—not just in volume and profits, but 'in terms of economic, social, and environmental value added, exceeding consumer expectations in benefit of its clients, workers, shareholders, and communities where it operates.'

Step 3: Definition of strategic objectives. A major outcome of the workshop was the setting of 12 strategic objectives: three for the economic dimension, three for the environmental dimension, and six for the social dimension. The social dimension was further divided into internal objectives (related to the company's responsibility to employees and their families) and external objectives (involving responsibility to the broader society, including the promotion of responsible alcohol consumption). The objectives are shown in Exhibit 4.

Step 4: Measuring impact. In 2006, FIFCO introduced a balanced scorecard that the Department of Human Resources used as a means to align employee performance with strategic objectives. Under the triple-bottom-line strategy, FIFCO adapted this tool to monitor goal achievement along each of the three dimensions. The Director of the Human Resources Department, Scarlet Pietri, explained that 'based on the new company vision, we set the goal of migrating from a traditional Kaplan & Norton[1] scorecard to a triple-bottom-line model.'

The HR Department began by identifying those indicators already monitored at the plant level, which were consolidated in a macro indicator known as 'Eco-Florida' and used to evaluate the company's environmental performance (see Exhibit 5). 'The organization already had experience [with] measuring something besides purely economic variables,' commented Pietri. 'There is this idea that initiatives in the social and environmental areas can't be measured–that they are ethereal and not tangible like sales or profits, but that is just not true. We are measuring such indicators as water usage throughout Florida's operations.'

With the new sustainability balanced scorecard, the variable portion of employee annual compensation was tied directly to meeting economic, social, and environmental goals. In the case of the CEO, this variable portion was 65%. 'Top management has a very high percentage of variable compensation because we should *walk the talk*,' Mendiola commented.

Step 5: Accountability to society. As a publicly traded company, FIFCO made its financial statements available to the general public. After adopting a triple-bottom-line strategy, the company decided to communicate its social and environmental

---

1 Refers to the authors of the original book on the concept, *The Balanced Scorecard*, by Robert Kaplan and David Norton.

performance to its stakeholders. For greater credibility, the company chose to adopt the Global Reporting Initiative (GRI) standard. The GRI established uniform sustainability reporting practices worldwide, using grades of A, B, or C, depending on the number of indicators reported. When a plus sign (+) accompanied the grade, it meant that the company's sustainability reports were audited by an external firm.

The double crisis

In late 2008, the financial crisis affecting the US still seemed remote to most Costa Ricans. With their savings protected by a nationalized banking system with strong regulations, growing trade relations with China, a continuing influx of European eco-tourists, and an economy unburdened by defense expenditures, most citizens had little knowledge or concern as to what was happening on Wall Street. The first warning signs were the drop in exports of gourmet coffees and the sudden cancellation of construction projects on the beaches of Guanacaste, a preferred destination for US retirees. Then, the Costa Rican banks' international credit lines began to dry up. Still, as the December holidays approached, beer sales continued to flow smoothly. Mendiola and other FIFCO executives could leave on vacation for a well-deserved rest.

When Mendiola returned to work on January 5, 2009, he encountered a double crisis. Costa Ricans, aware of the credit shortage and the growing economic uncertainty, had cut back on consumption in the New Year. But it was the second crisis that had been the major contributor to this decline in beer consumption: On December 23, the National Congress had suddenly passed several articles of a new traffic law enforcing heavy fines and penalties for driving under the influence of alcohol.[2] Mendiola had been aware of the bill, which had been under discussion since March 2007 and which was aligned with his initiatives for responsible alcohol consumption. However, he had not expected approval for another 10 months.

The bill imposed penalties that were among the world's most severe. Penalties of up to 10 years' imprisonment could be imposed for driving under the influence of alcohol and causing physical injury to a third party. The law imposed the loss of one's driver's license for driving under the influence, plus fines that were equivalent to over a month's salary of a typical middle-class Costa Rican.

In the face of this double crisis, Mendiola asked FIFCO managers to find savings and efficiencies in their respective areas. The goal was to maintain the same operating profit as in 2008, which meant reducing total operating costs by 20%. In February 2009, they presented an eight-point plan to: (1) increase operating efficiency; (2) reduce non-strategic costs; (3) improve employees' productivity; (4) negotiate better input prices; (5) rationalize capital investments; (6) strengthen the client and consumer base; (7) protect cash; and (8) reduce risk, particularly in the company's Pacific real estate investments. The cost reductions meant laying off 430 employees,

2 *Proyecto de Ley, Reforma de los Artículos 44, 111, 123, 124 y 125 del Código Penal.*

in direct contradiction to the social (internal) dimension of the triple-bottom-line strategy. Mendiola asked Pietri for ideas to reduce the number of layoffs.

Implementation: 2009–11

One alternative to the massive layoff was to decrease the number of working hours, reducing everyone's take-home pay. Pietri discovered an article in the Costa Rican labor law that allowed for such a reduction, but only if employees unanimously voted to do so. A company appeal for solidarity was successful, and the layoffs, while not eliminated altogether, were reduced to 130 employees, which was the usual number that left the firm each year as a result of the company's rigorous performance review process. As a part of the reductions in working hours, the company closed on Fridays at noon. To further reduce salary costs, executives' variable pay was eliminated, which represented up to 50% of total compensation for top management.

In the face of the double crisis, Mendiola made an announcement to demonstrate FIFCO's commitment to the triple-bottom-line strategy: In 2009, the social dimension in the new corporate sustainability balanced scorecard would account for 30% of the company-wide performance evaluation, and by 2011, the environmental dimension would account for an additional 10%, and the economic dimension for the remaining 60%. In later years, the distribution would be 20% environmental, 30% social and 50% economic.

These percentages would apply to the corporation as a whole – including the CEO. Additionally, managers had a customized scorecard with indicators from the three dimensions that were relevant to their individual responsibilities. Managers' variable compensation was subject to the achievement of the goals established in the sustainability scorecard – at both the corporate and the individual levels. The goals established in the scorecard were firm commitments and did not change during the year. As Carvajal explained, 'We did not impose goals for our employees, but we set them together with our teams. After people became involved in the first stage of this process of change, the rest was a smooth ride. FIFCO managers are very serious about committing to goals.' Exhibit 6 shows an example of a sales manager's sustainability balanced scorecard.

By 2011, 580 of the company's 2,300 employees were included in the sustainability balanced scorecard, representing the top 13 – out of 24 – hierarchical levels in the company. Each year, FIFCO published annual sustainability reports under the standards of the GRI, audited by Deloitte. The company's first report, issued in 2010 (with data from 2009), was graded 'B'. Its second report, issued in 2011, was graded 'A+'. Out of 583 reports submitted worldwide in 2011, FIFCO's was one of only 135 companies (and 19 in Latin America) to achieve this grade.

The sustainability reports included a broad range of initiatives in non-economic dimensions. Three of the firm's programs, which both Mendiola and Sánchez believed were representative of the triple-bottom-line strategy, were: (1) responsible consumption; (2) a volunteer program, 'Choose to Help'; and (3) water neutrality. The first two programs belonged to the social dimension, while the third one was environmental. These programs addressed some of the firm's most visible footprints, according to the feedback gathered in the consultations and dialogue with stakeholders.

Responsible consumption

Stakeholders reported that the company's most highly visible footprint was excessive alcohol consumption. Data showed that alcohol consumption in Costa Rica, though infrequent, was associated with festive occasions where drinking could be excessive, sometimes resulting in automobile accidents or domestic violence (see Exhibit 7 for data on beer consumption in selected countries).

Since 1999, FIFCO has sponsored 'designated driver' campaigns in which groups of friends going to party at night would select one of their numbers, who would not consume alcohol, to drive back. Some company executives felt this was a passive approach, but they were unsure how to encourage responsible alcohol consumption without damaging business in the long term. Research on international best practices revealed a successful program, Éduc'Alcool, in Québec, Canada. According to José Pablo Montoya, manager of alcoholic beverages:

> These people have been able to enter into dialogue with government authorities and to establish programs for consumer education. When you look at the indicators for Québec vs. those for Costa Rica, you see that Québécois have a higher consumption per capita than Costa Ricans, but with a more moderate consumption pattern. We found in Educ'Alcool a model that we should replicate because it will allow us to continue growing as an industry while minimizing the social footprint of excessive alcohol consumption.

Based on the Canadian experience, in 2009, FIFCO conducted a baseline study to measure patterns of alcohol consumption in Costa Rica and has monitored changes in these consumption patterns annually. The company also launched a campaign entitled 'Moderation as a Value', with the goal of reinforcing moderation as a value within the Costa Rican culture, not only as it pertains to alcohol consumption. This campaign was launched through a strategic alliance with the Ministry of Health, with FIFCO inviting other participants in the alcoholic beverage industry to participate in the creation of a Costa Rican organization equivalent to Educ'Alcool. The Department of Corporate Relations and the strategic business unit for alcoholic beverages coordinated all of these activities. The former was in charge of the educational component and of managing relations with stakeholder groups; the latter was responsible for sales and marketing of the company's major brands (some of these activities are described in Exhibit 8).

In one case, a promotional campaign for one of FIFCO's beers was canceled because the theme of the campaign ('pay for one, take three') was inconsistent with moderation. Juan Chinchilla, a sales representative, estimated that around 7–8% of beer sales at festive occasions were lost by eliminating this type of promotion. This decision created some confusion and discontent in the Sales and Distribution Division, whose members were responsible for achieving both the 'frequency of consumption' goal and the sales goal established in the sustainability balanced scorecard. There were tensions among members of the sales force, who were expected to meet short-term volume quotas while also promoting moderation.

'Choose to help' program

Florida developed a volunteer program called 'Choose to Help' because it gave employees an array of options for performing community service. According to FIFCO managers and employees, this program added a human element to the triple-bottom-line strategy by allowing FIFCO staff to 'live the company's footprint'. Some believed that it was through this volunteer program that FIFCO consolidated its social and environmental practices through an array of 12 programs that captured the essence of the triple-bottom-line strategy.

'Choose to Help' was officially launched after a devastating earthquake destroyed the home of a FIFCO employee in January 2009. The company provided time off and resources so that co-workers could rebuild the house. This effort was expanded to help other families in the region and soon involved 1,100 employees – including CEO Mendiola – who donated a total of 8,880 hours as volunteers in the reconstruction of 13 houses near the earthquake's epicenter.

Following this emergency response, the company developed a portfolio of strategic projects. Any volunteer project had to contribute to a given social or environmental goal of the firm's triple bottom line. For instance, the project 'aqueduct in the indigenous community of Gavilán Canta' contributed to the goal of water neutrality (described below). The project 'remodeling the driving education center' contributed to the goal of highway safety (see Exhibit 8 for more information on the road safety program).

In most of the volunteer programs included in the portfolio of options, FIFCO coordinated efforts with other businesses, NGOs or government organizations to leverage the project's impact. In the Gavilán Canta project, for example, the company partnered with *Acueductos y Alcantarillados*, the government organization responsible for providing water services to the population. For the remodeling of the driving education center, FIFCO partnered with the Ministry of Public Works and Transport. In both cases, the government institutions were in charge of the daily maintenance of the infrastructure, as it was public property.

By 2011, the company's employees were providing two days (16 hours) of voluntary work each year. Participation in this program was scheduled during working hours and was compulsory for all staff members – including the CEO. 'Volunteer hours' was an indicator included in every employee's individual balanced score-card. FIFCO's annual number of volunteer hours reached 48,715 in 2011, showing a significant increase over 2009 (when it was just below 25,000 hours) and making it Costa Rica's number one company in corporate volunteerism. FIFCO's volunteers were known as the 'blue tide' because they would arrive uniformed with their blue company T-shirts.

The volunteer program contributed not only to achieving social and environmental goals, but also to increasing the identification of the employees with the company's values and with the triple-bottom-line strategy. 'We no longer see volunteer activities as a sacrifice, but as a duty,' a company financial analyst explained proudly. According to an organizational climate survey done by Price Waterhouse Coopers, among FIFCO's five values, 'responsibility' showed the largest improvement between 2007 and 2009, increasing from 56 to 74%. The survey also showed that cultural alignment increased from 53 to 61%. FIFCO directors attributed a great deal of this improvement to the 'Choose to Help' program (see Exhibit 9 for more information on the volunteer program).

As observed in the volunteer and responsible-consumption initiatives, FIFCO often engaged in cross-sector partnerships, either with governments or with NGOs, to complement efforts to implement its social initiatives. Through these relationships, the firm accessed technical know-how, increased the scale of its projects, and increased the probability that the project would continue operations for the long run. Along these same lines, FIFCO was a member of the *Asociación de Empresarios para el Desarrollo* (AED), the most important organization promoting corporate social responsibility in Costa Rica. AED's members included some of the biggest local and multinational corporations in the country. Among the objectives of this association were the promotion of management systems to support socially responsible business models and the channeling of its members' social investment through public-private alliances. FIFCO has been represented on the Board of AED since its foundation and has played a strong role in sharing its know-how with other members. Membership in AED offered the company an opportunity to join efforts with other organizations and, thus, leverage its impact in Costa Rican society.

Becoming water neutral

Water was a strategic resource for FIFCO, as it was used not only in the composition of its products, but also in its production process. Water usage also had significant environmental implications for the communities in which FIFCO operated. Therefore, the company set a goal to become water-neutral in 2012.

FIFCO used the method known as 'measure–reduce–compensate' to achieve this and other environmental goals, such as carbon neutrality and the reduction of solid waste. The company followed three steps: (1) monitor the current situation and measure the operational footprint; (2) reduce usage of the resource to the lowest possible level; and when further reductions were no longer possible, (3) compensate by generating or saving the resource externally, outside company operations.

In Mendiola's first year as CEO, FIFCO consumed 14 liters of water for every liter of beverage produced, according to the plant-level indicator used at the time. Efforts to reduce water consumption began immediately, reaching 8:1 by 2008. These efforts were accelerated with the introduction of the triple-bottom- line strategy. By 2011, the figure stood at 4.72:1, approaching the world benchmark of 3.5:1, which FIFCO adopted as its own goal.

To compensate for water usage in its operations, FIFCO used the *Water Footprint Assessment Manual*, published by the Water Footprint Network, which included definitions and accounting methods. Using the Manual, FIFCO implemented community initiatives for water compensation, such as the construction of the aqueduct Gavilán Canta, mentioned above. As a result of this project, 500 villagers no longer had to walk more than 2 km to access clean water.

Another way to compensate water usage was through a national program of environmental services, through which private owners of forest areas who undertook conservation projects received payments. FIFCO selected 449 hectares (1,123 acres) of forest in the upper basin of the Segundo River and 370 hectares in Santa Cruz as areas for providing environmental services.

The future

Having received global recognition as a Sustainability Champion and reviewed the achievement of goals for 2011 (shown in Exhibit 10), it was now time to consider the next great company goal. Mendiola was preparing for the upcoming annual retreat at which the entire management team would be present. He needed to establish a new long-term goal for FIFCO; if he did not, the company could lose momentum. FIFCO had become goal-driven, and the triple- bottom-line strategy could stagnate without a clear objective for the next two years. In the worst-case scenario, the progress made could be lost.

One option was to promote the triple-bottom-line strategy among the company's suppliers and/or its distribution channels, thus ensuring that the gains made by the company were not lost in other parts of the total farm-to-final-customer value chain. It was also a way to continue the 'evangelization' process outside the company's boundaries. However, it would be necessary to develop a business case for the Board of Directors and for the entire management team, not all of whom would agree that this was the responsibility of the company.

The company had already developed a manual of social responsibility for suppliers and a code for responsible suppliers and had even evaluated 90 suppliers with sustainable business practices. Sánchez commented:

> Before the triple bottom line, we had an ABC for our suppliers, which told us how much they bought and how important their material was for the uninterrupted operation of our business. Now our ABC tracks which among these suppliers least affect our water and carbon footprints because we want to work with these suppliers.

On the distribution side, FIFCO worked with networks of large retail chains such as Walmart and AutoMercado, a Costa Rican supermarket chain. At the other end of the spectrum, the company distributed its products to thousands of small liquor stores and traditional mom-and-pop stores, called *pulperías*, located throughout the country. FIFCO had already begun point-of-sale recycling initiatives with all types of retailers, and the employees of some outlets even participated as volunteers in recycling programs.

Some supporters of the triple bottom line within FIFCO, while not opposed to spreading this philosophy to business partners in the value chain, believed that priority should be placed on further consolidating the strategy inside the company.

EXHIBIT 1
Florida Ice & Farm Company, S.A. and Subsidiaries: statements of income and expenses, 2003–11 (years ending September 30, in billions of Costa Rican colones)

Statements of income and expenses	2003	2004	2005	2006	2007	2008	2009	2010	2011
Sales:									
Beer and beverages	68.8	75.1	93.2	116.8	163.7	198.6	208.2	231.1	258.7
Foods	–	–	–	4.4	27.7	33.4	34.4	34.4	35.8
Real estate	–	–	–	–	12.3	45.6	33.4	22.3	19.9
Other	0.0	0.0	0.6	1.1	0.8	2.1	1.7	2.0	2.6
Total sales	*69.0*	*75.4*	*93.8*	*122.3*	*204.6*	*279.7*	*277.8*	*289.8*	*317.0*
Cost of goods sold:									
Beer and beverages	19.9	21.8	33.8	42.6	64.1	77.2	81.6	85.9	95.9
Foods	–	–	–	3.3	19.8	24.0	25.9	25.1	26.0
Real estate	–	–	–	–	4.1	22.4	14.6	10.0	9.7
Other	0.0	0.0	0.5	0.7	1.2	1.6	1.4	1.4	1.7
Total cost of goods sold	19.9	21.8	34.3	46.7	89.2	125.1	123.5	122.4	133.3
Gross Profit	*49.1*	*53.6*	*59.4*	*75.6*	*115.3*	*154.6*	*154.3*	*167.4*	*183.7*
Sales and marketing expenses	24.1	22.3	25.6	33.2	47.8	64.4			
Administrative expenses	8.7	8.3	9.6	10.9	21.8	32.3			
Total operating costs	32.8	30.6	35.2	44.1	69.6	96.6	95.6	101.1	112.8
Operating profit	*16.4*	*23.0*	*24.2*	*31.5*	*45.7*	*58.1*	*58.7*	*66.3*	*70.9*
Other income / expenses (net)	64.6	0.0	0.8	3.2	16.1	–11.4	–11.2	–4.8	–6.8
Profits before taxes	*81.0*	*23.0*	*25.1*	*34.7*	*61.8*	*46.7*	*47.5*	*61.5*	*64.1*

Statements of income and expenses	2003	2004	2005	2006	2007	2008	2009	2010	2011
Taxes	3.5	6.8	6.5	8.1	13.6	14.1	15.8	21.9	22.1
Net after-tax profits	*77.5*	*16.2*	*18.5*	*26.6*	*48.2*	*32.6*	*31.6*	*39.5*	*42.0*
Less: minority interests	1.2	2.9	3.4	4.8	10.5	0.4	0.7	12.8	12.8
Net profits for shareholders	*76.3*	*13.3*	*15.1*	*21.8*	*37.7*	*24.2*	*22.9*	*26.7*	*29.2*

Note: The extraordinary income in 2003 was due to gains in the sale of shares.

Exchange rate, average (Sept.–Sept.)	388.2	427.5	466.8	503.0	518.1	533.0	566.1	542.2	506.6

Source: Financial statements published on FIFCO's webpage (www.florida.co.cr); Exchange Rate: Banco Central de Costa Rica (www.bccr.fi.cr).

EXHIBIT 2
Florida Ice & Farm Company, S.A. and Subsidiaries: Balance Sheets, 2003–11 (years ending September 30, in billions of Costa Rican colones)

Balance Sheets	2003	2004	2005	2006	2007	2008	2009	2010	2011
Assets:									
Cash	7.2	3.2	1.6	3.0	6.3	7.5	6.7	34.3	54.3
Financial assets	–	–	–	39.3	15.3	12.9	29.1	12.6	–
Accounts receivable	6.7	8.2	10.4	17.9	24.1	34.7	28.7	29.1	30.6
Inventories	11.7	8.2	8.8	16.0	25.1	34.7	32.3	31.3	34.0
Properties for sale (short-term)	–	–	–	–	13.8	7.6	5.4	2.1	1.7
Other current assets	80.6	62.0	64.7	3.0	5.5	8.0	9.2	9.5	20.6
Total Current Assets	106.3	81.6	85.4	79.2	89.9	105.4	111.4	118.9	141.2

Balance Sheets	2003	2004	2005	2006	2007	2008	2009	2010	2011
Plant and equipment; real estate	61.4	59.9	57.7	65.6	161.1	171.6	183.6	168.2	172.0
Other fixed assets	37.8	54.9	63.2	100.5	148.7	158.9	167.4	157.7	156.3
Total Fixed Assets	99.2	114.8	120.9	166.1	309.8	330.5	351.0	326.0	328.3
Total Assets	**205.4**	**196.4**	**206.3**	**245.4**	**399.7**	**435.9**	**462.3**	**444.9**	**469.5**
Liabilities and Capital:									
Short-term debt	5.0	3.8	5.1	37.9	74.2	44.3	16.3	12.4	18.8
Accounts payable	9.6	7.2	8.2	8.2	19.8	20.1	14.0	16.6	22.4
Other current liabilities	7.9	9.7	12.1	17.1	45.4	31.1	25.8	30.9	27.2
Total Current Liabilities	22.5	20.7	25.4	63.2	139.4	95.5	56.1	59.9	68.4
Long-term debt	25.2	12.8	9.5	6.0	30.6	87.8	124.3	108.6	108.6
Deferred taxes	–	–	–	–	4.9	12.8	16.1	9.1	10.8
Other long-term liabilities	6.4	8.0	9.4	13.2	0.0	0.0	0.0	0.0	0.0
Total Long-Term Liabilities	31.6	20.8	18.9	19.2	35.5	100.6	140.4	117.8	119.4
Capital shares in circulation	39.2	38.5	39.1	39.0	38.8	38.8	38.8	38.3	38.2
Additional paid-in capital	0.0	0.4	0.1	0.1	0.1	0.1	0.1	0.1	0.1
Reserves	5.9	6.0	28.8	33.0	63.2	61.8	73.8	58.7	61.5
Undistributed profits	82.4	79.4	80.5	74.7	97.6	108.8	119.5	134.8	145.3
Minority interest	11.7	13.0	13.4	16.2	25.2	30.3	33.7	35.3	36.7
Other capital	12.0	16.9							
Total Capital	151.2	154.3	161.9	162.9	224.9	239.7	265.8	267.2	281.7
Total Liabilities and Capital	**205.3**	**195.8**	**206.2**	**245.3**	**399.7**	**435.9**	**462.3**	**444.9**	**469.5**
Exchange rate US$, as of Sept. 30th	407.77	446.98	486.40	519.73	516.39	549.59	582.49	502.55	508.36

Source: Financial statements published on Florida Ice & Farm's webpage (www.florida.co.cr); Exchange rate: Banco Central de Costa Rica (www.bccr.fi.cr).

EXHIBIT 3
Florida Ice & Farm Co.: business units and major brands

DIVISION	CATEGORY	BRAND
Alcoholic Beverages	Beer	Imperial, Imperial Light, Pilsen, Bavaria Gold, Bavaria Light, Bavaria Dark, Heineken, rock Ice, Rock Ice Limón y Kaiser.
	Flavoured Drinks	Smirnoff Ice, Bomboo y Cuba Libre.
	Wines	Concha y Toro
Non Alcoholic Beverages	Water	Cristal
	Fruit Drinks, Nectars, Te,	Tropical, Tampico, Kern's, Lipton
	Carbonated	Pepsi, Pepsi Light, 7 UP, Evervess, Mirinda, Milory
	Others	Maxi Malta, Gatorade, Maxxx Energy y Adrenalina
Food	Tomato Sauce and Pasta	Kern's
	Beans	Ducal

Source: Adapted from Florida Ice & Farm's triple bottom line presentation, April 2012.

EXHIBIT 4
Florida Ice & Farm Co.: strategic objectives and goals

Dimensions		Goals	Strategic Priorities		
1. Environmental		Improve Florida's environmental performance	1. Efficient use of water resource	2. Efficient use of energy and decrease of transmission of greenhouse gases	3. Proper management of solid waste
2. Social	Internal	Improve the quality of life of our employees and their families	1. Aim Culture: Live the company's values	2. Occupational health and safety	3. Talent Development
	External	Have a positive impact in the communities where we operate	1. Promotion of responsible alcohol consumption	2. Social Strategic Investment	3. Transparency and Ethics
3. Economic		Generate economic value for our shareholders and other stakeholders	1. Creation of economic value	2. Market Leadership	3. Growth in sales and profit

Source: Florida Ice & Farm's annual sustainability report, 2010.

EXHIBIT 5
Eco-Florida: macro indicators for environmental goals

Indicator	Specific Metric	Environmental Goal
Water consumption	• hl water / hl produced	Become water neutral in 2012
Consumption of Electric and Thermal Energy	• kWh o Mj / hl produced	Become carbon neutral in 2017
Emissions of Greenhouse Gases	• Ton CO_2 / hl produced	
Post-Industrial Waste	• Kg / hl produced	Become a leader in solid waste management
Packaging Recovery Post-consumer Non Returnable	• % of packages sent to the market	
Environmental Policy / ISO14001	• Certification award	

Source: Florida Ice & Farm's annual sustainability report, 2009.

EXHIBIT 6
Example of FIFCO's Sustainability Balanced Scorecard

As shown below, all employees were able to keep track of their performance and that of their subordinates regularly through the company's intranet system.

Sustainability Balance Scorecard for Sales Manager, Costa Rica

For example, for this person, 15% of his balanced scorecard corresponded to corporate goals, while individual performance was weighted 85%.

| Corporate Result | Individual Result | Combined Result |

The next section/screen of the Intranet details all the indicators that the employees have on their balanced scorecards. An example of one of Florida's employees is presented as follows (just as reference):

Indicator	Weight	Goal_80	Goal	Result	Score	Accomplishment	Objective	Perspective	Dimension
0307 – Star (ECO – Planta)	10%	80	86	86	100%	10%	Keep processes in harmony with the environment	Internal processes	Environmental
0251 – Execution of projects	10%	80	100	95	95%	9.5%	Assess performance of HR	Learning and Growth	Economic
0065 – Budget compliance	5%	1473.96	1.431,03	1.436,32	97,54%	4,88%	Reduction of costs and expenses	Financial	Economic
0095 – Savings and productivity plan	5%	238.29	219.25	345.42	120%	6%	Reduction of costs and expenses	Financial	Economic
0317 – Star: quality	5%	60	65	68	120%	6%	Develop successfully new products	Internal processes	Economic
0301 – Operational performance: bottles	10%	57	61	60	95%	9.5%	Efficient production	Internal processes	Economic
0302 – Operational performance: cans	10%	59	63	62.2	96%	9.6%	Efficient production	Internal processes	Economic
0304 – Overall productivity (brewery)	5%	7500	7850	7347	0%	0.0%	Efficient production	Internal processes	Economic
0310 – Audit TPM: maintenance	10%	65	70	73	120%	12.0%	Efficient production	Internal processes	Economic

0310 – Audit TPM: G.autonomy	5%	71	76	76	100%	5.0%	Efficient production	Internal processes	Economic
0102 – Satisfaction of the employees	10%	80	100	100	100%	10.0%	Build/shape a goal corporate culture	Learning and Growth	Social
0204 – Frequency of accidents at work	5%	4	3.2	1.72	120%	6.0%	Build/shape a goal corporate culture	Learning and Growth	Social
0320 – Volunteerism	5%	14	16	16	100%	5%	Forging corporate culture	Learning and Growth	Social
0135 – Findings of internal audit not resolved on time	5%	80	95	100	100%	5%	Forging corporate culture	Learning and Growth	Social

Source: Florida Ice & Farm's balanced scorecard system, April 2012.

EXHIBIT 7
Data on beer consumption

Beer consumption per capita in Latin American countries (liters / total population)

Country	2008	2009
Argentina	40.22	12.65
Bolivia	35.56	33.74
Brasil	52.79	45.21
Chile	35.88	35.55
Colombia	42.61	41.40
Costa Rica	35.39	32.71
Ecuador	35.04	37.98
El Salvador	12.01	11.17
Guatemala	11.44	10.48
Honduras	14.88	15.48
Mexico	60.64	59.76
Nicaragua	17.82	16.38
Panama	65.71	62.36
Paraguay	35.33	37.97
Peru	43.17	39.72
Dominican Republic	39.81	38.38
Uruguay	25.17	25.54
Venezuela	89.95	81.15

Average, Latin America: 37 liters / total population.

Source: Adapted from Cerveceros Latinoamericos, Industry Statistical Information: Index 2010.

Patterns of alcohol consumption, Costa Rica vs. Québec

Country/Region	Costa Rica[3]	Québec[4]
Consumers (%)	57%	82%
Dangerous Consumption	4%	2%
Occasional Excessive	16%	3%
Consumption (drinks/per time)	5	2.5
Frequency (days/week)	1.75	4
Association	'Party'	'Pleasure'

Source: Florida Ice & Farm's triple bottom line presentation, April 2012.

3 Data provided by Facultad Latinoamericana de Ciencias Sociales (FLACSO)
4 Data provided by Éduc'Alcool, Quebec

EXHIBIT 8
Marketing Activities in FIFCO's Responsible Consumption Campaign

- **Moderation as a value:** In the period 2009–10, FIFCO launched a campaign with the claim 'moderation: our next step,' in alliance with the Ministry of Health and several media. This initiative was very successful because, according to an external firm, the audience reached was 93.7%–89% of the people who watched a commercial remembered the central message, and more than 75% of them considered it relevant.

- **Formula 2 3 4 0:** A campaign to promote responsible consumption among adults, by explaining the different guidelines for men and women. Also, there are groups of individuals for whom '0' applies, meaning that they should not consume alcohol at all. For example, pregnant women, teenagers under 18 and car drivers. FIFCO used mainly brochures, posters and billboards to reach the target audience.

- **Beer Expert Program:** To train Florida's employees to promote moderation and responsible consumption. By 2011, more than 300 employees from the areas of marketing, sales, and beer manufacturing had graduated from this program.

- **Initiatives with customers:** Florida launched several campaigns to promote responsible consumption in the distribution channels. For example, at more than 200 points of sale, it implemented the program 'I am responsible, I do not sell alcohol to people under 18.' Additionally, the company created another program called 'Responsibility in action' to encourage their customers (liquor stores, groceries, others) to reduce dangerous consumption.

- **Highway Safety Programs:** Florida worked in alliance with the Ministry of Public Works and Transport to develop several initiatives as part of the 'Choose to Help' program. For example, Florida invested more than US$100,000, and 100 employees collaborated with volunteer hours, to rebuild the center for driving education and to offer road safety lessons, especially oriented to children.

Source: Adapted from Florida Ice & Farm's annual report, 2010–11.

EXHIBIT 9
Data on the 'Choose to Help' Volunteer Program

How does the program work?

- FIFCO has a variety of projects to choose from in the social and environmental fields.

- Employees also propose projects that they consider relevant and strategic.

- The company offers two working days per year to everybody to do volunteer service.

- The indicator 'volunteer hours' is included in the social dimension of the balanced scorecard of every single employee of the company.

- After every activity, the Manager of Social Investment carries out a survey.

Proud of the achievement of his division, Arnold Prada, Supply Chain Manager, explained that his team was highly motivated:

*'According to the 'Choose to Help' program, every employee has to complete at least **16 hours of volunteer service**, during their working schedule. Last year, the supply chain team completed 939 additional hours'*

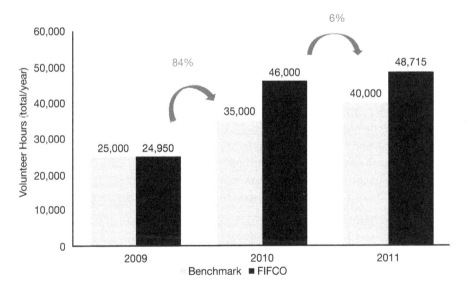

Source: Adapted from Florida Ice & Farm's triple bottom line presentation, April 2012.

EXHIBIT 10

Matrix of Goal Achievement – Year 2011

Strategic Objective	Results 2011	Savings vs. 2010	Unit Cost	Economic Impact 2011 (US$/year)	Additional Comments
Reduce the environmental footprint and become the first neutral company in Central America					
Efficient use of water resource (hlwater/hlproduced)	5.0E (Costa Rica)	1,156,836	0.013 US$/hl	15,198	Savings from water distribution and treatment. It does not reflect the impact on the cost of water, as FIFCO pays a concession fee.
Efficient use of energy and decrease of carbon emissions					
Thermal Energy (MJ/hlp)	161.12 (Costa Rica, 83.8 (Guatemala)	(1)			
Electric Energy (KWh/hlp)	10.95 (Costa Rica, 8.79 (Guatemala)	208,161	0.053 US$/kWh	11,033	
Emissions of CO_2 (tonCO_2/hlp)	0.0163 (Costa Rica, 0.0095 (Guatemala)	(1)			

Proper management of solid waste

Reduce to zero our post-industrial waste (Kg/hlp)	0.119 (Costa Rica)	0.100 (Costa Rica)	24.509 US$/MT	610,843	Disposal cost avoided by not sending waste to a landfill. It does not include transportation costs.
	98.5% waste recovery			549,342	Income from selling the recoverable post-industrial waste. It does not include post-consumer waste.
With the support of our customers, we recycle 100% of our post-consumer packaging	42.10%	31% (in 2010)		–128,917	Recycling post-consumer waste has an independent P&L statement. In 2011, revenues were US$ 2.6 million, but the overall operation showed a loss of $130K.

Improve the quality of life of our employees and their families

Occupational health and safety (incidence and severity)	Incidence: 2.68%, severity: 0.72 days (2)	Incidence: 3.8%, severity: 0.8 days (in 2010)		180,000	Decrease in the amount of the insurance premium for the past six years.

(1) No savings were reported between 2010 and 2011.

(2) Incidence is the percentage of employees that suffered an accident while working. Severity is the number of working days the employee lost due to the accident.

Source: Florida Ice & Farm, May 2012.

APPENDIX A
Briefing on Costa Rica (2011)

During the past 60 years, Costa Rica has enjoyed political stability and a consolidated democratic regime. The government abolished the army in 1949 and invested heavily in health and education. As Latin America's oldest democracy, Costa Rica has been an oasis of stability in a region that has been constantly degraded by war. The 1987 Nobel Peace Prize awarded to former President Oscar Arias for his role in the Central American peace accords is a point of pride for Costa Ricans and confirms their general appreciation for peace.

Costa Rica has consistently been among the top Latin American countries in the Human Development Index (HDI), ranked 69th in the world in 2011. It was also cited by the United Nations Development Program (UNDP) in 2010 as one of the countries that has attained much higher human development than other countries at the same income levels. Its health care system is ranked higher than that of the United States, despite having a fraction of the US GDP. By the year 2000, social health insurance coverage was available to 82% of the Costa Rican population. The literacy rate was 94.9%, one of the highest in Latin America. Elementary and high schools are found throughout the country, in practically every community. Universal public education is guaranteed in the constitution. Primary education is obligatory, and both preschool and high school are free.

Due to the country's political stability and relatively high education levels, as well as the fiscal incentives offered in the free-trade zones, Costa Rica has attracted one of the highest levels of foreign direct investment per capita in Latin America. Costa Rica used to be known mainly for its production of bananas and coffee. Even though coffee, bananas, pineapples, sugar, lumber, wood products and beef were still important exports in 2011, such industries as electronics, pharmaceuticals, financial outsourcing, software development, and ecotourism have become the primary industries in the country's economy in recent years. Since 1999, tourism has earned more foreign exchange than the combined exports of the country's three main agricultural exports.

In 2011, Costa Rica was highlighted by UNDP for being a good performer on environmental sustainability, and for having a better record on human development and equality than the median of their region. The country is ranked fifth in the world, and first among the Americas, in terms of the 2012 Environmental Performance Index. According to the New Economics Foundation, Costa Rica ranks first in the Happy Planet Index and is the 'greenest' country in the world.

Costa Rica developed a system of payments for environmental services by which the government offers incentives to farmers or landowners in exchange for managing their land to provide some sort of ecological service. In May 2007, the Costa Rican government announced its intentions to become 100% carbon neutral before the year 2030.

Costa Rica Basic information

Land area	51,100 km²	
Capital City	San José	
Neighboring Countries	Panama (South) Nicaragua (North)	Pacific Ocean (West) Caribbean Sea (East)
Population	4.4 m (based on the 2000 census)	
Official Language	Spanish	
Currency	1 colón (C) Average exchange rate in 2011, C508.4:US$1;	

Comparative economic indicators 2010

Economic Indicators	Costa Rica	Guatemala	Nicaragua	Honduras	El Salvador
Nominal GDP (US$ m)	35.8	41.2	6.4	15.4	21
Real GDP growth (%)	4.2	2.8	4.5	2.8	1.4
GDP per head (US$ at PPP)	10,650	7,187	3,039	3,806	6,398
Consumer prices (end-period; %)	5.8	5.4	9.2	6.5	2.1
Lending interest rate (av; %)	17.1	13.3	13.3	18.9	7.6
Exports of goods fob (US$ bn)	9.4	8.6	3.2	5.7	4.6
Imports of goods fob (US$ bn)	−13	−12.9	−4.8	−8.6	−8.2
Cur-account balance (US$ m)	−1,299	−878	−963	−955	−488
Debt stock (US$ m)	8,593	14,340	4,787	3,748	11,069

Source: Economist Intelligence Unit.

Protecting our oceans
Sustainability at Holland America Line[*]

Murray Silverman

Holland America Line (HAL) was proud of its reputation as a sustainability leader in the global cruise industry. Bill Morani, V.P. Safety & Environmental Management Systems, was responsible for ensuring that the company and fleet complied with safety and environmental regulations and policies. He had been with HAL since 2003 following a 25-year career in the U.S. Coast Guard. In light of the maritime industry's significant environmental impacts and the complex and rapidly evolving regulatory environment, Bill was thinking about the company's current initiatives in order to prioritize the areas that should be emphasized in the future. Bill's thinking was interrupted as Dan Grausz, Executive V.P., Fleet Operations, came into his office waving an article about a Stena Line ferry that claimed that the two helical turbines on the deck of one of their ferries was achieving cost-effective reductions in fuel use. Dan was the leader of the Fuel Conservation Committee, and he reminded Bill that wind turbines on the ship's deck was one of the 56 initiatives in the spreadsheet tracking their priority in being considered for adoption. However, this initiative had been assigned a very low priority, and Dan asked Bill to report back to the Fuel Conservation Committee (FCC) as to whether time and resources should be expended in reconsidering or piloting it.

---

[*] Also published in Parsa, H.G., Narapareddy, V., Jang, S., Segarra-Oña, M., and Chen, R.J.C., (Eds), "Sustainability, Social Responsibility, and Innovations in Tourism and Hospitality," Apple Academic Press, 2014.

Bill was particularly proud of the progress HAL had made in increasing fuel efficiency. HAL had committed to reduce its fuel use (on a per passenger berth – per nautical mile traveled basis), and thus it's associated carbon emission intensity by 20% between 2005 and 2015. They achieved this goal by 2011. Reductions in the quantity of fuel used to sail each guest on a voyage reduced HAL's carbon emission intensity as well as the intensity of emissions of sulfur and nitrous oxides (SOX and NOX) and particulate matter (PM). Regulations relating to SOX, NOX, and PM were becoming a major issue for the cruise industry, as there was increasing concern about their health and environmental impacts. According to Bill:

> Fuel conservation is our 'go-to' strategy. It is a win–win. By consuming less fuel, we are not emitting as much exhausts containing green house gases and other pollutants, while reducing HAL's fuel costs, and by the way, the money saved through fuel conservation can help offset the increased cost of cleaner fuel.

Bill put aside his thinking about broader sustainability priorities in order to look into the wind turbine idea.

Our oceans

Holland America Line (HAL) and the cruise industry business models rely on the oceans as their most important resource. The unspoiled waters and coral reefs at port destinations are a major attraction for passengers. Our oceans cover 71% of the earth's surface and they provide food in the form of fish and shellfish, they are used for transportation and for recreation, such as swimming, sailing, diving, and surfing. They are a source of biomedical organisms that help fight disease. And very importantly, the ocean plays a significant role in regulating the planet's climate. The oceans are an integral part of the world's climate system, absorbing CO_2 and heat. The oceans and the atmosphere work together in defining our weather patterns.[i] Unfortunately, our oceans face many threats:

Overfishing: More than half the planet depends on the oceans for its primary source of food, yet most of the world's fisheries are being fished at levels above their maximum sustainable yield. Furthermore, harmful fishing methods unnecessarily kill turtles, dolphins and other animals and destroy critical habitat.

Pollution: There are numerous sources of ocean pollution. An enormous amount of oil has been accidentally spilled from ships. While this in itself is destructive to aquatic plant and animal life, the threat from land-based activities is also great. Eighty percent of all pollution in seas and oceans comes from land-based activities.[ii] More oil reaches the ocean each year as a result of leaking automobiles and other non-point sources than was spilled by the Exxon Valdez.

Eutrophication: Another serious ocean threat is algal blooms which form and spread in coastal areas due to nutrient overloading primarily as a result of fertilizer and topsoil runoff and sewage discharges in coastal areas. As the algae die and decompose, the water is depleted of available oxygen, causing the death of other organisms, such as fish.

Black and grey water: The shipping industry, as well as recreational boats, discharge black water (human waste) and grey water (water from galley sinks and showers) at varying distances from shore. Cruise ships are outfitted with equipment that treats the black and gray water prior to overboard discharge.

Ocean acidification: Global warming is primarily driven by the increasing accumulation of CO_2 in the atmosphere due to the burning of fossil fuels. On the positive side for the earth's ecosystem, the oceans absorb about one third of this anthropogenic carbon, reducing the atmospheric warming potential. However, the CO_2 absorbed is converted into carbonic acid, which increases the acidity of the ocean. The current rate of ocean acidification is unprecedented, and the increase in acidity dissolves the carbonates needed by organisms such as corals and oysters, thereby threatening their survival. It is estimated that acidification is a major contributor along with ocean warming to the loss of 20% of our coral reefs, and that by mid-century; we may lose another 50%.[iii]

Ocean warming: Global warming is also increasing the temperature of the ocean. Increasing ocean temperature leads to significant marine ecosystem change, influencing the generation of plankton, which forms the base of the ocean's food web. Coral reefs are also endangered as they are extremely sensitive to temperature change. Over 90% of marine species are directly or indirectly dependent on these reefs.[iv]

Tourism: While tourism generates vast amounts of income for host countries, it can have negative social and environmental side effects. The most significant impacts are in the heavily visited coastal areas. Sewage and waste emanating from the local residents, resorts, hotels, restaurants, and the housing that supports the tourism related employees can find their way directly or indirectly into the bays and ocean. Even when there is municipal infrastructure, the sewage system can become overwhelmed or inadequate, resulting in seepage or dumping into the ocean. Also, careless diving, snorkelling, and other tour activities can damage coral reefs.

Ocean protection

The oceans are a global commons that is not under the control of a single nation, except for the territorial waters of coastal nations. There are a number of formal institutions and instruments that provide national governments the opportunity to cooperate in managing the ocean commons. These agreements may be bi-lateral, regional or global. Examples of these agreements include the UN Convention on the Law of the Sea (UNCLOS), which is a comprehensive treaty establishing protocols for the use and exploitation of the ocean and its resources. The International Whaling Convention (IWC), which implements the International Convention for the Regulation of Whaling, regulates the hunting of great whales. There are many other agreements and conventions, but they all apply only to nations that sign them, and even then there can be variations in enforcement.[v]

Cruise industry

According to the World Tourism Organization (WTO), tourism has become one of the largest and fastest growing economic sectors in the world.[vi] Taking a cruise is a popular tourist experience and the cruise industry is one of the fastest growing sectors of the tourism industry. Prior to the mid-20th century, ships focused on transporting customers to a particular destination. The modern cruise industry traces its beginnings to the early 1970s in Miami, USA with cruises throughout the Caribbean. The industry created a reasonably priced opportunity for many people to experience a resort-type vacation. Sometimes, cruise ships are referred to as floating hotels or marine resorts, because like land resorts, they have rooms, restaurants, entertainment, shops, spas, business centers, casinos, swimming pools, and other amenities.

Cruise ships travel worldwide in every ocean, and frequently visit the most pristine coastal waters and sensitive marine eco-systems. Cruise packages typically include more than one destination. The most popular destinations are the Caribbean, the Mediterranean, a number of European ports, the Bahamas, and Alaska. There are approximately 2,000 ports capable of receiving cruise ships. The amount of time spent at a destination can vary from one-half day to many days, depending on the design of the cruise package. The length of cruises can vary from two days to over two weeks, with an average length of about seven days. Destinations vary from tropical beaches, like Cozumel, to nature-based destinations, such as Alaska, while others might feature historical and culturally rich locations such as Istanbul. The cruise product is incredibly diversified, based on destination, ship design, on-board, and on-shore activities, themes, and cruise lengths. Cruise accommodations and amenities differ and are priced accordingly. A typical classification of cruise types ranges from budget to conventional to premium and lastly to luxury.[vii] Exhibit 1 elaborates on the differences between these categories. The passenger capacity of cruise ships tends to be larger at the budget and conventional categories and varies from a few hundred to over 5,000 passengers.

The popularity of cruising is reflected in its growth. Since 1980, the industry has had an annual passenger growth rate of 7.6%. Between 1990 and 2010, over 191 million passengers have taken a cruise.[viii] Twenty four percent of the American population has cruised. As demand grew, the industry responded by building more cruise ships. As of 2012, there were 256 cruise ships.[ix] Newer ships tend to be bigger, they include innovative amenities, such as planetariums and bowling alleys, and they are being designed to conserve fuel.

The typical cruise passenger is predominately Caucasian (93%), average age is 46 years, well educated, married (83%) with an average household income between (US$90–100k).[x] The leading factors in the customer decision to select a cruise package are the destination and the price. Customers tend to be very price sensitive. It does not appear that many customers factor a cruise line's environmental practices into their choice of cruise lines.[xi] The uniqueness of the experience also ranks highly. The customer can choose from luxury, premium, conventional, and budget offerings based on the packages being offered and the price. The packages are highly differentiated based on destination and the amenities associated with the ship. Ninety percent of the bookings come through travel agents.[xii]

Industry structure

The cruise line industry is a 30 billion dollar a year global industry. Three major cruise companies dominate the industry, and in 2012 controlled 84.3% market share based on number of passengers: Carnival Corporation (51.6%), Royal Caribbean Cruises Ltd. (21%), and Norwegian Cruise Line (7.1%).[xiii] The major cruise companies each have a number of brands, allowing them to operate within the different pricing segments. The market shares of the brands of Carnival, which includes HAL, are listed in Exhibit 2 along with the market shares of other cruise lines. Many of HAL's and Royal Caribbean's brands were a result of acquisitions. The resulting consolidation of the industry led to the high level of market share concentration. However, this level of concentration was not viewed as anti-competitive by the Federal Trade Commission, because cruise ships are viewed as part of the resort industry, rather than as an independent cruise industry. Carnival Corporation had 2011 revenues of $15.8 billion and averaged net income to revenue of 13.0% over the three years 2009–11. Royal Caribbean had 2011 revenues of $7.5 billion and averaged net income to revenue of 6.1% over those three years.[xiv]

There are a number of Cruise Line Associations. The largest is the Cruise Line Industry Association (CLIA), whose membership includes 22 of the world's largest cruise line companies, accounting for 97% of the demand for cruises.

The cruise lines have the ability to compete with each other on the basis of a highly diversified set of offerings. Much like hotels, they offer different levels of comfort and style, all priced accordingly. In addition, cruise lines can vary destinations, cruise lengths, ship themes, and amenities in the packages they offer. To the envy of traditional hotels, the major cruise lines operate at 100% occupancy levels. They do this through a marginal pricing strategy, adjusting prices downward as the date of departure approaches.

There are major barriers to entry and exit in the industry due to the high cost of purchasing ($300–500 million) or selling a single cruise ship and the large investment required to operate a cruise line. In terms of the supply chain, there are many sellers to choose from in terms of food, supplies, equipment, and fuel. On the other hand, ship builders are few and are in a strong negotiating position. Cruise ships need many employees. There might be as few as 2–2.5 passengers for each employee. While there is an ample supply of cabin stewards and other lower skill jobs, there is a shortage of qualified deck and engineering officers.[xv]

Regulations

The mechanisms governing the shipping industry are complex and multi-layered. Shipping activities are regulated by a mixture of the international law of the sea and the laws of various nations. The country where a ship is registered is called the flag state. The flag state is obligated to ensure that the ships it registers comply with regulations set down in international conventions and agreements to which the flag state is a signatory. The International Maritime Organization (IMO) plays an important role in developing regulations relating to shipping.[xvi] The IMO is the United Nations' specialized agency responsible for improving maritime safety and preventing pollution from ships. Their regulations relate to safety, labor standards, and the environment. Even though a ship may be registered in a flag state that has not ratified a particular IMO convention, that ship must conform to the conventions adopted by nations it visits. Since almost all cruise ship ports are in nations that have ratified the IMO regulations, cruise ships must abide by IMO regulations.

Sustainability in the cruise industry

There is a wide range of environmental and social aspects and potential impacts associated with cruise ship operations. There are discharges to water and to air, enormous amounts of waste are generated and there are environmental aspects associated with inputs such as packaging and food sourcing. Social aspects relate to employees, cruise customers, and impacts on destination communities. The environmental aspects and impacts are displayed in Exhibit 3.

Prior to 2000, each of the three major cruise companies listed above had been convicted of violations of U.S. water quality laws. In response to these convictions, the Cruise Line Industry Association (CLIA) developed Cruise Industry Waste Management Practices and Procedures.[xvii] CLIA members have adopted these voluntary environmental standards, which exceed the requirements of U.S. and international laws. Formal adoption is reflected by a cruise line including the requirements in the company's Safety Management System (SMS). As a result of these standards and an industry-wide effort to be responsible environmental citizens, the cruise industry has dramatically improved its environmental performance.

However, some cruise lines perform better than others in the environmental and social arena, because CLIA does not describe the manner in which the voluntary standards are to be implemented by their members or impose consequences for failing to incorporate them. Also, there may be a failure to adhere to an adopted voluntary standard due to equipment failure or operator error. Lastly, the standards do not address every environmental issue. In comparing performance across cruise lines, HAL has been recognized as a top performer.

Holland America Line and sustainability

HAL was founded as a shipping and passenger line in 1873 and offered its first vacation cruises in 1895. Over its first 136 years, HAL has carried over 11 million passengers. In 1989, HAL became a wholly owned subsidiary of Carnival Corporation. HAL maintains its own identity, operating its own fleet and managing its marketing, sales, and administrative support. In 2011, HAL operated 15 mid-size ships and expected to carry 750,000 passengers to 350 ports in 100 countries. HAL operates ships with passenger capacities in the 1200 to 2100 passenger range. HAL is recognized as a leader in the industry's premium segment. HAL has more than 14,000 employees and is headquartered in Seattle, Washington, USA.[xviii] Holland America has received a number of awards for environmental sustainability and responsible tourism. In 2006, HAL was awarded the Green Planet Award, which recognizes eco-minded hotels, resorts, and cruise lines for outstanding environmental standards.[xix] This award was based on their ISO 14001 certification and the installation of shore power plug-in systems on three ships. In 2008, Virgin Holidays awarded HAL the Responsible Tourism Award based on reducing dockside emissions by 20%, increasing recycling by 50% and instituting a training program to avoid 'whale strikes'.[xx] HAL was named the World's Leading Green Cruise Line at the World Travel Awards in London in 2011[xxi] and they received a 2010 and 2012 Rear Admiral William M. Benkert Gold Environmental Protection Award from the U.S. Coast Guard.[xxii] HAL does not advertise its environmental credentials or accomplishments to potential customers, nor do any of their competitors.

In 2009, HAL released its first sustainability report covering activities from 2007–09. Other Carnival Corporation subsidiaries also developed sustainability reports and were among the first in the industry to do so. Their sustainability report used the Global Reporting Initiative's (GRI) G3 Guidelines as the framework for their report. They include a GRI content index so that readers can see where GRI categories are covered in the report. The data in this baseline report was not independently verified, although this was not unusual among first time GRI reporters. Their environmental management system (EMS) was recertified in 2009 and 2012 as meeting the ISO 14001 environmental standards.

Discharges to water

Exhibit 4 diagrams the various discharges associated with a cruise ship. The primary discharges to water include black water (sewage), gray water (from showers, sinks, laundry, and the galley), and bilge water (potentially oily water leaked from engines and equipment that accumulates in the bilges). Black water is an issue because it contains pathogens, including fecal coliform bacteria that needs to be removed before being released into the environment. Untreated blackwater can cause serious contamination of fisheries and shellfish beds, resulting in a general contamination of the food chain and a risk to human health by transmitting infectious diseases.

On most cruise ships, sewage is treated using a marine sanitation device (MSD) that disinfects the waste prior to discharge. While regulations require the use of marine sanitation devices (MSDs), there is a newer technology, Advanced Waste Water Purification Systems (AWWPS) that are capable of producing water effluent that is as clean or cleaner than that produced by many municipal treatment plants.[xxiii] HAL was instrumental in developing the AWWPS technology for use in cruise ships. The first installation was on the ms Statendam in 2002. These systems use a combination of screening, maceration, biodigestion, ultrafiltration, and ultraviolet light to go a quantum leap beyond MSDs. Approximately 40% of cruise ships have AWWPSs and more are being added every year. Holland America is a leader in this area, as 12 of their 15 ships have AWWPSs.

MARPOL (International Convention for the Prevention of Pollution from Ships) and U.S. regulations require that treated sewage (MSD or AWWPSs) be discharged at least 3 nautical miles (nm) from shore and untreated sewage at least 12 nm from shore. In addition, there are no discharge zones (NDZs) that limit discharges in certain areas. MSD discharges by HAL are at least 12 nm from shore.

Graywater can contain a wide variety of pollutant substances, including oil and some organic compounds, detergents and grease, suspended solids, nutrients, food waste and small concentrations of coliform bacteria. In the U.S., graywater was not considered a pollutant until recently. Current regulations prohibit the discharge of graywater within 3 miles of the coast in California and Alaska. CLIA voluntary standards specify a distance of at least 4 miles from the coast. There do not appear to be conclusive studies as to the safest distance from shore to discharge black water or gray water.[xxiv] Regulators require that discharged bilge water be less than 15 ppm (parts per million) while the vessel is en route and not operating in a special area. HAL was also a leader in improving bilge water treatment prior to overboard discharge.

HAL also reduces the amount of water used and discharged through various water conservation strategies. In 2009, HAL used their EMS to set a target to use 7% less water than in 2008. They exceeded the target using 9% less water through a number of approaches, including low-flush toilets, low flow shower heads and faucets, specialized pool filters, etc. In 2010, HAL passenger growth was 9.8%, but overall water use rose by only 1.8%.[xxv]

Solid and hazardous waste

Cruise ship waste streams can be either hazardous (chemicals from dry cleaning or photo processing, solvents, paint waste, etc.) or non-hazardous (food waste, paper, plastic, glass, etc.). The industry has grown 7.6% per year between 2000 and 2009, but has cut its waste almost in half.[xxvi]

The potential impact from pollution by solid waste on the open ocean and coastal environment can be significant, with a diversity of effects and consequences, including aesthetic degradation of surface waters and coastal areas, entanglement of sea birds, fish, turtles, and cetaceans, which may result in serious injury or even death by ingestion or asphyxiation, and nutrient pollution derived from continued disposal of food wastes in restricted areas.

HAL's disposition of solid waste breaks down as 26% going ashore primarily to landfills, 16% recycled to shore, 39% incinerated on board, and 19% (food waste and ground glass) discharged at sea. Recycled items include glass, paper, cardboard, aluminum, steel cans, and plastics. On HAL ships, paper and cardboard are shredded and are most often incinerated to reduce the fire load carried by the vessel. Food waste that has gone through a pulper is discharged more than 12 nm from shore.

In 2006, HAL set objectives to reduce solid waste offloads by 15% and to increase materials recycled ashore by 10%.[xxvii] Between 2007–08, solid waste disposed ashore increased by 5% and the total amount of solid waste recycled ashore increased by 86% attributable to fleet personnel properly segregating materials. The total quantity of waste generated by HAL during 2009 was 28% less than during 2008. The amount of material incinerated decreased by 27% in this period. Some of their waste management initiatives included replacing highly toxic perchloroethylene dry-cleaning with a non-toxic technology, developing a paint and thinner recycling program, and implementing a list of approved chemicals to reduce the use of toxics. HAL donates many partially used products and reusable items (mattresses, toiletries, linen, clothing, etc.) to non-profits.

Supply chain issues

Exhibit 3 shows that the primary inputs for a cruise are food, packaging materials, fresh water and fuel. Fresh water is needed to clean and prepare food, clean kitchen equipment, wash guest and crew linens and clothes, and to maintain engine room equipment. HAL used their EMS to target 7% less water use between 2008 and 2009 and they exceeded that target and used 9% less water. HAL has been working with their vendors to reduce packaging and this is reflected in their solid waste reduction.

One important supply chain issue with food is the sustainability of the seafood served. In 2010, HAL partnered with the Marine Conservation Institute (MCI) to protect marine ecosystems.[xxviii] MCI is a non-profit organization working with scientists, politicians, government officials, and other organizations around the world to protect essential ocean places and the wild species in them. The HAL/MCI program is entitled 'Our Marvelous Oceans' and includes the purchasing of sustainable seafood to be served on board, the development of a series of video programs about the oceans to be shown to guests and support for MCI to provide grants to graduate students and young scientists engaged in historical marine ecology. As part of the sustainable seafood program, MCI evaluated over 40 species of fish for HAL. MCI classified fish options within each species for HAL as best choice, good choice, not sustainable and need more information. Best choice seafood items are abundant, and caught or farmed in an environmentally friendly way. Good choice items are evaluated by MCI as acceptable although there may be some environmental concern. In those cases best choice alternatives are sought. For the 'not sustainable' category, HAL discontinued purchases of those items. When more information was needed, HAL went back to the suppliers, and in many cases where there was a sustainability issue, suppliers worked hard to find sustainable alternatives for HAL. In a few instances, HAL had to eliminate specific menu items, but in some cases they were able to find an acceptable substitute for a menu item they wanted to retain (e.g. sustainably fished dover sole caught with hook and lines). HAL embraced this program because there was strong interest at the top management levels and even though purchasing costs were higher.[xxix]

Social sustainability issues

The cruise industry also has social aspects in the areas of guest experience, employee satisfaction, and impacts on port communities visited by cruise ships. HAL's 800,000 guests are provided an opportunity to have a unique vacation, traveling by water to beautiful and interesting destinations, and they rate the cruise line very highly on follow-up surveys. In terms of employees, HAL makes considerable effort to be a socially responsible employer. Their sea going workforce was 81% Filipino and Indonesian, who are away from home 3–10 months of the year, working seven days a week. All of the Filipino and Indonesian employees work under a collective bargaining agreement. The International Labor Organization in Switzerland sets standards which the CLIA supports. Benefits for HAL employees include health care, room and board, paid vacation, sick leave, compassionate leave, and preparation of cuisine from their homeland. Seventy-two percent of HAL's more than 14,000 crew, officers and shore-side employees were covered by collective bargaining agreements in 2009.[xxx]

Community impacts associated with port visitations have complex social and environmental aspects for HAL and other cruise lines. When the cruise ship docks, thousands of passengers disembark, and it is a boon to merchants and the local economy. Many port destinations are economically dependent on tourists and cruise ships. However, the cruise line passengers can engender perceptions of income inequality and have other cultural impacts. Also, human health can be impacted by air pollution from SOX, PM, and NOX emitted from the ship's stacks. About 9–14% of a cruise ship's emission occur in ports (depending on the type of ship), as some of the ship's diesel engines are used to power lights, refrigeration units, pumps and other equipment.[xxxi]

Coastal water pollution is primarily an indirect impact associated with the cruise ships. While the cruise lines follow established regulations and voluntary standards that minimize the risk to the coastal waters, the number of passengers engaging in shore excursions in combination with tourists staying at the local resorts and hotels can place an excessive burden on the local municipal sewage treatment systems. Overflow from those systems or leaching from injection wells that are drilled to contain the sewage can enter the coastal water leading to algal blooms and pollution that degrade the coral reefs and coastal ecosystems that are the raison d'être for visiting the destination.

Another issue is the environmental footprint of the shore side vendors and tour operators (boating, snorkelling, and diving) that cater to the guests. The cruise lines responses to shore-side issues are referred to as destination stewardship. In 2003, CLIA partnered with Conservation International (CI) to establish the Ocean Conservation and Tourism Alliance with the goal of addressing the shared responsibilities among cruise lines, governments, civil society, and shore operators to manage the growth of tourism in sensitive ecosystems. An example of CI's efforts in partnership with the Coral Reef Alliance is the Mesoamerican Reef Tourism Initiative (MARTI), a stewardship initiative involving Carnival and Royal Caribbean cruise lines.[xxxii] MARTI is intended to protect the natural resources that draw tourists to Mexico, the Caribbean, Belize, and Honduras. MARTI partners meet in a multi-stakeholder format that includes private sector, government, and non-governmental organizations to develop solutions to port related environmental issues.

Emissions to air

Cruise ships generate the energy they need for propulsion as well as the electricity needed for lights, refrigeration, HVAC, and other equipment. Approximately 60% 0f the energy generated goes for propulsion, 15% HVAC, 10% lighting, 5% refrigerators and freezers, and 10% to other systems.[xxxiii] Engine exhaust is the primary source of ship emissions. The most significant gases are CO_2, NOX, SOX and particulate matter PM. The major concern with CO_2 is global warming. The primary concern with SOX, NOX and PM, is air pollution in coastal areas.

The primary fuel used by cruise ships is heavy fuel oil (HFO). Distillate and low sulfur fuel oil (LSFO) offer an alternative to HFO. The price of these lower sulfur fuels fluctuate, but they are expected to cost between 10 and 50% more than HFO.[xxxiv] Burning LSFO or distillate fuel reduces SOX and PM pollution, but the carbon footprint of these fuels is about the same as HFO. HAL relies primarily on HFO, but changes in national and international regulations in 2015, will require an increase in use of more expensive distillate fuel. In 2011, about 4% of fuel use at HAL was distillate.[xxxv] (See Exhibit 7: Fuel use and efficiency). Considering that fuel costs can be on the order of 15% of operating expense, increases in fuel cost would have a major impact on the industry.

CO_2 emissions

There is a high level of agreement that global warming is undermining the complex web of natural systems that allows life to thrive on earth. The CO_2 emissions from the burning of fossil fuels accounts for most of the increase in greenhouse gas (GHG) concentrations. Approximately 2–3% of the global total of CO_2 emissions comes from shipping, mostly from the 50,000 merchant ships plying the ocean.[xxxvi] The 350 cruise ships contribute in a small way to this problem. In comparison to shipping, CO_2 emissions from aviation contribute 2%, road transport 21%, and 0.5 % from rail.[xxxvii] According to the IMO, there is 'significant potential to reduce GHG through technical and operational measures.' The IMO estimates these measures could reduce emissions rate by 25% to 75% below 2009 levels (see Exhibit 5). Of course, not all of these measures are technically feasible and/or cost effective for the cruise lines, especially in the short term. Ship retrofit is very expensive, so design changes need to be built in up front. Some ships are getting as much as 7–10% fuel reduction from coatings.[xxxviii] Speed reductions can significantly increase fuel efficiency. A 10% reduction in speed can provide an energy saving of 19%.[xxxix] Just like with driving an automobile, ship size and speed is the most critical defining parameter with respect to fuel consumption.

Holland America Line's response to its GHG impact has been to reduce fuel use through:

- More energy efficient equipment
- More energy efficient ships
- Energy conservation
- Shore power
- Circulate monthly fuel use data to encourage competition between vessels
- Sharing best practices from high performing ships
- Providing monetary incentives to senior shipboard staff to encourage fuel conservation practices

These options not only conserve fuel and reduce GHG, they also reduce the amount of SOX, PM, and NOX because less fuel is burned. Exhibit 6 shows fuel use at HAL between 2007 and 2009. Fuel use overall increased due to an expanding fleet and passenger growth, however, on a normalized basis, the fuel used per available lower berth on the ships steadily decreased over that period.

SOX and NOX

The maritime industry accounts for approximately 4% and 7%, respectively, of global SOX and NOX emissions,[xl] of which a small proportion is attributable to the cruise industry. Combustion of HFO produces sulfur dioxide and particulate matter Sulfur dioxide reacts with other substances in the air to form acid rain, which falls to earth as rain, fog, snow, or dry particles. Some may be carried by wind for hundreds of miles. Acid rain causes deterioration of cars, buildings, and historical monuments; and causes lakes and streams to become acidic and unsuitable for many fish. PM may cause serious human health problems, including respiratory diseases, neurological damage, birth defects, or cancer. Emissions from cruise ships are of concern while a ship is at port, close to residents of coastal communities. NOX causes a wide variety of health and environmental impacts. Ground-level ozone (smog) is formed when NOX and volatile organic compounds (VOCs) react in the presence of heat and sunlight. Children, people with lung diseases such as asthma, and people who work or exercise outside, are susceptible to adverse effects such as damage to lung tissue and reduction in lung function.

The health and other environmental impacts associated with SOX, PM, and NOX emissions have been under intense regulatory scrutiny. International regulations (MARPOL) in 2000 lowered sulfur limits in fuel to 4.5% and for 2012 to 3.5 %, and for 2020, global sulfur limits are set at 0.5%. However, certain national and regional regulations have put reduced sulfur emissions on an even shorter time line. Emission Control Areas (ECAs) are being established that impose very tight limits on sulfur, NOX and PM for ships entering those areas. For example, sulfur limits are restricted to 1.0% levels already in the Baltic and EU rules will cap sulfur at 0.1% by 2015. Significant reductions in NOX are also being mandated. Australia, New Zealand, and Hong Kong have voluntary measures, likely to develop into ECAs by 2015. The industry is experimenting with seawater scrubbers in the stacks, which would remove a high level of SOX and PM. However, it is not yet clear as to whether the use of seawater scrubbers will be a less expensive option than low sulfur fuels. In any case, increasing regulatory pressure to reduce SOX, PM and NOX will have a significant financial impact on HAL and the rest of the cruise industry.

Managing fuel conservation at HAL

In 2005, HAL's parent, Carnival Corporation, set an ambitious corporate goal of increasing fuel efficiency as measured by the amount of fuel used per lower berth per nautical mile by 20% by 2015. In order to address the need to reduce fuel use, HAL had established a Fuel Conservation Committee in 2007 that systematically identified and assessed fuel reduction opportunities based primarily on projected fuel savings and return on investment (ROI). The committee was very effective in adopting successful initiatives based on established financial criteria, and HAL reached their 2015 target in 2011. (See Exhibit 7: Fuel use and efficiency.)

Bill participated in the weekly Fuel Conservation Committee[xli] meeting in Seattle, which explored and implemented various fuel conservation initiatives. In 2012 the committee was evaluating close to 50 initiatives. These initiatives fell into five broad categories, a majority of which required capital investments in new and modified equipment:

- Sailing and maneuvering (6 initiatives): Many of these initiatives involve the use of software to optimize speed and maneuvering.

- Modifying or adding equipment (28 initiatives): A wide variety of initiatives such as upgrades of air conditioner chiller control systems.

- Operational improvements (8 initiatives): Initiatives such as running one sea-water cooling pump while in port.

- Monitoring various sources of energy consumption (10 initiatives): Initiatives such as installation of KWh meters in electrical substations to monitor the energy consumption of various users.

- Waste Heat recovery (4 initiatives): Initiatives such as adding an additional heat exchanger to reuse high temperature waste heat for potable water heating

The committee's spreadsheet included estimates of potential savings from each initiative and the cost per ship. Typically, the estimates of savings were measured in terms of percentage of overall fuel budget. For the 38 initiatives for which estimates had been made, 13 would save 0.25% fuel or less, 16 save between 0.26% and 0.99%, nine might save more than 1.0%. The committee also tracked whether each initiative was proven or assumed to be viable and its stage of implementation (study, funding required, implemented, or discontinued). If the committee decided that a proposed fuel conservation initiative should be implemented, it was pilot tested on a single ship. Performance was tracked and if the results met investment criteria, the initiative would be eligible to be rolled out to other ships. Finally, based on all of this information, the committee assigns a priority (1, 2, or 3) to each initiative. Because there is a limited capital budget available to pursue fuel conservation projects, even initiatives with a priority of 1, might not be implemented, or might not be implemented fleet wide.

Because of the unproven nature of the wind turbine initiative, and skepticism on the part of HAL's engineering department personnel, the Fuel Conservation Committee had long ago assigned a priority '3' and an estimated fuel savings of less than 0.25%. Wind turbines can be horizontal (HAWT) or vertical axis (VAWT). However it appeared that VAWT were most appropriate on ships as they can withstand much higher wind speeds, and are significantly more efficient than HAWT.[xlii]

Bill read the article about Stena Line, a ferry line operating a travel service between Britain, Holland, and Ireland. He learned that Stena Line estimated that the two turbines installed on Stena Jutlandica would generate about 23,000 kWh per year, equivalent to the domestic electricity consumption for four normal homes during one year. (See Exhibit 8 for a photo of Stena Jutlandica.) This was equivalent to a reduction in fuel consumption of between 80 and 90 tons per year.[xliii] Bill began to inquire internally at HAL about the wind turbine idea, and one of his direct reports had received unsubstantiated information from a third-party that the Stena Line installation was projected to be very cost effective and that contrary to intuition, the turbines reduced aerodynamic drag on the ferry. Bill also found another article describing how Hornblower Cruises planned to launch the Hornblower hybrid to take passengers on sightseeing, dinner, and social events in New York Harbor.[xliv] This 600-passenger vessel would incorporate helical wind turbines, solar panels, and hydrogen fuel cells in addition to its diesel engine. The company believed the combination of alternative power generators would result in fuel savings that justified the investment.

Bill consulted with Pieter Rijkaart, former Director of New Builds, who had led the design and build of almost all of HAL's current fleet. Pieter mirrored the skepticism expressed by other engineers. For example, the engineers noted that a cruise liner is much larger and more streamlined than a ferry, raising questions about the applicability of the Stena Line performance results. There were also cost issues. A pilot test on one ship would require a large up-front investment in addition to the cost of the turbine, as it would have to be anchored to the deck and tied into the electrical grid on the ship. There were also major aesthetic concerns. Cruise ships are designed to have a beautiful appearance, and having bulky wind turbines on the deck could be an eyesore. Lastly, the amount of energy supplied by the wind turbines would account for an extremely small percentage of the ships energy needs.

Bill wondered whether there were intangible benefits associated with the use of wind turbines. HAL had already demonstrated a proactive interest in alternative energy initiatives. HAL had installed heat reflective film on windows to reduce the transfer of heat to the interior, and thus reducing the load on air conditioners. At a cost of $170,000 per ship, and a projected fuel savings between 0.5–1.0%, three ships had this technology installed and other ships awaited funding.[xlv] Also, HAL had adopted an initiative involving the pumping of used cooking oil into the fuel line. In 2010, HAL reused 51,000 liters of used cooking oil. This very low cost option resulted in both the reduction of fossil fuel and avoidance of the disposal cost of drums of used cooking oil. Wind turbines represented another opportunity for HAL to explore using alternative energy. While this could contribute to HAL's reputation as a sustainability leader in the industry, Bill did not believe that reputation should be factored into a FCC decision. According to Bill: 'We don't talk about whether something will get good press.' While the turbines would produce only a very small amount of the electricity used on the boat, they would contribute to reduced fuel use. Bill did not have enough information to estimate ROI or payback. Given that there were dozens of other proposed initiatives in the FCC spreadsheet, he wondered whether it made sense to expend FCC effort on this initiative. On the other hand, Bill said, 'I would be concerned that we could be missing an opportunity.' Bill was eager to pull together his thinking on the turbine initiative for the upcoming FCC meeting so that he could get back to longer-term thinking about the sustainability priorities facing HAL.

Discussion questions

1. From the viewpoint of the cruise line companies, do you believe that the industry will be more or less attractive in the future? Explain your thinking. How will sustainability issues and regulations impact industry attractiveness?

2. Who are the key stakeholders in relation to HAL's sustainability issues. What is the influence of each in terms of their potential impact on HAL?

3. What are the most significant environmental issues facing Holland America Line? In what ways has Holland America gone beyond compliance in its environmental initiatives?

4. What are the most significant social issues facing Holland America Line?

5. Bill Morani has asked for your assistance in assessing what action to take with respect to the wind turbine initiative. What would you recommend?

6. What are the challenges facing Bill Morani and Holland America in moving their sustainability agenda forward?

Acronyms used in the case

AWWPS	Advanced Waste Water Purification System
CI	Conservation International
CLIA	Cruise Line Industry Association
CO_2	carbon dioxide
FCC	Fuel Conservation Committee
HAL	Holland America Lines
HAWT	horizontal axis wind turbine
HFO	heavy fuel oil
HVAC	heating, ventilation and air conditioning
IMO	International Maritime Organization
IWC	International Whaling Convention
MARTI	MesoAmerican Reef Tourism Association
MCI	Marine Conservation Institute
MSD	marine sanitation devices
NOX	nitrous oxide
PM	particulate matter
SOX	sulfur oxide
UNCLOS	United Nations Convention on the Law of the Sea
VAWT	vertical axis wind turbine
VOC	volatile organic compounds
WTO	World Tourism Organization

EXHIBIT 1
Characteristics of cruise line segments

Budget Segment

- Low-price

- Appealing to youth and lower income population segments

- Small ships with a minimum of on-board facilities

- Leading cruise lines in this segment include Louis Cruise, Travelscope, Thompson, Island Cruises, Pullmantur and Fred Olsen

Contemporary Segment

- Most popular and profitable segment based on application of economies of scale

- Offers resort-type facilities with a strong emphasis on on-board activities and services, such as beauty shops, golf, ice skating, etc.

- Well adapted to families with children

- Broad target market with "something for everyone"

- Cruise lines in this segment include Royal Caribbean International, Carnival Cruises, Norwegian Cruise Line, Disney, MSC, P&O and Costa

Premium Segment

- A somewhat more sophisticated product than contemporary- better suited to repeat cruise passengers

- Clientele in the over-40 age group

- Itineraries featuring rarely visited ports

- Cruise lines in this segment include Celebrity Cruises. Holland America Line, and Oceana Cruises

Luxury Segment

- High style luxury with emphasis on the destination and on-board facilities

- Exclusivity, with fewer passengers and a much more formal atmosphere

- Spacious accommodations

- Clientele: couples and singles with a taste for super luxury resorts on land, with no facilities for children

- Longer itineraries (10 days or more) and unusual ports and places

- Cruise lines in this segment include Radisson Seven Seas, Silversea Cruises, Seabourn Cruise Line and Crystal Cruises

Source: Cruise Tourism: Current Situation and Trends, 2010, WTO.

EXHIBIT 2
Share of worldwide passengers and number of ships: 2011

Parent company	Brand	Share of worldwide passengers (%)	Number of ships
Carnival Corporation and PLC (CCL)	Carnival Cruise Line	21.1	24
	Costa	7.2	17
	Princess	6.4	16
	AIDA	4.4	8
	Holland America	3.7	15
	Other CC Lines	6.4	23
	TOTAL CC Lines	49.2	103
Royal Caribbean Cruises, Ltd. (RCCL)	Royal Caribbean International	17.0	22
	Celebrity	4.7	11
	Other RCCL Lines	2.1	7
	TOTAL RCCL	23.8	40
Norwegian		7.1	11
MSC Line		5.8	12

Source: Cruise Market Watch 2011, www.cruisemarketwatch.com/market-share.

EXHIBIT 3

Environmental Aspects and Potential Impacts from Cruise Ship Operations

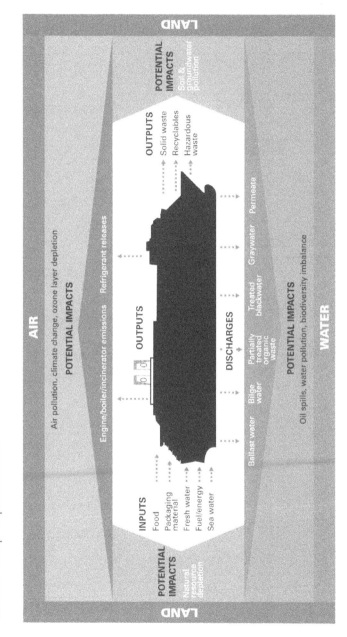

AIR

Air pollution, climate change, ozone layer depletion

POTENTIAL IMPACTS

Engine/boiler/incinerator emissions   Refrigerant releases

INPUTS
Food
Packaging material
Fresh water
Fuel/energy
Sea water

OUTPUTS

DISCHARGES

Ballast water   Bilge water   Partially treated organic waste   Treated blackwater   Graywater   Permeate

POTENTIAL IMPACTS

Oil spills, water pollution, biodiversity imbalance

WATER

OUTPUTS
Solid waste
Recyclables
Hazardous waste

POTENTIAL IMPACTS
Soil & groundwater pollution

LAND

POTENTIAL IMPACTS
Natural resource depletion

LAND

Source: Holland America Lines.

EXHIBIT 4
Where does cruise ship waste go?

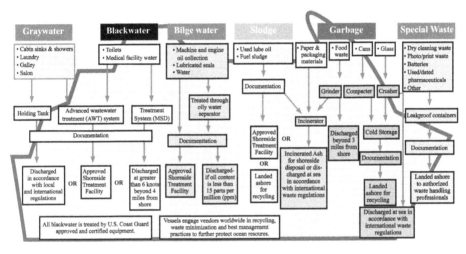

Source: Cruise Line Industry Association.

EXHIBIT 5
Assessment of potential reductions of CO_2 emissions from shipping using known technology and practices

	Saving of CO_2	Combined within category	Overall combined
DESIGN (new ships)			
Concept, speed and capability	2% to 50%*		
Hull and superstructure	2% to 20%	10% to 50%	
Power and propulsion system	5% to 15%		
Low-carbon fuels	5% to 15%		
Renewable energy	1% to 10%		
			25% to 75%
OPERATION (All ships)			
Fleet management	5% to 50%		
Voyage optimization	1% to 10%	10% to 50%	
Energy management	1% to 10%		

*Reductions at this level would require reductions of operational speed.

Source: Second IMO GHG Study 2009, UN International Maritime Organization.

EXHIBIT 6
Fuel use at Holland America Line

Measure	Units	2007	2008	2009
Heavy Fuel Oil (HFO) use	Metric Tonnes (MT)	435,806	442,362	446,765
	Kg/ALB-km*	0.1011	0.1163	0.1141
Distillate fuel use**	MT	5,730	5,230	4874
		Direct GHG emissions		
Carbon dioxide	MT	1,395,571	1,407,527	1,420,216
Equivalent (CO_2-e)	Kg/ALB-km	0.3883	0.3862	0.3628
		Other emissions		
Nitrogen oxides (NOX)	MT	28,327	29,093	29,357
	Kg/mile	21.2	22.2	21.2
Sulfur oxides (SOX)	MT	19,411	18,606	18,606
	Kg/mile	14.5	14.2	13.4
Particulate matter (PM 10)	MT	523	537	542
	Kg/mile	0.391	0.411	0.392

* Kg/ALB is a measure of efficiency agreed upon by all of Carnival Corporation's operating lines. It is the quantity of fuel used in kilograms divided by the available lower berths in the fleet times the number of kilometers traveled by the fleet.

** Distillate fuel is used in the diesel electric generators in geographic regions as specified by laws and regulations.

Source: Holland America Line 2009 Sustainability Report, p.65.

EXHIBIT 7
Holland America Line fuel use and fuel efficiency 2007–11

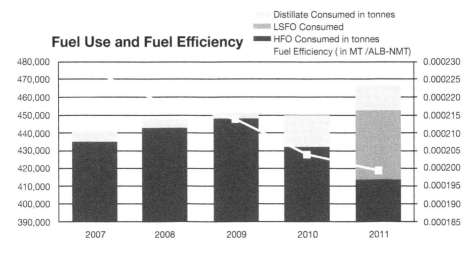

Source: Internal Holland America document.

EXHIBIT 8
Wind turbines on Stena Jutlandica

Source: Courtesy of Stena Line Scandinavia AB.

Notes

i www.savethesea.org/resources/briefings/governance.php, accessed April 10, 2012.

ii ibid.

iii Interview with Rick MacPherson, Conservation Programs Director at the Coral Reef Alliance on March 7, 2012.

iv www.savethesea.org/resources/briefings/governance.php, accessed April 10, 2012.

v www.seaweb.org/resources/briefings/governance.php Important agreements relating to the global oceans are described here. Accessed May 5, 2012.

vi The World Tourism Organization (UNWTO) is the United Nations agency responsible for the promotion of responsible, sustainable and universally accessible tourism. www.unwto.org.

vii Berlitz Complete Guide to Cruising and Cruise Ships 2011, Douglas Ward, www.berlitzcruising.com.

viii 2011 CLIA Cruise Market Overview, Cruise Line International Association, Inc., p.1, accessed on May 25, 2012 from cruise.org/regulatory/clia_statisticalreport.

ix www.cruisemarketwatch.com/capacity, accessed on April 20, 2012.

x www.windrosenetwork.com/The-Cruise-Industry-Demographic-Profiles.html, accessed on April 20, 2012.

xi www.thevacationgals.com/best-cruise-ships-of-2011.

xii Cruise Tourism: Current Situation and Trends, World Tourism Organization, Madrid Spain, 2010, Section 4.1.

xiii www.cruisemarketwatch.com, accessed May 20, 2012.

xiv Carnival Corporation & PLC, 2011 Annual Report and Royal Caribbean Cruises Ltd., 2011 Annual Report.

xv email exchange with Tina Stotz, Manager, Sustainability and ISO Systems Management, July 20, 2012 and Bill Morani, VP Safety & Environmental Management Systems.

xvi For information about the IMO, go to www.imo.org/About?pges/Default.aspx, accessed on June 15, 2012.

xvii Interview in Washington, D.C, at the Cruise Line Industry Association with Michael Crye, Executive Vice President, and Bud Darr, Director of Environment and Health Programs on February 15, 2012. The CLIA Waste Management Practices and Procedures can be accessed at www.cruising.org/regulatory/cruise-industry-policies/cruise-industrys-commitment-environment.

xviii Holland America Line 2009 Sustainability Report. www.hollandamerica.com/about-best-cruise-lines/Main.action?tabName=Sustainability#.

xix www.boards.cruisecritic.com/archive/index.php/t-457134.html, accessed August 1, 2012.

xx www.bloomberg.com/apps/news?pid=newsarchive&sid=aLw6DFDEovrI, accessed August 1, 2012.

xxi www.worldsleadingcruiselines.com/about-us/press-room/holland-america-news/holland-america-line-receives-second-benkert-environmental-award.aspx, accessed August 1, 2012.

xxii www.markets.on.nytimes.com/research/stocks/news/press_release.asp?docTag=2012 05221327PR_NEWS_USPRX___SF11884&feedID=600&press_symbol=83500, accessed August 1, 2012.

xxiii CLIA at 35, p.20.

xxiv Post and Courier, Charleston, S.C., 2011, www.postandcourier.com.

xxv Email exchange with Tina Stotz, May 23, 2012.

xxvi   www.ethicaltraveler.org/2010/01/sustainability-in-the-cruise-industry, accessed August 1, 2012.

xxvii   Data relating to waste management can be found in Holland America's Sustainability Report (2009).

xxviii Interviews with Lance Morgan at Marine Conservation Institute and Tina Stotz at HAL, Fall 2011. Also, see www.marine-conservation.org/what-we-do/program-areas/how-we-fish/holland-america/sustainable-seafood.

xxix   Ibid.

xxx   Holland America Line 2009 Sustainability Report.

xxxi   Internal HAL document.

xxxii   www.conservation.org/fmg/articles/pages/greening_tourism.aspx.

xxxiii Holland America Line 2009 Sustainability Report.

xxxiv   www.maritimeuk.org/2012/01/marine-fuel-sulphur-content.

xxxv   Email correspondence with Tina Stotz and Bill Morani at HAL.

xxxvi   www.marisec.org/shippingfacts//worldtrade/index.php?SID=ca4a0dfa59eac4d7f4ed c87fefd82b4d.

xxxvii Second IMO GHG Study 2009, UN International Maritime Organization, London 2009.

xxxviii Interview with Michael Crye and Bud Darr at CLIA.

xxxix   Second IMO GHG Study 2009, UN International Maritime Organization, London 2009, p.176.

xl   www.dieselnet.com/standards/inter/imo.php.

xli   Information relating to the FCC is based on internal documents and interviews with HAL managers.

xlii   www.colonizeantartica.blogspot.com/2008/01/vertical-axis-wind-turbines.html.

xliii   www.stenaline.com/en/stena-line/corporate/media/press-releases/wind-power-on board-a-ferry.

xliv   www.engadget.com/2010/12/02/hornblower-hybrid-ferry-relies-on-eco-friendly-trifecta-hydroge.

xlv   Internal HAL document.

Part II
Managing stakeholder relationships

CASE 6

Hunghom Peninsula in Hong Kong (A),* (B) and (C)

A realistic call for corporate social responsibilities

Terence Tsai and Shubo Philip Liu[1]

The Hunghom Peninsula was firstly built up under Hong Kong government's PSPS (Private Sector Participation Scheme) to help meet the Government's housing supply target. The real estate market shrank significantly during the construction of Hunghom, and in order to ensure the stability of market, the Government decided to suspend the scheme altogether and put it up for sale. Two developers, New World Development Company Limited (NWD) and Sun Hung Kai Properties Limited (SHKP), which had been engaged in the construction of Hunghom, came forward to take ownership and proposed three options for further development of the project – status quo, renovation to fit middle-range private housing standards

* Hunghom Peninsula in Hong Kong (A): A Realistic Call for Corporate Social Responsibilities, T. Tsai and S.P. Liu, ASIAN CASE RESEARCH JOURNAL, Vol. 14, Issue 1, 117–140. © 2010 World Scientific Publishing Co.

1 The authors wish to thank the research fund granted by China Europe International Business School which supported this research.

or redevelopment as a luxury property after demolition. The decision to demolish was not a good one as balance needed to be achieved for satisfying the concerns of many different stakeholder groups, such as the government, NGOs, neighboring residents and the general public. Ever mindful of the ever-changing real estate market of Hong Kong and with an obligation to maximize shareholders' return, NWD and SHKP were perplexed in searching for an optimal solution.

Hunghom Peninsula background

Built on the Hunghom waterfront area, which was regarded as one of the best urban areas in Hong Kong, Hunghom Peninsula was a government-subsidized housing development project under the PSPS. This project was once a controversial topic: some perceived it as a good deed by the government towards lower-income residences while others pointed out that the project was unpractical and the idea ill-conceived in land-strapped Hong Kong. The construction of the Hunghom Peninsula was completed in August 2002, comprising seven blocks with 2,470 residential flats, 494 car parking spaces and shopping facilities.

Hong Kong property market

Property-related industries, especially the property development industry, is one of the most essential engines of Hong Kong economy. With high economic growth in the 1980s and the 1990s, together with the limited supply of flats, land values and property prices in Hong Kong rose to a sky-high level.

Needless to say, contribution of land sales to the Hong Kong government's revenue was significant. Unlike most of the governments' other revenue sources, land sales to the Hong Kong government consistently contributed over 20% of the total government revenue throughout the 1990s. For example, in 1995–96 before the Asian financial crisis, the Hong Kong government raised over HK$62 billion from land transactions. This represented 32% of total government revenue.

At the same time, the affordability ratio based on mortgage repayment amounts over average household income remained high. From 1990 to 1996, the ratio was 67% on average. By the end of 1995, a small-sized flat (40 m^2) in an urban area cost 70% of the monthly income of an average household in terms of monthly mortgage repayment. This compared unfavorably to the 40–50% of monthly mortgage repayment of household income which was considered by banks to be affordable at the maximum. Compared to Europe and North America, the mortgage ratio was 35% of the average household income.[2]

2 The Government's High-Land-Price Policy: *Can Hong Kong People Afford It?* - Christine Loh and Citizen's Party, 8 May 1997.

HOS and PSPS

In view of the highly priced private properties, the Hong Kong government introduced the Home Ownership Scheme (HOS) in 1978. The plan was to assist eligible households (mainly lower income households and public housing tenants) to purchase housing properties at a reasonable and discounted price relative to the market. The PSPS was subsequently introduced in 1979 to supplement HOS by permitting the participation of private developers. Unlike HOS flats which were owned by the Housing Authority (HA), PSPS developments were owned by private developers.

Under the PSPS, private developers were invited to tender for housing sites on which they were required to build flats conforming to certain specifications stipulated by the government. Like other government land sales, the land title of a PSPS site was vested in the developer. The developer held the legal title to the land lot, owned residential units and car parking spaces, and commercial facilities were built under the same lease. Under the Conditions of Sale for PSPS projects, HA was called to nominate eligible parties to purchase flats from the developers within a specified period. In the event that flats were unsold at the end of the period, HA was obliged to purchase the flats at a guaranteed price.

Property market values reached a peak in mid-1997. But the boom ended quickly and Hong Kong was hit by a series of market downturns as a result of unfavorable global economic conditions in the late 1990s. Demands for private residential flats fell drastically and property prices in general experienced a sharp fall. The government policy makers became anxious because they assumed that the major downward price adjustments in the private residential property sector were the direct impact of HOS. In order to correct the mistake and to restore confidence of the public and the investors in the property market, in November 2002, the Hong Kong government decided to indefinitely cease the HOS/PSPS project, and the sales of such flats from 2003 onwards, to address the imbalance between supply and demand of the private residential property sector.

The negotiation

The construction of the Hunghom Peninsula was completed in August 2002. However, PSPS sales, given the aforementioned scenario, were then suspended by the government. Under the PSPS agreement with the private developers, HA was obliged to purchase all the flats at a guaranteed price. After the suspension of the Hunghom Project, HA was reluctant to re-acquire the PSPS flats, and this agitated private developers. As a result, in July 2003, the developers of Hunghom Peninsula initiated litigation against the Hong Kong government and the Hong Kong Housing Authority. In December 2003, the government finally agreed to negotiate with the developers.

Not long after the beginning of the negotiation, in February 2004, an agreement was signed between the developers and the Government: in the modified Conditions of Sales, the 2,470 flats of Homhung Peninsula were allowed to be sold in the open market. The developers consented to surrender their rights to receive the payment of guaranteed sales at HK$1,914 million from HA and instead paid a premium of HK$864 million to the government for the lease modification. The Conditions of Sale restricted the development on the lot to a gross residential floor area of 1.55 million square feet and any redevelopment would have to be in accordance with the master layout plans approved for development. By then, Hunghom Peninsula had been officially transformed into a private residential property of the developers[3].

Hong Kong political environment

After the Asia financial crisis in 1997, the economy of Hong Kong struck a downward spiral. The attack of SARS in 2003 worsened the situation. Being the backbone of the local economy, the property market suffered heavily. With the economic recession followed by a drastic fall in property prices, there was a vigorous rise in bad debts of mortgage loans and an ever-increasing unemployment rate. On top of these, incidences reflecting an inept Civil Service, such as the chaotic opening of Chek Lap Kok Airport and the complete U-turn of the housing policies within just five years, further diminished the local communities' confidence in the government. Hong Kong people grew skeptical of their government's new policies.

Moreover, many were critical that selected local real estate tycoons had such strong bargaining power in negotiating with the Government, so the deal was felt to be unfair. Some thought that the decisions made by the Government were biased towards the tycoons and there was thought to exist a collusion between the Government and the tycoons.

The situation deteriorated further after the election of the Legislation Council (LegCo) in 2004. The newly elected councilors, in siding with the best interests of the general public, urged the government to disclose the truth. Hunghom Peninsula was yet again cast in the spotlight when Hon Ronny Tong, Legislative Councilor, repeatedly raised sharp and critical questions of the LegCo and demanded 'honest' replies from Mr Michael Suen, the Secretary for Housing, Planning and Lands,[4] with regard to the case of the Hunghom Peninsula

---

3 LC Paper No. CB(1) 350/04-05(04), Legislative Council, HKSAR, 2 Dec 2004.
4 Website of the Housing, Planning and Lands Bureau of the Government of the HKSAR, 2005 Press Releases, 23 May 2005.

The two developers

Hunghom Peninsula was jointly held by Sun Hung Kai Properties Limited (SHKP) and New World Development Company Limited (NWD) on an equal basis.

Sun Hung Kai Properties Limited (SHKP)

SHKP became publicly listed in 1972 and was one of the largest property companies in Hong Kong. It specialized in premium-quality residential and commercial projects. SHKP was committed to upholding conservative financial policies and maintaining high liquidity and low leverage. Its net assets value on 31 December 2004 was HK$138,000 million (as at 30 June 2004: HK$135,239 million). The fixed assets value at 31 December 2004 was HK$98,843 million (as at 30 June 2004: HK$98,839 million).[5] The group was also one of Hong Kong's largest landowners, with a land bank of around 42.9 million square feet.[6]

SHKP devoted a considerable amount of effort to fulfilling its corporate social responsibility goals. It showed a strong commitment to the community and actively supported social activities and education. It was a Platinum Contributor to the Corporate & Employee Contribution Programme of the Community Chest and the winner of the Community Chest's highest fundraising honour in Corporate Challenge for nine consecutive years in Hong Kong. Furthermore, it participated in the One Company–One Job Programme and the Youth Pre-Employment Training Programme pioneered by the Hong Kong government. It also offered free office space to not-for-profit organizations like ORBIS.

> The Group is committed to maintaining high standards of ethics, corporate governance and effective accountability mechanisms in every aspects of its business. Conducting business in a socially responsible and honest manner serves both the Group's and shareholders' long-term interests.[7]

In addition to being committed to the community, it was keen on protecting the natural environment.

> Protecting the environment is a high priority for the Group, and environmental considerations play a part in all aspects of its operations.

SHKP was committed to developing green space in urban areas, to make optimized use of natural light and to apply energy and water saving fixtures and facilities in its buildings. SHKP also enacted environmental policies with respect to design, construction, material sourcing and property management and used green construction principles in the early stages of its property developments. These

---

5 Unaudited interim report December 2004 of SHKP.
6 Corporate website of SHKP, 20 Apr 2005.
7 Extracted from the corporate website of SHKP, 20 Apr 2005

measure included reduction of construction waste and the use of eco-friendly construction materials and green techniques.

Aside from the provision of eco-friendly facilities, the company also actively took part in a number of environmental conservation activities in Hong Kong such as being a Business Environment Council Member, joining the Social Recycling Scheme of the Social Welfare Department and participating in the project to rebuild and upgrade the Tsing Yi Nature Trails.

New World Development Company Limited (NWD)

NWD was a Hong Kong-based leading conglomerate and had been listed in Hong Kong since 1972. The company was active in property, infrastructure, services and telecommunications with its major business in developing private real estate properties. Its net assets value as of 31 December 2004 was HK$55,798 million (as at 30 June 2004: HK$54,405 million). The fixed assets value as of 31 December 2004 was HK$33,771 million (as at 30 June 2004: HK$33,898 million).[8]

As with SHKP, NWD was keen to give the impression that it was a socially responsible company.

It had shown strong support to the community:

> We recognize we are an integral part of the communities in which we operate and are committed to doing our shares as a responsible corporate citizen.[9]

NWD sponsored HK$40 million[10] in the design and construction of the Avenue of Stars at Tsimshatsui East in 2003. It also keenly participated in events and functions organized by non-profit organizations. For instance, it jointly launched the 'Create a New World for Children' Corporate Alliance Campaign with UNICEF in 2003.

The options

The management team of the consortium formed by NWD and SHKP was to determine the fate of Hunghom Peninsula after they had paid an additional premium of HK$864 million to the government to turn the original government subsidized housing estate into a private property. The developers proposed three options for their next step.

---

8 Extracted from the corporate website of SHKP, 20 Apr 2005 [8] Unaudited interim report December 2004 of NWD.

9 Extracted from the corporate website of NWD, 20 Apr 2005.

10 Corporate website of NWD, 20 Apr 2005

1. Status quo

This was the least destructive to the environment and the simplest option to implement as it was without any modifications. Also this plan met the two developers' environmental standards, but the commercial result was not expected to be fully realized because the existing layout and facilities were originally designed to suit PSPS housing estate standards, not standards for luxurious private property. Thus it could not meet the expectation of the market and the financial return was thought to be very limited.

2. Renovation and reconfiguration

The second option was to renovate and enhance the buildings without tearing them down. Partial interiors, external walls together with the unit layouts were to be changed, and enlarged windows and more living spaces were to be added in the renovation specifications. Developers believed that the renovation could bring in a modest profit in a shorter time frame relative to Option 3.

3. Demolition and redevelopment

The last option was to knock down the never-occupied project and then redevelop Hunghom Peninsula into a brand-new luxurious real estate property using premium design and materials. Based on a comprehensive market survey, this option was expected to bring a far above average profit for the developers.

The developers wished to act entirely within their legal and contractual rights at every stage, and they understood fully that the demolition would require approval to change the master layout plan. With the additional land premium to be received as well as the increase in income from the stamp duties and rates with the change of Hunghom Peninsula into higher grade flats, the government would not resist this proposal. The developers expected Option 3 to maximize their investment return. However, they would need to devote a substantial amount of investment and they had to bear the risk of waiting for at least three years before the new construction could be finished.

Also, the demolition and redevelopment process would generate intensive pollution to the environment of an already very crowded Hong Kong City: imagine 200,000 tons of construction waste that could fill some 4,000 double-decker buses in all. Another reason why Hong Kong people should hate this option is the lack of a landfill charge legislation in Hong Kong. It would be the taxpayers who would pay the HK$25 million landfill cost. In addition, residents who lived near the construction area, especially pupils and teachers of Ma Tau Chung Government Primary School, would have to tolerate the noise and air pollution from the demolition and redevelopment.

The future development of Hunghom Peninsula had become a hot topic of public discussion. All concerned parties were eagerly awaiting the developers' final decision.

B

Following NWD and SHKP's year-long intensive study and careful market analysis, the consortium decided to demolish and redevelop Hunghom Peninsula. They believed this approach could bring profit maximization to their shareholders. To address public concerns of possible environmental issues which might arise from the project, the developers planned to implement a comprehensive construction materials recycling programme to supplement the redevelopment plan. Everything appeared to be well under control when suddenly the unexpected happened: after the announcement of the demolition plan, neigbouring residents, schools, communities and environmental organizations in Hong Kong flocked to Hunghom Peninsula shouting in loud and strong voices against the decision and bringing mounting pressure on the developers.

The spokesperson for the Hunghom Peninsula project commented that the development, which began as a PSPS project, was a mismatch of land resources and it would be a huge waste without fully utilizing the prime site to its potential.

> The Hunghom development began as a PSPS project to help meet the government's housing supply target, and the original plan for this prime site is now clearly at odds with Hong Kong's future development needs. To make optimal use of Hong Kong's scarce land resources is the right decision.

> Redeveloping Hunghom Peninsula not only helps in creating over a thousand new jobs, meeting market demand for premium land, raising government revenue from increased stamp duty and rates, and stabilising Hunghom's housing prices. In addition, the project will improve the landscape of the waterfront with a new green design coupling with more open space and better environment.

> In correcting the mismatch in land resources, we demonstrate to our next generation that if a mistake was made, one should have the courage to put it right. Moreover, our comprehensive green construction program also helps raise the next generation's awareness of protecting the environment.

The developers believed that a full redevelopment was the best option as it would offer the benefits of a much improved comprehensive planning using premium design and materials, as well as incorporating facilities that would meet or even exceed the environmental standards of a private estate.

> We appreciate the controversy surrounding the project and the redevelopment plan was a difficult decision for us. We understand public concerns about the environmental issues, and we also attach great importance to the development needs. As a result, we have carefully studied various options for almost a year, hoping to find a solution that can meet Hong Kong's development needs, addresses community concerns and balance all interests.

To address public concerns of possible environmental issues that might arise from the project, a construction material recycling program was built into the redevelopment plan:

> Up to 95% of the construction materials will be recycled to minimize wastage. Hydraulic crusher, instead of conventional breakers, will be used with a view to significantly reducing noise and dust created by the demolition works. Of the 190,000 tons of construction debris, only a few thousand tons will be transported to the landfill. This is about one-thousandth of the waste handled by Hong Kong landfills last year. Although the legislation on landfill charge has yet to come into effect, we have committed to donating an amount matching the landfill charge to support the promotion of greenery projects in Hong Kong. In addition, the proceeds from the sale of recyclable and reusable materials will be donated to support environmental projects.

The developers would invite representatives from the Kowloon City District Council, Ma Tau Chung Government Primary School (Hunghom Bay), the Hong Kong Polytechnic University and its residence halls, Whampoa Garden owners' committees as well as green groups to form a Concern Group, which would provide a platform for all concerned parties to be briefed regularly concerning the project's status and the implementation of environmental measures. A hotline and a dedicated e-mail address would also be set up for public enquiry.

The developers hailed their decision with a spirit of transparency, sincerity and responsibility.

> From the time we bid for the project to making today's decision to redevelop the site, every step we took is within the law. The decision is also reasonable and fully reflects that we have acted responsibly to our shareholders.
>
> Redeveloping Hunghom Peninsula is a major investment for the consortium, and the fact that we are implementing a comprehensive recycling programme only adds to the investment risk. Nonetheless, we are willing to spend more time and money on the project. The investment decision is our vote of confidence in Hong Kong's future.
>
> The redevelopment plan has been conceived with the principles of balancing the interests of society and our shareholders, as well as our commitment to be good corporate citizens. We believe our decision will create a win–win situation," the spokesperson concluded.

Stakeholders' reactions

Intense public concern was aroused soon after the developers officially announced their decision. Green groups were major objectors. The first response of five local major environmental groups, namely The Conservancy Association, Friends of the

Earth (HK), Greenpeace, Green Power and WWF Hong Kong, was to sign a joint petition to voice their strong objections to the demolition plan. They accused the developers of showing absolutely no environmental concerns. According to the environmentalists, the demolition would generate a volume that equaled the total amount of 15 days of settlement waste for all of Switzerland. The green groups also pointed out that the plan was not in line with sustainable development that the Government had been promoting. In fact, it was also revealed there was no landfill charge legislation to demand that polluters bear the pollution handling charges to the city. As a result, all taxpayers would have to pay for this landfill charge, which was estimated to be HK$25 million. Environmentalists asserted that it was a blow to the principle of environmental justice that the polluters would not adequately pay their share.

Hong Kong's educators also stepped forward to show strong objections to the plan. They were worried that this influential event in which the rich maximized their profit at the cost of endangering environment could set a bad example and bring negative influence on the younger generations and twist the moral and educational values. Principal of Ma Tau Chung Government Primary School, Ms Agnes Choi Sook-chun said: 'Destruction of the towers would set a negative example to children. Should we think of money only?'

The Hong Kong Professional Teachers' Union then joined force with Friends of the Earth (HK) and a local radio station to organize a drawing competition for children to express their feeling towards the demolition plan (see Exhibit 9). Another joint effort was writing competitions among primary and secondary students. As well, primary school teachers joined the environmentalists in a protest against the demolition bid.

Staff and students at Ma Tau Chung Government Primary School (Hung Hom Bay), which was located just 15 m away from the buildings, were particularly concerned by the developers' decision. In fact, the 1,000 pupils were among the most directly affected as they had eye witnessed the 'rise and possible fall' of Hunghom Peninsula. Principal Agnes Choi Sook-chun said: 'We are concerned about the many effects of demolition such as air and noise pollution, and a great amount of rubbish.' Mo Choi was also worried that dust from demolition works could impact students' health and result in illnesses, such as asthma and bronchitis. The school gathered 7,000 signatures from pupils, parents and friends opposing demolition of the towers.

However, not everyone in the community objected to the demolition plan. For example, some of the 10,000 private premises owners living near Hunghom Peninsula supported the plan. Even though pollutants from the large-scale demolition project might discourage people from buying the nearby premises, this was only regarded as a short-term effect. In the long run, with the 2,470 flats redesigned into more luxury configurations, surveyors anticipated a strong recovery in the market.

As one of the major stakeholders in this controversial incident, the Hong Kong government reached an agreement with the two developers on the modification premium after months of negotiation. However, environmentalists and the public vigorously accused the government of making a serious mistake in allowing the demolition of the Hunghom Peninsula estate. In the midst of the public outcry, the Government issued a letter to the developers reminding them that any redevelopment must be in accordance with the estate's master layout plans. Several government officials also publicly commented on the issue. The Director of Environmental Protection Department wrote to the developers urging them to abandon the demolition plan. The Director of Lands took a reserved position about approving any modification that might be required for the proposed development. Another government minister also was critical of the waste and that the project was in violation of environmental protection principles. An executive councilor described the plan as a big joke that would only benefit the property developers. In its defense, the Government announced that it would shortly release all exchanges of correspondences of Hunghom Peninsula and hand over them to the Legislative Council.

Like with other eye-catching topics, the media, especially the print press, played a very significant role throughout. The local newspapers were full of coverage when the developers announced their plan to pull down the residential blocks. The newspapers provided continuous coverage of the intense public opposition aroused among environmentalists, government officials, legislators, teachers, pupils, etc., and focused their strongest criticism upon the two developers in terms of social responsibility and the huge profit the developers might earn without a full consideration of environmental protection.

The developers were facing a tough situation. They believed that they were making a sound legal business decision while being confronted with fierce opposition from the general public and environmental protection groups. *Should they proceed with their original demolition plan or retreat?*

C

On 10 December 2004, in an unprecedented move, the developers, NWD and SHKP, issued a joint statement acknowledging that the decision to tear down the never-occupied project to make way for luxury flats had generated significant controversy and caused discord in the community, thus the plan would be withdrawn. The developers explained that they placed greater concern for community harmony and had therefore decided to change their plans for demolition in favor of exploring the option of renovation and reconfiguration, as well as enhancement of estate facilities in general.

The developers defended their responsibilities to their shareholders:

> As public companies, the developers are accountable to their shareholders. The latest decision also works in their favor, since renovation and reconfiguration, along with facility enhancement, could produce a profit in a shorter period of time and avoid taking an investment risk for three to four years.

Moreover, the developers stressed that they did not want to precipitate an assault on private property rights and freedom of contract, as this would impair the business environment in a free economy.

> The two developers have acted entirely within their legal and contractual rights at every stage of their dealings with Hunghom Peninsula. The decision to change the demolition plan was made after taking into account prevailing circumstances and listening to public opinion. We have tried to understand and balance all interests with this decision.

The developers restated their proposed green construction programme and community involvement plans to minimize the impact of any future work on the neighborhood. On 12 December 2004, the protest originally organized by the environmentalists and the teachers against the demolition bid was dramatically reorganized into a mass celebration.

EXHIBIT 1
Hong Kong property price index

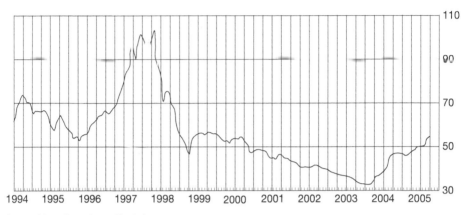

Source: Hong Kong Centa-City Index.

EXHIBIT 2
Estimated cost of "Old" Hunghom Peninsula

	HK$Million
Tender price in Sep 1999 with gross floor area* of 1.33 million sq ft.	583
Premium paid on Feb 2004 for lease modification to sell as private housing with gross floor area* of 1.55 million sq ft.	864
Construction cost and interest expenses	2,000
Total	3,447

* Gross floor area is the area that was allowed for flat development under the contract

Source: Mingpao Daily, December 2004.

EXHIBIT 3
Estimated construction costs

	HK$ / sq ft.*
Internal renovation and reconfiguration costs	900
Redevelopment costs (demolition, re-built and interest expenses)	1,500
Additional premium for modification to master layout plans	2,000

* HK$ per square feet of gross floor area

Source: Hong Kong Economic Times, December 2004.

EXHIBIT 4
Estimated selling prices

	HK$ / sq ft.*
After internal renovation and reconfiguration (c.f. Whampoa Garden)	4,000
After redevelopment (c.f. Laguna Verde and Harbourfront Landmark)	8,000

* HK$ per square feet of sellable floor area, the area that can be sold to buyers. It can be assumed that gross floor area = 80% of sellable area.

Source: Centanet, April 2005.

EXHIBIT 5
Financial highlights of two developers

	SHKP 6 months ending 31 December 2004 (HK$ M)	NWD 6 months ending 31 December 2004 (HK$ M)
Turnover	11,278	11,520
Profit from operations	4,096	1,140
Profit before taxation	6,332	1,161
Taxation	642	453
Profit after taxation	5,690	1,708

Source: www.shkp.com/zh-HK/Pages/annual-interim-reports.

EXHIBIT 6
The entrance of Hunghom Peninsula

Source: www.img.readtiger.com/wkp/zh/Hunghom_Peninsula_Entrance.jpg.

EXHIBIT 7
Hunghom Peninsula before renovation

Source: www.img.readtiger.com/wkp/zh/Hunghom_Peninsula_Entrance.jpg.

EXHIBIT 8
Hunghom Peninsula in renovation

Source: www.starphotohk.com/hk-place/2006/20060616-HunghomPeninsula01-600.jpg.

EXHIBIT 9
An article from Hong Kong Professional Teachers' Union

The following article 'Don't let our children cry at night' on the Hunghom Peninsula Incident was written by Legislative Councillor the Hon. Cheung Man-kwong, who is the president of Hong Kong Professional Teachers' Union. The article, written in Chinese, was first published in Ming Pao on November 12, 2004. Friends of the Earth (HK) had this article translated into English. (www.foe.org.hk/newsletter/newsletter_112004_page3.html; March 22, 2009)

Don't let our children cry at night

The Hunghom Peninsula Incident exposes humankind's arrogance and greed.

While our Government is still trying to pacify public outcry against its selling of Hunghom Peninsula at knock-down price to private developers, the developers declare that they will be demolishing the seven brand-new towers.

What the developers are telling us is: 'everything has its price'. As long as it makes money, Hunghom Peninsula could be bought, and could be levelled as well.

Hunghom Peninsula, unlike our heritage buildings, does not have a history. Unlike Victoria Harbour, Hunghom Peninsula does not register [in] our collective memory.

What the developers are attempting to accomplish are: shutting off the 'noise' of green groups, softening councillors' critical stance at the legislative chamber, keeping government officials' lips sealed, and diverting academics' attention. All these will enable a speedy euthanasia for Hunghom Peninsula.

But will this euthanasia be a speedy and painless one? Ma Tau Chung Government School, which is the next-door neighbour of Hunghom Peninsula, has its students collected 7,000 signatures to petition against this proposed demolition.

It is the children making the developers realise that they may not be able to translate everything into monetary terms.

Their voices are the ones that cannot be ignored.

Twelve years ago, a 12-year-old Canadian girl Severn Suzuki delivered her six-minute speech in front of world leaders at the 1992 Earth Summit. And her speech received a standing ovation.

Suzuki said, 'I'm only a child and I don't have all the solutions, but I want you to realise, neither do you! You don't know how to fix the holes in our ozone layer. You don't know how to bring salmon back up a dead stream. You don't know how to bring back an animal now extinct. And you can't bring back forests that once grew where there is now desert. If you don't know how to fix it, please stop breaking it!... Well, what you do makes me cry at night. You grown ups say you love us. I challenge you, please make your actions reflect your words'.

A folk tale originating from South America has it that: in the midst of a hill fire, human beings, birds, insects and all animals all flee for their lives. But a humming-bird remains and carries water with his beak. He pours tiny drops of water over the hill fire. People laugh at him, saying: 'What are you trying to do?' The hummingbird says: 'I'm doing what in my capacity can be done'.

Suzuki was also doing what in her capacity could be done. And so are the children of Ma Tau Chung Government Primary School

So how can we adults remain reticent about it? How long can we keep our silence?

Modernizing Dharavi
If you build, will they come?

Abhijit Roy and Mousumi Roy

Looking outside from his office at West Bandra overlooking the Arabian Sea, Mr Mukesh Mehta sighed; he recalled when he first had the dream of creating a Modern Dharavi – free of slums, where the poor, hardworking people will finally be able to enjoy a better quality of life and be integrated with the mainstream citizens. Throughout the history of the world, migrants have moved to the urban areas in search of a better life – his goal is to provide a decent standard of living to the people in this urban slum of over 600,000 residents. He shared this dream with his family too. His son, Shyam, was very enthusiastic and regarded him as a 'versatile' person who is capable of serving both the rich and the poor, while his wife considered him a 'confused' person.[1] He is, however, dedicated to pursue his dream of oocing that his heroes are living a far better life in a revamped Dharavi, free of slum.

Mr Mehta has been the management consultant for Dharavi Redevelopment Project (DRP)[2] for more than seven years to date. The project was supposed to break ground a long time ago. However, there were many stakeholders related to this project and several issues needed to be resolved. This has caused unavoidable delays in every step of the way. Mr Mehta has already overcome many hurdles presented by different governmental and nongovernmental organizations. However, the toughest resistance has come from the slum dwellers and their leader, Mr Jockin Arputham, the Director of National Slum Dwellers Federation.

How can Mr Mehta convince them that this redevelopment plan is radically different from the many other earlier plans which haven't improved the lives of slum dwellers significantly? The media has been following up all news regarding

Dharavi's redevelopment plan over the years. They are watching the progress of DRP not just in Mumbai, or in India, but throughout the whole world – waiting, and expecting it to materialize soon. Will Mr Mehta's dream of a modern urban center at Dharavi come true? Will it be possible that the slum dwellers would enjoy a better life style and integrate with other citizens of Mumbai? Is it possible to re-create sustainable urban developments from the existing slums around the world? Only time will tell...

Historical background of Dharavi

Dharavi competes with Karachi's Orangi Township to be the largest slum in Asia.[3] It is located in the middle of Mumbai, the largest metropolis and the financial, commercial, and industrial center of India. Mumbai generates approximately 5% of India's GDP and contributes to approximately 23% of the country's tax revenues.[4] Furthermore, it accounts for 25% of industrial output, 70% of the maritime trade in India and 70% of the capital transactions in India's economy.[5] It is home to the major financial institutions of India such as the Reserve Bank of India, the Bombay Stock Exchange, the National Stock Exchange of India, as well as the corporate headquarters of most of the Indian-based multinational corporations. Furthermore, the city is also the home to the largest film and television industry in the world, popularly known as 'Bollywood.'

In the past few decades the people from surrounding rural areas came to Mumbai to make a better living and contributed to the fast growth of the economy and make the city a potpourri of a kaleidoscope of communities and cultures. The current population of the city is more than 13 million and is predicted to reach 27 million by 2020, to become the second largest urban area in the world after Tokyo.[6] The real estate prices in Mumbai are among the top five in the world. Mr Mukesh Ambani, one of the top five richest people[7] in the world has recently built the world's first billion dollar home in this city. However, more than 60% of the Mumbai residents live in the slums.[8]

Dharavi was originally a mangrove swamp by the creek, formed by the Arabian Sea. It was first settled by *Koli* fishermen in the early 20th century.[9] However, the creek dried up over time and new immigrants started to build on the lands emerged from the dried out swamps.[10] It is surrounded by two of Mumbai's main train lines, the Western and Central railways along its borders and the river, Mithi, to the north. It is so close to the city's airport that the passengers from the airplane could see the tin roofs of Dharavi while landing.

EXHIBIT 1
A bird's eye view of Dharavi during the Day

Source: www.dharavi.org/D._Photos.

EXHIBIT 2
Dharavi at night

Source: www.journeyidea.com/dharavi-slums-a-diamond-in-the-rough.

The new financial center at Bandra-Kurla is located only a mile away from Dharavi. The central location and availability of transportation made Dharavi a highly desirable place for slum dwellers to live and work. A total of 535 acres[11] of Dharavi, which is approximately the two-thirds the size of Central Park in New York, is occupied by about 600,000 people. Rural immigration from different parts of India made Dharavi a truly diverse community. Artisans from Gujarat in the potters' colony, Muslim tanners from Tamil Nadu, embroidery workers from Uttar Pradesh, and many other different groups have contributed significantly to the financial growth of Mumbai.

Numerous vendors and artisans opened their shops in this self-sufficient neighborhood. The average household income in this community is between Rs. 3,000[12] and Rs. 15,000 per month. The small businesses of these slum dwellers generate $700 million to $1 billion in revenue annually. An estimated number of 15,000 single room factories are recycling a major portion of city waste, such as plastics, car batteries, computer parts, food processing, garments, and other materials to create new products for the markets. Their products are sold not only in Mumbai and other Indian cities, but also in international markets. The residents here enjoy a higher income and more prosperous lifestyle compared to the rural life they had before.

EXHIBIT 3
Examples of current small industries in Dharavi

Source: www.dharavi.org/D._Photos.

Clockwise from top left recycling computer keyboards, drying bread chips, making plastic pipes, and clay pottery

EXHIBIT 4
Inside view of Dharavi

Source: www.ngm.nationalgeographic.com/2007/05/dharavi-mumbai-slum/jacobson-text/1.

Access to clean water and public sanitary system are unavailable in Dharavi, since the whole area was built illegally on government land. The locals have no choice but to buy the essential amenities, such as water and electricity mostly from illegal sources by paying a premium price. Stealing electricity from public utilities is a common practice in this neighborhood. There are a few public toilets available; however, most of them are broken or filthy. Other public services such as medical office, hospital, or post-office are also unavailable. Its location and poor drainage system made it susceptible to floods during rainy seasons. The narrow alleys are always dark. The dirt and garbage are dumped here every day. The pollution generated from some of the local industries, such as tanneries and potteries, are causing very unhealthy living conditions here.

EXHIBIT 5
Outside boundary of Dharavi

Source: www.journeyidea.com/dharavi-slums-a-diamond-in-the-rough.

However, these garbage- and pollution-creating small factories are the sources of their income. Many communities with different culture and religious beliefs continue to live together in Dharavi rather peacefully. There are 27 temples, 11 mosques and 6 churches for the local residents. Recently, an ATM from a major bank has opened here. There are about a dozen schools for local children. Most of the children start earning income as soon as they are able to do so. However, some parents have high aspirations for their children, even in the adverse conditions. They continue to pursue higher education in order to enroll in esteemed professions such as medicine and engineering.

EXHIBIT 6
Education is valued by many families in Dharavi

Source: www.dharavi.org/D._Photos.

Over the years different projects were funded by the World Bank and Bombay Urban Development to solve housing problems for the poor slum dwellers. Different schemes such as PMGP (1985), SRD (1991), and SRS (1995)[13] were introduced by government agencies, NGOs, and public donors like the UN and World Bank. In the mid-1990s, the Maharashtra state government established a new organization called the Slum Rehabilitation Authority (SRA), headed by the Chief Minister of Mumbai. It gave the slum dwellers protection for their homes against private developers, who were encroaching upon the slum areas to make a profit from the highly priced real estate of Mumbai. Meanwhile, the World Bank attached the conditions of requiring proof of rehabilitation and resettlement of slum dwellers in exchange for monetary aid for slum development. In 2004, the Chief Minister of Maharashtra declared its mission to 'transform Mumbai as a world class city with a vibrant economy and globally comparable quality of life for its citizens' by 2013. The Mumbai task force was formed and a detailed report on 'Transforming Mumbai into a World-Class City' was prepared jointly by a local organization called Bombay First and international consulting firm called McKinsey Company. Their report listed the strategies for the next 10 years, with short- and long-term goals. The project was divided in five sub-groups and the total cost of the project was estimated to be at $40 billion over 10 years.

EXHIBIT 7
Dharavi development proposed sector map

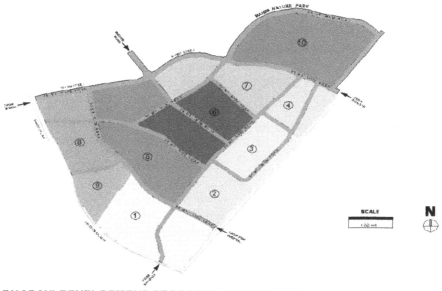

DHARAVI DEVELOPMENT PROPOSED SECTOR MAP

The number of sectors has now been consolidated from ten to five sectors.

The past Prime Ministers of India have always been sympathetic to the slum dwellers in Dharavi. In 1985, Mr Rajiv Gandhi, the Prime Minister at that time, allocated Rs. 350 million to state government to improve the housing, sanitary and public services in Dharavi as a report documented that only 162 water taps and 842 toilet seats were available for nearly 300,000 residents. It took more than a decade to provide better housing with improved facilities to a limited number of lucky residents in Dharavi. After a few changes in political party in India, another Prime Minister, Dr Manmohan Singh, in 2004, aspired to transform Mumbai to a modern city with a good quality of life similar to Shanghai in China. To convert his vision to a reality, he committed to pay $2 billion over five years to rebuild Mumbai as a traffic- and pollution-free, world class city without slums. With the full support of central government, the state government and the Mumbai Task Force established the Mumbai Development Fund, which was financed by the public donors, such as the World Bank, IMF, USAID, AIILSG, Urban Management

Program for the UN, UN-INHABITAT, etc., civic societies, such as, Bombay First, AGNI, etc, and the private sector, like national and multinational corporations. The state and central government have been working together to attract capital for investments from the financial/capital markets, private sector, civic society, and the donor community.

Dharavi redevelopment plan and Mr Mehta

Dharavi's prime location[14] and its contribution to Mumbai's economy made it an ideal slum redevelopment project. Government of Maharashtra hired Mr. Mukesh Mehta, an architect and project management consultant to radically redesign Dharavi. His proposal, called the Dharavi Redevelopment Plan (DRP) has three main objectives:

- First and foremost, to improve the living condition of the slum dwellers and to maintain their occupation, unless it is hazardous for the environment

- To create a radical plan in which Dharavi will be rebuilt as a whole, instead of earlier piece-by-piece approach. This plan tried to avoid moving the slum dwellers to a multi-storied building without making any significant change in the overall planning of Dharavi. It had been done before, but that housing turned out to be vertical slums. The holistic approach of assimilating other citizens, businesses, and service providers from Mumbai to co-exist, to live and work with slum dwellers, is the backbone of this plan. The new urban center of Dharavi will provide a better and sustainable way of life for the citizen of Mumbai as a whole and will be an exemplary slum redevelopment project to the other cities of the world.

- To make a feasible scheme that will benefit all stakeholders of Dharavi. Its central location, proximity to the financial district of Mumbai, commuting access to many areas by two main train lines, and proximity to the main airport make it an asset to many people and organizations. The DRP was planned to provide future benefits to each of the stakeholders to create a win–win situation for all.

The master plan for *DRP* presented an eco-friendly, self-sustainable, and modern development, which incorporated the five principles of HIKES (health, income, knowledge, environment, and socio-cultural development). Mr Iqbal Chahal, one of the state official commented that once this $2.1 billion project is built, it would be the best place to be in Mumbai.

Mr Mukesh Mehta was born in Mumbai into a wealthy family. He was the youngest son and was predicted by an astrologer to be the most successful person in his family. His parents raised him lavishly. Later, as an adult, he was sent to the USA for higher studies. Mr Mehta studied architecture at the Pratt Institute in Brooklyn. He managed his father's steel business successfully and later decided to open his own real estate development business in the most expensive North Shore area of Long Island. He lived among the affluent in Long Island and built private multi-million dollar homes for them. When he was hired as a consultant for the first slum development project at Dharavi, he considered it a financial opportunity. He was aware of the few extremely rich people, who lived in mansions with a life-style of the rich world, and the too many poor, who lived in *zopadpatti*, with awful living condition in the same city. However, after he stayed in his office in Dharavi for six months to have a first-hand idea about the project, his mentality changed. He remembered that his father, like the poor people in Dharavi, came to Mumbai from a little village, in search of a better life. His father also shared a small room (*chawl*) with others in his early days in the city. He empathized with the hard working and honest people of Dharavi, who work sometimes 15 hours a day to make a living – they suddenly became his heroes. He wanted to make a difference in their lives; to give them the opportunity of the better lives they deserved.

Mr Mehta's argument against past failures of slum improvements is that this was not only the housing problem – it was also about human resources. Unless the development projects are planned with a holistic sustainable approach, as described by HIKES, to find ways in assimilating slum dwellers with the mainstream people, the plan would bound to be a failure. He compared how the immigrants in the USA start mostly as financially poor and struggle hard with a strong belief that one day they'll achieve a piece of the American dream. Over time they integrate in the melting pot of the American society. He wanted to provide the same opportunity to the slum dwellers, not to be looked down upon, but to gradually be a part of the middle-class society in Mumbai.

His master plan includes 535 acres of land to be re-built in five sectors over seven years. The eligible slum dwellers, whose names were established in the electoral roll by the year 2000 will receive 225 sq. ft housing unit per family, free of cost, and will have the option to buy more at the construction cost. Thirty-five percent of the total 325 acres of building construction will be sold to outside businesses and service providers, while 65% will be used for providing free housing to approximately 57,531 families. Temporary residences will be provided to these families during the construction phase. To improve transportation, the existing roads will be widened and new roads will be built. The train line will be connected to this community to facilitate the commuting process. The plan has provision for hospitals, schools, colleges, post offices, police stations, shopping malls, parks, art galleries, a theater, a cricket museum, and more. The state government has provided an incentive for developers as FSI index (the ratio of total floor area to the plot size) of 4 for the free housing, compared to 3.1 for municipal and government land and 1.3 for private lands. The projected cost, estimated to be $2.3 billion, will be divided into five contracts for five sectors. Winning bidders will receive the development rights from the government by paying a 'premium'. According to Mr. Mehta, the 'premium' may be as high as $1 billion, which will be collected by the state government from developers' profit.

Dharavi's stakeholders

DRP is a very high profile redevelopment project, which is being watched at national as well as international level. There are many stakeholders also who are involved with this project over the years. They are as follows:

- Dharavi Slum Dwellers
- Political leaders, government officials and ministers at central, state and local level such as mayors, members of parliament (MPs), members of legislative assembly (MLAs), etc.
- The Planning Commission and other government agencies, like MAHADA, MMRDA, MCGMCivic societies such as citizen action groups, and many NGOs
- International donors such as World Bank, IMF, etc.
- Builders and developers involved in this project.
- The citizens of Mumbai

Mr Mehta's philosophy for creating a successful development project is to meet the interests of all stakeholders involved in the project. It is hardly possible to build anything without benefitting all parties involved. Hence, he particularly aimed to ensure that this project, once built, will create a win–win situation for everyone involved. For example, the slum dwellers will get free housing and public services such as clean water and a sanitation system – an overall improved quality of life. The builders and developers, on the other hand, will make enormous profits by selling 35% of the building facilities to other interested buyers at an extremely high real estate price of Mumbai. The citizens of Mumbai will have a new modern suburb with modern facilities to explore and enjoy. The local and state government will be benefitted by obtaining a modern urban center at Dharavi and also will obtain different types of premiums and taxes from the developers and future users of the facilities. The political leaders will be able to keep their vote bank, since the slum dwellers will not be moved away. The civic societies' and NGOs' mission of uplifting poor slum dwellers from their inhuman living conditions will be accomplished. The international donors will be satisfied, since the success of this project will provide them with proof that their monetary aid is helping to improve the quality of lives of many poor and they will be able to use this project as an example of how to upgrade human living conditions in other cities in the world. Even the Mumbai Airport Authority and the passengers will enjoy a beautiful skyline, instead of the images of tin roofs, while landing. Mr Mehta's son, Suman, considers Dharavi as a pilot project for upgrading slums in a sustainable way. So, its success will promote similar redevelopment project for urban slums all around the globe.

Hurdles on the way...

The extremely high budget and radical design of this project created many questions and confusions for its stakeholders. Maintaining communications among them and resolving the personal conflicts of each individual and organization have turned out to be a very lengthy process. Mr Mehta communicates with 14 different organizations in the government and distributes many posters and pamphlets to all related parties. However, different organizations for slum dwellers, such as NSDF (National Slum Dwellers Federations), Mahila Milan, and NGOs, such as SPARC[15] (Society for the Promotion of Area Resource Centers) are actively involved in protecting the interests of slum dwellers. Some of the slum residents are also ambivalent about the project.

Many slum development projects have been planned over the years. However, lives of the slum dwellers haven't improved significantly. This may be another of those projects, concocted by political leaders, government, and developers to fulfill their own interests. Mr Mehta has met personally with the slum dwellers in Dharavi to present his plan in detail and listened to their objections and worries. For example, the khumbers or potters represent the soul of Dharavi, where people make new things out of thrown-out rubbish. They worry that their business will be harmed if they have to move to a small place of 225 sq. ft area, in one of the floors of a multi-storied building; they won't have enough space or sunlight for drying their pots in the sun. They have been living there for generations and think of themselves as rightful owners of the land. However, Mr Mehta has tried to convince them that they lost ownership in 1974. The brick kilns they use for their work are also causing pollution – a nearby hospital has started complaining that the smoke is causing harm to patients with pulmonary ailments. The leather tanners are also not happy about the fate of their future. Since the tanneries produce pollutants, they will not be allowed to continue their business at that location.

Another person, who already owns 400 sq. ft does not see any gain from getting 225 sq. ft free of cost, since she earns monthly rent by subletting part of her property to a furniture maker and renting out her basement. Hence, some of the slum dwellers are asking to raise the area from 225 sq. ft to 400 sq. ft. Many of them are not comfortable thinking of living in a floor away from the ground in a multi-storeyed building, where they have to ride an elevator and may be forced to pay a fee for riding it. The notion of having a personal toilet is not exciting to Dharavi dwellers, who currently share the toilets with many others. One of the residents pointed out that Mr Mehta is dreaming his own dream, which he and other Dharavi residents may not want to be part of. Even, Dharavi Development Authority's chief executive Mr Gautam Chatterjee is apprehensive about the future of the slum dwellers in new development. He is afraid that they will lose their identity of entrepreneurs and will end up being the peons, drivers, and maids for the rich people who will pay premium prices for rest of the development.

The most outspoken person in this debate is Mr Jockin Arputham,[16] who is a life-long slum activist and an expert on Dharavi. He is the founder and director of

National Slum Dwellers Federation (NSDF) and represents the interests of the slum dwellers in Dharavi. He was born into a wealthy family and lived a good life as a young boy. He went to a school run by Catholic nuns. However, his family was faced with financial difficulties when he was teenager. He taught himself to become a good carpenter and moved to Mumbai in search of a better life. He started a school for street children. Slowly over time he emerged as a leader of the poor slum dwellers. He gave them a voice, and helped them to organize protests in fighting back against eviction from their settlements by local and state authorities.

His main objection was that Dharavi's people were not informed about the Dharavi Redevelopment Plan. He is a supporter of bottom-up approach of redevelopment, rather than top-down approach, as has been the case in Dharavi.[17] He pointed out that the tender has been called and the bidders have submitted their bids without any initial survey statistics – this is not a standard norm. Mr Arputham is concerned about the eligibility issue since according to his estimate only 35% of the current residents are eligible for free housing as per government plan. He is apprehensive about the rest of the Dharavi residents who are currently renting the lofts and the basements. His other complaint is that Mr Mehta's plan does not mention the future of many Dharavians, such as rag pickers, who are helping in recycling the city garbage and keeping the city clean, or *idliwallahs* – who make more than half a million *idlis*[18] each day in Dharavi, and sell them all over the city. Another of his concern is that will the builders be trustworthy to provide what is promised? The developer may just give them a hallway with a toilet at the end for everyone to use instead of their own apartment. Will the slum dwellers be charged with some kind of monthly fees in future, and does Mr Mehta have any idea how much is that going to be? He reflects the concerns of the Dharavi residents towards the powerful and rich builders and developers who so far have not built any goodwill from their earlier housing projects for the poor. He mentioned that the developers required obtaining 60–70% consensus from people according to SRA. He is demanding 80% consensus instead, in order to make any progress on this project. He also wants to see that slum dwellers get a fair share of the profits that the developers will make, considering the current estimate of Dharavi's real estate is $10 billion[19,20]. At this point, neither slum dwellers, nor Mr Arputham are convinced that this project will bring them many of the publicized facilities. The slum dwellers would like to see improvement in their living conditions, however, they are not ready to accept this proposal, since so many of the issues still remain unresolved. They demand appropriate social justice and will not compromise for anything less.

Rebuttal and conclusion...

Mr Mehta denies the allegation of not communicating with slum dwellers. He had an office in Dharavi and he met many of the residents to present his plan and listened to their complaints. He also had been communicating with 16 different agencies to get his projects approved. He has provided many pamphlets and posters have been passed around about the project. He also mentioned that the local, national, and international media have been provided with information since the beginning of this project. Regarding the 80% consensus demanded by Mr Arputham, the state government[21] claimed that consensus is not required for Dharavi, since it is a government-sponsored project. However, a window of 30 days was given to register any complaints. Exhibit 8 shows the timeline for this project. Mr Mehta is communicating with all interest groups including 14 agencies from government and NGOs as well as the residents of Dharavi to get to the next step – selection of the bidders for this project.

EXHIBIT 8
History of hurdles in the Dharavi Redevelopment Project

HISTORY OF HURDLES

2004: State plans Dharavi redevelopment project
June 1, 2007: Global tenders for expression of interest invited. Nineteen consortia selected
March 2009: Following global slowdown, five companies exit the project citing lack of clarity and delay in implementation
July 7, 2009: Expert committee debunks Dharavi Project, passes adverse remarks against consultant Mukesh Mehta. Calls the scheme 'sophisticated land grab'.
October 16, 2009: Of 14 bidders, only 7 submit the Memorandum of Understanding they have signed with their foreign partners.
October 16, 2009: BMC submits a preliminary survey report stating that 63% of Dharavi residents are ineligible for houses under the project.
February 2, 2010: A sub-committee of secretaries recommends that sector-wise redevelopment of Dharavi take place
June 11, 2010: Mhada submits proposal to the state seeking to redevelop Sector 5 of Dharavi.

SECTOR-WISE DISTRIBUTION OF POPULATION IN DHARAVI

Sector	Population
1	1,400
2	4,400
3	12,600
4	11,300
5	9,300

Source: www.dharavi.org/D._Photos.

However, he knows in his heart that it is the slum dwellers and Mr Arputham, who need to be convinced that he shares their dream – a better life and a part in the society with their own identity.

Is he the 'versatile' individual that his son, Shyam, thinks he is, capable of serving both the rich and the poor, or is his wife's characterization of him as a 'confused' person a more appropriate metaphor? If he rebuilds Dharavi, will the residents come? Can he win their hearts in the end…?

Notes

1 Urban age India: Mukesh Mehta, Part 1 & 2 Available at: www.youtube.com/ watch?v=KWj09_94wR0. Accessed 18 February 2011.

2 Available at: www.dharavi.org/Dharavi_Advocacy/I._Government_Documents/Expres sion_of_Interest_Dharavi_Redevelopment_Project. Accessed on 18 February 2011.

3 Available at: www.timesofindia.indiatimes.com/city/mumbai/Karachi-is-Asias-largest-slum-not-Dharavi UNDP/articleshow/1070202.cms. Accessed 18 February 2011

4 Bunsha, D. (2004), 'Developing Doubt', *Urban Development, Frontline,* Vol. 21, No 12.

5 "Navi Mumbai International Airport" (JPG). City and Industrial Development Corporation (CIDCO). www.img214.imageshack.us/img214/2299/dscn7619ql4.jpg. Accessed 18 February 2011.

6 Available at: www.citymayors.com/statistics/urban_intro.html.

7 Available at: www.richestmen.info/4.php. Accessed 18 February 2011.

8 WHO (2002), *Mumbai slums dwellers' sewerage project goes nationwide,* Bulletin of the World Health Organization, 80(8), 684.

9 Edwards, S.M. (2001), *The Gazetteer of Bombay City and Island,* Reprint. First published in 1909. New Delhi, Cosmo, 3 volumes, 1396 pages.

10 Sharma, K. (2000), Rediscovering Dharavi: Story from Asia's Largest Slum, Penguin Books.

11 Source: *Slum Rehabilitation Authority,* www.sra.gov.in. Accessed 18 February 2011.

12 Rs. 49 is approximately equal to $1 in 2011.

13 PMGP: Prime Minister Grant Project; SRD: Slum Redevelopment; SRS: Slum Redevelopment Scheme.

14 Available at: www.wn.com/Dharavi_Slum_Development. Accessed 18 February 2011.

15 Available at: www.sparcindia.org/docs/alliance.html. Accessed 18 February 2011.

16 Arputham Jockin (2008), "Developing new approaches for people-centered development", *Environment and Urbanization* 20, 319.

17 Jockin A. An offer of partnership or a promise of conflict: Slum dwellers' views on development plans for Dharavi and for Mumbai international airport. Available at: www.pubs .iied.org/pdfs/G02314.pdf.

18 "Idlis" are inexpensive South Indian savory cake popular throughout India. The cakes are usually two to three inches in diameter and are made by steaming a batter consisting of de-husked fermented black lentils and rice.

19 Urban age India: Jockin Arputham, Part 1 & 2 Available at: www.youtube.com/ watch?v=KWj09_94wR0. Accessed 18 February 2011.

20 Available at: www.wn.com/Dharavi_Slum_Development. Accessed on 18 February 2011.

21 Jacobson, M. (2011), *Mumbai's Shadow City.* Available at: www.ngm.nationalgeographic .com/2007/05/dharavi-mumbai-slum/jacobson-text/1.

Lululemon's commitment to the environment

A tangle of seaweed, suppliers, and social responsibility

A. Erin Bass and Rebecca J. Morris

It was the morning of Wednesday, November 14, 2007. The article on the front page of the *New York Times* Business Section read '"Seaweed" clothing has none, tests show.' The story asserted that one of Lululemon's product lines, Vitasea®, which purported to contain a seaweed fiber designed to release marine amino acids, minerals, and vitamins into the skin upon contact with moisture, contained no such element. Both Chip Wilson, Chairman and Founder of athletic wear retailer Lululemon, and Robert Meers, Lululemon's CEO, were about to embark on their first damage-control mission since the company's Initial Public Offering in July. This was the most widespread negative press Lululemon had received since going public, and the aftermath of the article would question Lululemon's product integrity, marketing and strategy, suppliers, and ethics. Lululemon's next move would be crucial to both its survival and reputation.

Lululemon's background

Lululemon Athletica Inc. (Lululemon), a yoga-inspired athletic apparel and accessories manufacturer and retailer, was founded in 1998 in Vancouver, Canada. In 2007, the company owned or franchised 81 stores internationally. See Exhibit 1 for store locations. Lululemon's mission was – to create components for people to live longer, healthier, and more fun lives, based on core values of quality, product, integrity, balance, entrepreneurship, greatness, and fun.

Lululemon produced high-quality, innovative products meant to inspire physical activity in yogis and athletes. The company created a manifesto to capture the essence of the Lululemon culture and inspire customers to consider changes to improve their own lifestyle. Ideas like 'a daily hit of athletic-induced endorphins gives you the power to make better decisions, helps you be at peace with yourself, and offsets stress'; 'that which matters the most should never give way to that which matters the least'; and 'successful people replace the words "wish", "should" and "try" with "I will"' were part of the manifesto and part of the Lululemon brand religion. The company targeted 'Super Girls'; the daughters of the 1980s 'Power Women'. These educated, hard-working women lived healthy lifestyles by working out, eating right, and taking care of themselves. Lululemon opened lines of men's clothing and accessories, but still remained highly dedicated to its core market of 'Super Girls'.

Lululemon's founder, Dennis 'Chip' Wilson, graduated with a Bachelor of Arts in Economics from the University of Calgary in 1980. He founded the surf/skate/snowboard company Westbeach Sports in the early 1990s, and sold it in 1997. At the age of 41, Chip started taking yoga classes and a year later, in 1998, he opened Lululemon's first store in Vancouver's trendy, upscale neighborhood, Kitsilano Beach. Wilson described his leadership style as 'run and let it be run', desiring a culture of autonomy and accountability among employees. Robert 'Bob' Meers joined Lululemon initially as a consultant in 2005 before accepting the role of CEO. The reorganization allowed Wilson to retain his positions as company Chairman and Chief Product Designer, while relinquishing his duties as CEO. Meers had a seasoned background in retail; serving as President of Reebok International and President and CEO of home décor designer, Syratech Corp.

Lululemon designed and produced technical athletic apparel for yoga, running, and dancing. The company initially became popular for its well-fitting black workout pants. In addition to workout pants, the company sold workout bras and tanks, shorts, capri pants, t-shirts, sweatshirts, jackets, and other pieces of apparel for men and women. The company also produced a line of accessories including water bottles, headgear, yoga mats and accessories, and yoga and gym bags. Lululemon took pride in using innovative materials to manufacture its products. The company's most well-known and often-used fabric was Luon®, a moisture wicking fabric that was used for most of its pants, shorts, tanks, and bras. A more innovative fabric the company used was Silverescent™, a fabric made with silver yarn, designed to eliminate bacteria and remove odor from the fabric. The average price for a pair of Lululemon pants was US$99, bra was US$48, tank was US$54, and jacket was US$98. Lululemon's line of accessories ranged from water bottles sold for US$25 to bags as expensive as US$88.

2007 proved to be a financially stellar year for Lululemon. Total assets had more than doubled, from US$48,492,745 at the beginning of 2007 to US$97,906,418 by the end of the 2007 fiscal year. Net revenue had increased during the same time period by 45.8%, while net income posted a 75.1% increase. A financial analysis for the company can be viewed in Exhibit 2. The company continued an aggressive expansion strategy, focused on development of the Canadian and US markets. Lululemon went public on the Toronto Stock Exchange on July 26, 2007 and was first listed on the NASDAQ on September 4, 2007 at US$36.87 per share. Stock information can be viewed in Exhibit 3.

Lululemon's plan for sustainability and corporate social responsibility

From its inception, Lululemon had extensive plans for incorporating sustainability into the overall strategy of the organization. Corporate social responsibility was at the heart of Lululemon. The company named its corporate social responsibility strategy 'Community Legacy', and Lululemon's business processes were centered on the five elements described in the Community Legacy initiative: community, people, sourcing and manufacturing, efficiency and waste reduction, and green building and spaces. Lululemon specifically focused on three elements of the Community Legacy initiative as it related to sustainability: sourcing and manufacturing, efficiency and waste reduction, and green building and spaces.

Sourcing and manufacturing was developed around a three-year strategy aimed at working with suppliers that not only shared Lululemon's vision and values, but that complied with Lululemon's Workplace Code of Conduct, developed internally by Lululemon executives. Lululemon was committed to only work with suppliers that were as concerned about the environment and human health as Lululemon. The company set a high level of expectations; therefore suppliers that wanted to work with Lululemon had to meet specific requirements, and were continuously audited by Lululemon to identify areas of weakness and opportunity. Lululemon created a Social Responsibility Compliance ranking to assess suppliers and manufacturing partners, and evaluated each partner out of a possible score of 100. The scorecard was broken down into three sections: labor practices, environmental responsibility, and health and safety.

Efficiency and waste reduction was also at the core of Lululemon's Community Legacy initiative and overall strategy. The five-year vision for this plan included a high level of product and process innovation to reduce environmental pollutants in garment manufacturing and retailing. The company worked on implementing an internal environmental guide and clause in the Workplace Code of Conduct for compliance by both Lululemon and its suppliers. In addition to constant innovation of design, packaging and shipping processes were constantly scrutinized in order to find the best possible way to decrease the company's environmental impact. Lululemon also implemented measurement tactics and benchmarks as indicators of the company's environmental footprint, and to identify areas where improvements could be made. Finally, Lululemon set up networks between itself and environmental experts and NGOs to facilitate idea sharing about process and product improvements, and to foster ongoing conversations about corporate social responsibility and environmental impact.

Green Buildings and Spaces was the final component of Lululemon's Community Legacy initiative. The company had a five-year vision for LEED (Leadership in Energy and Environmental Design) designed buildings and spaces for new construction, and motivated existing departments and retail locations to aim for zero waste and emissions through the implementation of an internal building guide and the Building Code of Conduct; which encouraged paperless communication along with recycling and paper reduction programs, natural building and maintenance materials sourcing, and existing facility retrofitting for improved energy efficiency. Lululemon set a corporate goal of 95% zero waste efficiency in operations by 2010.

Lululemon declared 'social responsibility is our DNA' and felt responsible to all stakeholders: employees, customers, vendors, suppliers, stockholders, and the environment. Lululemon further supported its commitment to social responsibility on its website: 'It is who we are and what we do and we will continue to further our mission of creating components for people to live longer, healthier and more fun lives... both for our guests, our employees, and our manufacturing partners.'

Smartfiber AG, SeaCell®, and Vitasea®

Smartfiber AG was a small, privately held German company based in Rudolstadt, Germany, with fewer than 30 employees. In July 2007, Smartfiber AG took over Sea-Cell®, a competitor, to expand its research, production, and marketing potential. Smartfiber AG developed, produced, and distributed the SeaCell® Lyocell fabric used in Lululemon's Vitasea® products.

Based on the Lyocell system of combining SeaCell® with cellulose material, Sea-Cell® contained a skin protective and anti-inflammatory seaweed additive. Lyocell was the seaweed fiber that was part of the SeaCell® fabric. Smartfiber AG claimed that SeaCell® caused an active exchange between the seaweed fiber and the skin, which activated wellbeing in those exposed to the fiber. The partnership between Lululemon and Smartfiber AG commenced in 2006 and the Vitasea® product line was born; made with 23% SeaCell®Pure, Smartfiber AG's purest form of the product. Smartfiber AG complied with Lululemon's Workplace Code of Conduct and had potential to offer a new, exiting relationship between the two companies: one built on environmental awareness, innovation, and trust.

Smartfiber AG provided Lululemon with every piece of information it needed about the SeaCell® fabric. The German company gave Lululemon information on the composition of SeaCell®, and the benefits of producing the Vitasea® product line with the SeaCell® fabric. The clothing line, mainly shirts and some undergarments, was sold with a product claim created by Lululemon and Smartfiber AG certifying that Vitasea® products release amino acids, minerals and vitamins directly into the skin. Lululemon further marketed the product, with knowledge relayed by Smartfiber AG, indicating that the vitamins and minerals released from Vitasea® products' contact with skin would:

- keep skin firm and smooth

- prevent the skin from drying out

- enhance blood supply to skin

- activate cell metabolism

- promote skin cell regeneration

- contain anti-viral or anti-bacterial properties

- sooth skin rashes

- reduce stress

- detoxify the skin

Lululemon employed its grassroots marketing efforts to communicate the benefits of Vitasea® products to customers. Through company spokespersons, termed 'Lululemon Ambassadors', store employees termed 'Educators', and corporate marketing efforts, Vitasea®'s product benefits were made known to all Lululemon customers. Vitasea® products were priced at a premium compared to other Lululemon products. Vitasea® t-shirts were sold at an average US$58, whereas other Lululemon t-shirts were priced at an average of US$48 per shirt. Vitasea® products represented 3% of Lululemon's total product line, and accounted for approximately 1% of sales.

The investor's tip

In late 2007, *The New York Times*, one of the largest newspapers in the world, received a tip about one of the NASDAQ's star performers: Lululemon. An anonymous investor, poised to short-sell the stock, tipped the newspaper of Lululemon's false Vitasea® product claims, and even had verification of the company's dishonesty through independent product testing. The investor explained that Chemir, an analytical lab specializing in investigational analytical chemistry, tested the product and found no trace of seaweed in the product's composition. Louise Story, a hedge-fund manager assigned to business and finance articles for *The New York Times* was appointed to get to the bottom of both the investor's and Lululemon's product claims.

The New York Times testing

Story researched Lululemon, Chemir, and Vitasea®. Her conversation with Carolyn J. Otten, director for specialized services at Chemir Analytical Services, solidified the need to investigate the trendy, yoga-wear retailer. 'Seaweeds have known vitamins and minerals, and we searched specifically for those vitamins, and we didn't see them,' stated Otten. With Chemir's findings in its back corner, *The New York Times* ordered an independent test of Lululemon's Vitasea® fabric by the McCrone Group, a premier microscopy resource base in Westmont, IL. The newspaper arranged a lab test of a blue Lululemon Vitasea® racer-back tank top composed of 70% cotton, 6% spandex, and 24% seaweed fiber to be tested alongside a gray J. Crew t-shirt. The McCrone Group's findings were less decisive than those of Chemir; the laboratory could not rule out seaweed as part of the composition of the tank top, but also could not substantiate Lululemon's claims that seaweed was in fact part of the tank top's composition.

The New York Times publication

The New York Times published the article, '"Seaweed" clothing has none, tests show,' on the front page of the newspaper's business section on Wednesday, November 14, 2007. Story's article saw immediate attention from investors, analysts, fashion enthusiasts, and businesses alike. Prior to this date, Lululemon had been the poster-child for social responsibility, community involvement, and hip, trendy clothing. The article's publishing caused speculation around Lululemon's integrity and reputation. Some critics felt that *The New York Times* acted unethically, publishing the article even though the tip came from an investor planning on shorting Lululemon's stock. Others questioned Lululemon's ethics and product quality.

NASDAQ: LULU, TSX: LLL

The New York Times article sent shockwaves through investor circles. Since Lululemon's initial public offering (IPO) on the NASDAQ, the stock had seemed unstoppable. The stock climbed from US$36.87 to US$58.00 in just seven weeks. Lululemon had also experienced similar increases in stock price on the Toronto Stock Exchange. The release of *The New York Times* article had a negative effect on Lululemon's stock. The stock price decreased 8% on November 14, 2007, and continued to decline for the next several weeks.

Lululemon's rebuttal

Before the article was published, Story spoke to Lululemon's founder, Chip Wilson, about the Vitasea® fabric. 'If you actually put it on and wear it, it is different from cotton,' Wilson stated. 'That's my only test of it.' Wilson was confident in the Vitasea® fabric, the supplier SmartFiber, and Lululemon's brand name. Wilson's and Lululemon's strategy was to ignore *The New York Times* article; however, a few short hours after publication, Lululemon executives and investors watched the stock tumble, an unseen occurrence since Lululemon's initial public offering a few months earlier. Shortly after, Wilson and Meers quickly arranged for Lululemon to conduct an impromptu Vitasea® product test of their own.

Lululemon's tests

Lululemon contacted its partner, SGS Group (SGS), an independent, Switzerland-based inspection, verification, testing, and certification company to conduct a special test on its Vitasea® products. An SGS lab in Hong Kong conducted the test on the night of November 14, 2007, and came to the same result this time as it had when the previous Vitasea® product testing was conducted in June 2007: the product contained Lyocell fibers consistent with Lululemon's product labels, based on special tests required to confirm the fiber's existence. Smartfiber AG also provided Lululemon with a statement supporting Lululemon's product labels and the contents of the Vitasea® fabric: 'SeaCell® is permanently incorporated in the spun fiber we provide to Lululemon and is of the highest quality. In addition, we conduct our own quality assurance procedures, including regular visits to production facilities, to ensure the manufacturer is producing products in strict compliance with our specifications as well as Lululemon's,' declared Gerhard Neudorfer, Sales and Marketing Director SeaCell® Fibers.

Lululemon announced on Thursday, November 15, 2007 at 9:00 pm ET via a press release that the content of the Vitasea® product line was consistent with independent laboratory tests. The press release outlined the results of SGS Groups' tests on Vitasea® conducted in December 2006, June 2007, and November 2007, and included statements from Lululemon supporting its Vitasea® clothing line and product claims. Meers further defended Lululemon's findings and brand: 'Product quality and authenticity are of the utmost importance to Lululemon. Integrity goes to the core of everything we do and is at the heart of our relationship with our guests. For this reason, we test our products for content using a leading testing facility. We absolutely stand behind our products, our processes and refute any claims in recent press reports to the contrary. Innovation and integrity are at the heart of Lululemon. We pride ourselves on innovative and technical design. We are committed to continually bringing new and cutting edge products to the marketplace.'

Lululemon's public relations tactic was received with mixed reviews. The press release earned the company headlines such as 'Lululemon says tests verify fabric's properties' and 'Lululemon CEO says new seaweed clothing tests should clear company's name,' but others were not as confident in Lululemon's claims. Investors, media, and industry critics concluded that Lululemon played with semantics in its press release, arguing that Lululemon, while contending that the clothing did contain a fiber derived from seaweed, remained quiet about the truth regarding the Vitasea® product claim: that the clothing releases amino acids, minerals, and vitamins directly into the skin.

Some Lululemon customers stood behind the brand's products. Toronto shopper Irene Nava stated 'I personally do not care – I just love the pants. I wear them all the time. I have ones for running, ones for yoga, ones for outside.' David Wilkinson echoed Nava's comments, 'I couldn't care less, because it is so comfortable.' Others felt that Lululemon had gone too far. Student Kristie Furlong, said 'I would probably still buy the regular [products], but [the Vitasea®] ones are more expensive, and I don't know that I would pay more anyway just for seaweed.'

The Lululemon brand name and reputation was now in question. The company had been known for its sustainability practices, respect to the environment, and innovative processes, but was now the center of an international controversy. Critics argued that the company should have just told the truth as it knew it, admitted that it made a mistake, and notified the public of corrective action, rather than creating a press release to defend its product.

Canada's government intervenes

After the article was published, the Competition Bureau of Canada, an independent Canadian law enforcement agency that investigated complaints and monitored businesses for fair practices, contacted Lululemon's corporate offices in Vancouver. On Friday, November 16, 2007, the Competition Bureau of Canada released a statement that Lululemon had agreed to remove all therapeutic claims from its Vitasea® clothing line sold in all Canadian Lululemon stores. 'The Bureau acted quickly to resolve this issue of significant consumer and marketplace interest,' said Andrea Rosen, Deputy Commissioner of Competition. 'Canadians are entitled to receive accurate information from businesses in order to make informed purchasing choices.'

The Bureau outlined that Lululemon had to eliminate the following product attribute claims from its Vitasea® clothing line:

- remove all tags and/or representations on tags that contain unsubstantiated therapeutic and/or performance claims of the Vitasea® technology from all stores across Canada;

- remove all references to the Vitasea® technology from its website and any in-store advertising;

- immediately inform all store managers and employees that they should not provide information on therapeutic benefits and performance claims of the Vitasea® technology to customers; and

- undertake a review of all promotional and marketing materials to ensure they comply with relevant legal requirements.

Lululemon's removal of the Vitasea® label

With pressure from the Competition Bureau of Canada, a falling stock price, and potential backlash from consumers, Lululemon removed the label storewide. This included not only the Canadian stores over which the Competition Bureau of Canada had jurisdiction, but Lululemon stores in the US, Japan, and Australia. The company was forced to remove all of the current Vitasea® merchandise, re-educate the store employees and ambassadors about the change in the Vitasea® product claims, redesign a new label, and manufacture all new Vitasea® products with the new claimless label.

How would those few days in November 2007 affect Lululemon's strategy going forward? For a company like Lululemon, fostered in creating a positive change in those that wear its clothing, the Vitasea® debacle was a huge setback. Did *The New York Times* act unethically by publishing the Vitasea® article?

Did Lululemon perform due diligence in testing SmartFiber AG's claims? With the myriad of suppliers Lululemon currently employed – how many of them were also providing the company with false information that had not been checked? Would Lululemon have to implement a random testing process to ensure the truth of its claims? Should Lululemon continue to carry the Vitasea® line?

Lululemon had a huge mess to clean up: many stakeholders wanted explanations about both Lululemon's inadequate testing and Chip Wilson's original comments to Louise Story of *The New York Times*. The holiday sales season was right around the corner – how would Lululemon repair its tarnished image? Lululemon's grassroots marketing strategy focused on conveying a message of health, happiness, and environmental awareness through its clothing to customers needed to be re-vamped – but how?

EXHIBIT 1
Lululemon stores and locations

LULULEMON ATHLETICA INC.

LULULEMON STORES AND LOCATIONS

	Corporate-Owned Stores	Franchise Stores	Total Stores
Canada	37	3	40
United States	30	4	34
Total International	4	3	7
Overall total, as of January 31, 2007	41	10	51
Overall total, as of February 3, 2008	71	10	81

EXHIBIT 2
Financial analysis, Lululemon Athletica, Inc.

	2/3/2008	1/31/2007	Variance		COMMON SIZE	1/31/2007	1/31/2006	Variance		COMMON SIZE
	USD	USD	USD	%		USD	USD	USD	%	
INCOME STATEMENT										
Revenues	274,713,328	148,884,834	125,828,494	84.5%	100.0%	148,884,834	84,129,093	64,755,741	77.0%	100.0%
Cost of Goods Sold	128,411,175	72,903,112	55,508,063	76.1%	46.7%	72,903,112	41,176,981	31,726,131	77.0%	49.0%
Gross Profit	146,302,153	75,981,722	70,320,431	92.5%	53.3%	75,981,722	42,952,112	33,029,610	76.9%	51.0%
Selling, General & Administrative Expenses	96,177,348	52,539,998	43,637,350	83.1%	35.0%	52,539,998	26,416,262	26,123,736	93.9%	35.3%
Income (Loss) from Operations	50,124,805	16,213,414	33,911,391	209.2%	18.2%	16,213,414	3,726,708	12,486,706	335.1%	10.9%
Net Income (Loss)	30,842,439	7,666,331	23,176,108	302.3%	11.2%	7,666,331	1,394,104	6,272,227	449.9%	5.1%
BALANCE SHEET										
Cash & Equivalents	53,339,326	16,028,534	37,310,792	232.8%	34.4%	16,028,534	–	–	–	22.2%
Receivables (ST)	4,431,556	2,290,665	2,140,891	93.5%	2.9%	2,290,665	–	–	–	3.2%
Inventories	39,092,208	26,628,113	12,464,095	46.8%	25.2%	26,628,113	–	–	–	36.8%
Current Assets	97,906,418	48,492,743	49,413,675	101.9%	63.1%	48,492,743	–	–	–	67.1%
Net Property Plant & Equip	44,038,565	18,175,944	25,862,621	142.3%	28.4%	18,175,944	–	–	–	25.1%
Total Assets	155,092,142	72,293,109	82,799,033	114.5%	100.0%	72,293,109	–	–	–	100.0%

	2/3/2008	1/31/2007	Variance	%		1/31/2007	1/31/2006	Variance	%
Accounts Payable	5,199,604	4,935,037	264,567	5.4%	3.4%	4,935,037	—	—	6.8%
Current Liabilities	35,821,551	31,938,590	3,882,961	12.2%	23.1%	31,938,590	—	—	44.2%
Total Liabilities	42,739,309	34,346,612	8,392,697	24.4%	27.6%	34,346,612	—	—	47.5%
Common Stock	466,847	442,908	23,939	5.4%	0.3%	442,908	—	—	0.6%
Total Equity	112,034,009	37,378,798	74,655,211	199.7%	72.2%	37,378,798	—	—	51.7%

RATIO ANALYSIS

Profitability Ratios	2/3/2008	1/31/2007	Variance	%		1/31/2007	1/31/2006	Variance	%
ROA % (Net)	26.91	—	—	—		—	—	—	—
ROE % (Net)	40.95	41.02	-0.07	-0.2%		41.02	—	—	—
ROI % (Operating)	66.55	—	—	—		—	—	—	—
EBITDA Margin %	21.28	13.99	7.29	52.1%		13.99	7.36	6.63	90.1%
Calculated Tax Rate %	40.16	53.68	-13.52	-25.2%		53.68	62.63	-8.95	-14.3%
Revenue per Employee	101,556	—	—	—		—	—	—	—

Liquidity Indicators	2/3/2008	1/31/2007	Variance	%		1/31/2007	1/31/2006	Variance	%
Quick Ratio	1.61	0.57	1.04	182.5%		0.57	—	—	—
Current Ratio	2.73	1.52	1.21	79.6%		1.52	—	—	—
Net Current Assets % TA	40.03	22.90	17.13	74.8%		22.90	—	—	—

	2/3/2008 USD	1/31/2007 USD	Variance USD	%	COMMON SIZE	1/31/2007 USD	1/31/2006 USD	Variance USD	%	COMMON SIZE
Asset Management	2/3/2008	1/31/2007	Variance	%		1/31/2007	1/31/2006	Variance	%	
Total Asset Turnover	2.4	—	—	—		—	—	—	—	
Receivables Turnover	81.07	—	—	—		—	—	—	—	
Inventory Turnover	8.29	—	—	—		—	—	—	—	
Accounts Payable Turnover	53.77	—	—	—		—	—	—	—	
Accrued Expenses Turnover	18.19	—	—	—		—	—	—	—	
Property Plant & Equip Turnover	8.76	—	—	—		—	—	—	—	
Cash & Equivalents Turnover	7.86	—	—	—		—	—	—	—	
Per Share	2/3/2008	1/31/2007	Variance	%		1/31/2007	1/31/2006	Variance	%	
Cash Flow per Share	0.57	0.39	0.18	46.2%		0.39	—	—	—	
Book Value per Share	1.66	0.57	1.09	191.2%		0.57	—	—	—	

EXHIBIT 3
Market information and dividends

LULULEMON ATHLETICA INC.

MARKET INFORMATION AND DIVIDENDS

Period End: Feb 03, 2008

	Common Stock Price (Nasdaq Global Select Market)	
	High	Low
Fiscal Year Ending February 3, 2008		
Second Quarter (from July 27, 2007)	$34.17	$24.92
Third Quarter	$60.70	$28.70
Fourth Quarter	$51.94	$25.00

Sources

2002 Economic Census Manufacturing Industry Series. Other Apparel Accessories and Other Apparel Manufacturing: 2002. Dec 2004. US Census Bureau. 14 Mar. 2009, www.census.gov/prod/ec02/ec0231i315999.pdf.

About Us > Community Legacies. *Lululemon.* 15 Nov. 2007. Internet Archive – WayBack Machine. 21 Aug. 2009, www.freerepublic.com/focuwww.web.archive.org/web/20070518124957/www.lululemon.com/about/media/news.

Alexander, Renee. Lululemon Athletica in shape. *BrandChannel.com.* 13 Feb 2006. Brand Channel, 20 Mar. 2009, www.74.125.95.132/search?q=cache:i77z2rl-xZwJ:www.brandchannel.com/features_profile.asp%3Fpr_id%3D271+lululemon+innovation&cd=1&hl=en&ct=clnk&gl=us.

Alter, Lloyd. NYTimes on Lululemon's 'Seaweed" Clothing: Lousy Chemistry, Lousy Journalism.' *Business & Politics*, 15 Nov 2007. Treehugger, 21 Aug. 2009, www.treehugger.com/files/2007/11/new_york_times_15.php.

Anderson, Diane. Stretching for Success: Lululemon Athletica reaches out to every corner of its customer base to design versatile yoga apparel. *CNNMoney.com.* 10 Oct. 2006. CNN, 20 Mar. 2009, www.money.cnn.com/magazines/business2/business2_archive/2006/05/01/8375911/index.htm.

Bissonnette, Zac. Lululemon underscores the strength of short sellers' research. *Blogging Stocks.* 14 Nov 2007. Blogging Stocks, 21 Aug. 2009, www.bloggingstocks.com/2007/11/14/lululemon-underscores-the-strength-of-short-sellers-research.

Competition Bureau takes action to ensure unsubstantiated claims removed from Lululemon clothing. *Competition Bureau – Lululemon Vitasea® Clothing.* 16 Nov. 2007. Competition Bureau of Canada, 21 Aug. 2009, www.cb-bc.gc.ca/eic/site/cb-bc.nsf/eng/02517.html.

George, Lianne. How Lululemon lost its balance. *Macleans.ca*. 06 Feb 2008. Macleans Magazine, 21 Aug. 2009, www.macleans.ca/business/companies/article.jsp?content=2008 0206_87890_87890.

Suppa, Julia. The Lululemon love affair. Digital Journal, June 16, 2008, www.digitaljournal .com/article/78230/The_Lululemon_Love_Affair.

Shaw, Hollie. The making of Lululemon; superheroines inspired company's founder to revolutionize women's yoga wear. *Financial Post*, 15 Feb. 2008: FP7.

Lazarus, Eve, The Tao of Lululemon. *Marketing Magazine* 113 6 (14 Apr. 2008): 22–27. Business Source Premier. EBSCO, 27 May 2008, www.search.ebscohost.com/login/aspx?dlrec t=true&db=buh&AN=31871319&site=bsi-live.

Lululemon Athletica, Inc. Annual Report. *www.shareholder.com*. 23 Feb. 2008. Shareholder .com a Nasdaq OMX Company, 13 Mar 2009, www.investor.lululemon.com/secfiling .cfm?filingID=909567-08-415.

Lululemon Athletica Inc. Lululemon Athletica Inc. Form 10-k. Edgar Online. 3 Feb. 2008. Edgar, 12 Oct. 2008, www.sec.gov/edgar.shtml.

Lululemon Athletica Officers and Directors. Lululemon Athletica, Inc, 17 June 2008, www .investor.lululemon.com/biodisplay.cfm?ubioid=19073.

Lululemon Manifesto. Lululemon Athletica, Inc. 22 June 2008, www.lululemon.com/culture/ manifesto/text.

Lululemon stock submerged by seaweed-wear doubts. *Reuters*. 15 Nov. 2007. Reuters, 21 Aug. 2009, www.reuters.com/article/hotStocksNews/idUSN1531911220071116.

Mayger, Joe. 9 Recession-proof stocks. www.cnn.com. 27 June 2008. CNN, 19 Oct. 2008, www .money.cnn.com/investing/dividends-income/2008/06/27/9-recession-proof-stocks.aspx.

Moffitt, Sean. Canada word of mouth discovery #5 Lululemon Athletica. *Buzz Canuck*. 18 Nov. 2006. Buzz Canuck, 20 Mar 2009, www.buzzcanuck.typepad.com/agentwild fire/2006/11/canada_word_of_.html.

Our Day-to-Day Greatness. *Lululemon*. Lululemon, 20 Mar. 2009, www.lululemon.com/ legacies/greatness.

Piller, Frank. The Consumer decides: Nike focuses competitive strategy on customization and creating personal consumer experiences – data about the Nike Plus Personalization System. Mass Customization & Open Innovation News, 26 Feb 2007, www.mass-customi zation.blogs.com/mass_customization_open_i/2007/02/the_consumer_de.html.

Shirt sham: Lululemon's Vitasea® is seaweed-less. *Fitsugar*. 16 Nov. 2007. Fitsugar, 21 Aug. 2009, www.fitsugar.com/810560.

Stewart, Monte. Lululemon boss rides creative wave. *Lululemon Blog*. 16 May 2008. Lululemon, 21 Aug. 2009, www.lululemonblog.com/2008/06/lululemon-blog-301st-post-interview.html.

Story, Louise. 'seaweed' clothing has none, tests show. *The New York Times*. 14 Nov. 2007. *The New York Times*. 21 Aug. 2009 <www.nytimes.com/2007/11/14/business/14seaweed .html?_r=2&hp&oref=slogin>.

Taylor, Susan. UPDATE 2-Lululemon to remove health claims from fabrics. *Reuters*. 16 Nov. 2007. Reuters, 21 Aug. 2009, www.reuters.com/article/companyNewsAndPR/id USN1638905320071117.

Team Research and Development. Lululemon Athletica, Yoga-Inspired Apparel. 2009. Lululemon Athletica Inc., 15 Mar. 2009, www.lululemon.com/community/rd_team.

Vaucher, Andréa. Lululemon Athletica's yoga-inspired sports attire positions itself for success. *The New York Times*. 9 Sep. 2007. *The New York Times*, 21 Aug. 2009, www.nytimes .com/2007/09/09/style/09iht-rlulu.7438175.html.

Wells, Jennifer. Lululemon tries activism on for size. *TheStar.com*. 17 Oct. 2007. *The Toronto Star*. 21 Aug. 2009, www.thestar.com/comment/columnists/article/267598.

Yahoo! Finance – LULU Lululemon Athletica, Inc. Yahoo! Finance. 13 Mar. 2009. NASDAQ, 14 Mar. 2009, www.finance.yahoo.com/q/in?s=LULU.

SeaCell See and Feel. *Topkapi Iplik*. Topkapi Iplik, 21 Aug. 2009, www.topkapi-iplik.com.tr/ EN/scell.html.

Part III
Sustainability as a source of differentiation strategies

CASE 9

Burgerville

Sustainability and Sourcing in a QSR Supply Chain

Darrell Brown, Phil Berko, Patrick Dedrick, Brie Hilliard, and Joshua Pfleeger

> Doing business locally out of the relationships that people had was really important to this company and the people who were running it. These family kinds of values and the relationships and the way that people interacted with each other was very important and it was important to keep the money in the communities where we were doing business and the better job we do of doing that the more money people have to spend in your business. So it's a circle that works very well. It's pretty basic economics, actually, and today we call it sustainability. Years ago they called it "that's the way you do business".
>
> *Jack Graves, Chief Cultural Officer, Burgerville*

Jack Graves is considering buying chicken. More precisely, Jack is considering *where* to buy chicken. He needs to make a recommendation to the purchasing team soon, and the decision is complicated. Jack is a long-time employee of the Burgerville restaurant chain, a quick-serve restaurant chain in the Northwest USA. Burgerville prides itself in being true to its long-held values while maintaining profitability and growth. Graves' primary job at Burgerville is to assure that the company's values are embedded in all its actions, including its relationships to its supply chain. His current concern is the dilemma of *which* values to promote. Burgerville sells chicken, lots of chicken. So the purchase of chicken has significant impacts on the social and environmental impacts of Burgerville's supply chain. Should Burgerville buy local, with the inherent social and environmental benefits, while paying attention to concerns about labor issues, animal treatment, and non-organic stewardship? Or should it find a supplier with some assurance that these potential problems are eliminated, regardless of location? Jack knows that Burgerville needs to address this issue soon, as the supply of chicken that is produced to Burgerville's high standards is small and there are sure to be competitors seeking the same products. He will have to weigh the company's values and make a recommendation soon.

As the Chief Cultural Officer of The Holland Inc., Burgerville's parent company, Jack Graves is constantly aware of the need to align the Burgerville culture and identity throughout all units of the business, including vendor partners (Exhibit 1). The chain's slogan: "Fresh. Local. Sustainable." proclaims its commitment to offering foods differently than other quick serve chains, with specific attention to where food is being sourced. Burgerville aims to deliver on this promise as often as possible, and has had success in the past.

Over the past decade, Burgerville has made a concerted effort to ensure its purchasing supports it values. As of 2009, over 70% of Burgerville's total spending on food products was from local suppliers, up from less than 60% in 2008 (Exhibit 2). With chicken, though, Graves was faced with some difficult questions and hard choices: can Burgerville find a local supplier who can provide a sufficient quantity and quality of breaded and plain chicken breasts and chicken strips at a cost comparable to the existing national brand supplier? Is buying local the most important decision to make for Burgerville and its image? Is the issue more than simply reducing the distance the food travels from origin to the customer? Are Burgerville customers willing to pay a premium for locally sourced chicken? It makes sense to purchase from local farmers who may then become loyal customers, but what if distant farms operate more sustainably than the local farms? Is there a sustainable chicken farm that could handle Burgerville's demand? These questions weigh on Graves's mind as he struggles to balance the chain's profitability with the company's values.

The company

George Propstra founded Burgerville in 1961 when he opened the first restaurant in Vancouver, WA (Exhibit 3). Propstra followed in the footsteps of his father, Jacob Propstra, a Dutch immigrant to the area, who founded and owned The Holland Creamery, primarily an ice cream producer. George ran his restaurant with the same principles that he had learned from his father – buy local ingredients, treat your employees well, support the local community, and serve fresh, never frozen, products whenever possible. Since 1961, the company, which is still owned by the family, has maintained these core philosophies.

Now operating 39 restaurants (Exhibit 4), and a mobile unit known as "The Nomad," in Washington and Oregon, Burgerville sources local ingredients as often as possible (Exhibit 5). Its seasonal items featured during the peak of the harvest emphasize Burgerville's attention to and creativity around local sourcing (Exhibit 6). Burgerville prides itself on emphasizing products that are grown or harvested with particular attention to environmental and social impacts. Specifically, Burgerville strives to select ingredients from suppliers that pay particular attention to the way in which their products are made or grown and to the people that work to produce those ingredients. Although it is not possible in all cases, they attempt do so by relying on standards such as those embodied by the Food Alliance, and attempt to select farmers, growers, and products that either already adhere to Food Alliance certification standards or are willing to adapt their practices to meet those certification standards (Exhibit 7). Many of these ingredients are sourced from farms in the Pacific Northwest, and the total annual spend on local ingredients for all Burgerville locations represented over US$13.2M (Exhibit 8). As a business that must maintain profitability, of course, Burgerville cannot always meet these stringent standards for every product it sells. It actively attempts to move closer to these standards in all products and processes as it continues to grow and evolve. The move to obtain a chicken product closer to the Burgerville core values is what currently concerns Jack.

Overall, Burgerville has embraced progressive environmental and social practices for years. In 2005, the company began purchasing wind energy credits equivalent to 100% of its yearly electrical usage, and recycling as much as it could. In 2007 it instituted a campaign to begin using compostable products in restaurants. By 2010, the program included all 39 restaurants with compostable cups, napkins, and food wrappers – 23 restaurants even had on-site access to composting – and it has diverted enough trash from landfills annually to save approximately $60,000 per year in hauling costs. This amounts to over 50% of Burgerville's divertible trash being recycled or composted. The percentage was increasing each month.

Burgerville prides itself in its attention to its employees as well. In 2010, Burgerville had over 1,300 employees, and provided health insurance coverage for all employees working 20 hours a week or more at a highly subsidized monthly price of $20 to the employee and an additional $20 for the employee's children. In addition, Burgerville actively participates in employee health and development programs and is known nationally for their "best practices" in employee treatment.

As a broad interest in "sustainability" increased in the United States, attention to and reporting about corporate social responsibility (CSR) began to rise throughout the economy. The quick-serve restaurant industry was no exception. At that time many quick-serve restaurants companies began to publish yearly reports of their environmental and social sustainability efforts, however Burgerville chose not to join this trend. Even though Burgerville had been conducting business in a way which emphasized its values since day one, it wanted to avoid being accused of "green-washing," or overemphasizing their CSR and environmental consciousness to generate sales. Burgerville, of course, wants to be sure to capitalize on the positive marketing benefits of activities inherent to their operations and company culture. Burgerville has received, and highlights, its considerable recognition from local, national, and industry media for its efforts related to unique, local menu items, employee and social programs, and environmental practices. This recognition is external validation of Burgerville's attempts to keep its corporate values evident in its actions (Exhibit 9).

Burgerville was started as a small, family-run operation, and its growth has not altered the values on which the company was founded. As the company grows, its commitment to its values remains central to its identity, meaning that Burgerville continues to treat its employees well, and commits to serving the highest quality product possible that can be procured from local farmers. This is Burgerville's heritage and it is the culture Jack weighs as he tries to make the right chicken-sourcing recommendation.

The industry

The quick-serve food industry originated as the drive-in restaurant in the 1940s. Offering food to patrons late into the night, drawing them in with attractive waitresses and bright neon lights, these drive-ins were the perfect locale for young customers to show off their cars, meet their friends, and enjoy a burger, shake, and fries. Early drive-in successes included McDonald's Famous Hamburgers and Carl's Drive-In Barbecue, which opened in 1940 and 1945, respectively. By 1948, the McDonald brothers, founders of McDonald's Famous Hamburgers, re-engineered the standard diner kitchen and processes to speed up production to meet increasing demand and to standardize the products of their increasing number of restaurants. The result is what is now known as the quick-serve restaurant, in which food is prepared quickly and made available for an inexpensive price. Included among these early fast food standards were smaller, more limited menus, and an assembly-line style of preparing food. With this new model, one attendant might grill (or even warm up) meat for a burger, while another added toppings and wrapped it for the customer, a third might prepare French fries, and yet another prepare milkshakes. Reducing the number of reusable dishes was also critical to this model, and most food was served in disposable wrappers. This fast, streamlined system was coined as the "Speedee Service System," and is considered the original model of the modern day quick-serve restaurant. Carl's Jr., McDonald's, Taco Bell, Burger King, Wendy's, Kentucky Fried Chicken and countless other restaurant chains have since based their production model on the Speedee Service System.[i]

The quick serve industry is typically known for intense competition, low prices, and enormous marketing budgets. Industry players compete by differentiating their products from those of their competitors, keeping the menu interesting in order to appeal to constantly changing consumer preferences, and maintaining low prices. For example, McDonald's innovated on the burger package in the 1990s by creating a box with a "hot" side and a "cold" side for the now discontinued McDLT. In 1997, Burger King spent $70m advertising their newly developed fries in order to attract consumers to the "best" fries in the market, and steer them away from competitor McDonald's.[ii] Taco Bell maintains differentiation by offering Mexican-style food that appeals to mainstream tastes. In 2009, the chain launched a menu item that included bacon to diversify its offerings and capitalize on parallel trends found in burger and fries quick-serve restaurants. Most of the national chains advertise "Dollar menus" or "Value meals" emphasizing the low cost of their offerings. Recent interest in issues of the social costs of poor nutrition and obesity add another dimension to which the industry players can differentiate their products, resulting in quick-serve companies competing on their ability to serve customers "healthy" foods. Currently, in addition to traditional fare, most national quick-serve chains advertise a limited selection of low-carb menus, "real" fruit smoothies, salads, and "kid-friendly" snacks such as apple slices.

Typical quick-serve industry sourcing

The quick-serve industry typically divides its food purchases into two categories – proprietary and conventional. Proprietary items are processed items that have been custom formulated for the equipment, packaging, standards, and menu items of a specific restaurant chain. The restaurant chains purchase these at a contract price, and they may include French fries, milkshakes, ice cream, meats, and toppings – any food items that are unique to a particular chain.

Conventional items are more commoditized and are generally used by a variety of different chains and generally include condiments, produce, and soft drinks. Prices for conventional items tend to be market based and negotiated through corporate offices. Many restaurant chains enter into long-term agreements with suppliers to ensure a steady supply of the quantities needed at a predictable price. These agreements often put downward pressure on prices, reducing total costs to purchasing chains, either increasing the profit margins of the final products to the restaurants or reducing the costs to the ultimate restaurant consumer, or both.

In recent years, the practices of national and global quick-serve companies have come under considerable criticism. A number of chains have been criticized for forcing supplier prices down so far that wages paid to farm laborers are below subsistence levels.[iii] In response to the reputational damage that a supplier's business practices can do to the chains, McDonald's circulated a "Code of Conduct for Suppliers" in 2000.[iv] This document aims to address the social issues that surround the relationship restaurant chains have with their suppliers, and includes standards for:

- Compliance with local laws
- Prohibition of prison, forced, and child labor
- Compensation
- Work schedule

- Discrimination
- Working conditions
- Inspections by supplier personnel
- Inspections by restaurant personnel

Similar concerns about the treatment of animals throughout the supply chain of quick-serve restaurants resulted in public responses to mitigate potential damage to corporate and industry reputations. For example, Burger King responded in 2007 with guidelines for their suppliers regarding care, housing, transport, and slaughter of animals.[v]

Sourcing issues also are an area of concern for the quick-serve industry. In India, McDonald's demand for lettuce encouraged farmers to adjust their agricultural practices to grow lettuce year-round rather than only during the winter months to provide for McDonald's needs. While this allowed for McDonald's locations in India to source local produce, this decision also affected the overall agricultural industry within the affected areas of India, as it changed the production of formerly grown produce.[vi]

Local sourcing

The concept of promoting local food systems has recently gained popularity, partially as a counter to the results of an agri-food industry dominated by a few firms. The goal of the "local food movement" is to shift away from globalized networks of distribution and revert to local communities supported by, and supportive of local production. Local food systems provide primarily what is readily accessible in the local geographies. This movement hopes to contribute to economically sustainable, environmentally less damaging, and socially supportive communities. Local food systems generally minimize "food miles," support farms able to patronize the businesses to which they supply product, and rely on, and pay, local labor. Beyond the potential advantages of local food quality, the local food movement tends to encourage more socially and environmentally sustainable food production and sourcing through intentional spending.

Changes in food system preferences are characterized by consumer interest in many forms, ranging from a wide variety of third party certifications for 'organic' or 'sustainable' products to a dramatic increase in the number of local farmers' markets, springing up all around the United States. The total number of farmers' markets in the United States and Canada has grown by over 20% from 2006 to 2009, to nearly 6,000 total markets.[vii] Beyond the level of individual households, the local food movement has reached a point at which it calls for participation from larger entities to source their food products with particular attention paid to the "locality" of those products, striving to maximize the foods that are grown locally.

One metric commonly used to evaluate local food is the "food mile." In essence, food miles are an expression of the distance that a food product travels geographically from the point of its origin to its final destination.[viii] Food miles may use actual miles traveled, or may calculate a carbon value for a product in the form of the emissions generated during the transport of a product along each step in its supply chain. This metric, if known, allows consumers to become aware of the impact that food choices may have on the environment and allows them to alter their personal environmental impact by choosing products that have as many or few food miles as desired.[ix] For example, a consumer in Denver, Colorado, wishing to reduce her personal carbon footprint might choose to eliminate bananas from her diet, since they cannot be grown in the Intermountain West, and must come from a farm in the Caribbean or Central America. Ideally, individuals will consume only foods that they get from retailers who make concerted efforts to stock local foods or at smaller farmers' markets or community-supported agriculture services, where consumers buy directly from farmers and artisans.

Bringing food to Burgerville

Burgerville locations are typically run by a manager and two assistant managers. This management team is responsible for placing orders for their own restaurants from Burgerville authorized distributors, who make deliveries directly to the stores three times per week. The accompanying invoices are sent to the corporate office, where they get paid. This direct delivery eliminates the need for a commissary, which would distribute foodstuffs internally among Burgerville locations.

Burgerville, like other quick serve restaurants, constantly refines its menu items. Unlike many of its competitors, however, for Burgerville this refinement includes adding vegan and vegetarian options, fish, and limited time offer seasonal items. The company began offering these rotating menu items based around seasonal foods in 2008 and have begun asking local "foodies," and celebrity chefs to create new offerings. Typical items include entrée sandwiches or side order items such as "The Roasted Turkey & Cherry Chutney Wrap" (Exhibit 10), developed by Allison Hensey, director of The Oregon Environmental Council. A percentage of the proceeds for this particular item benefit the Council, supporting the "healthy foods and farms" program and promoting the environmental stewardship and economic vitality of Oregon's farmers and ranchers. Additional seasonally rotated items include fresh, local berry milkshakes, fried portobello mushroom wedges, fried asparagus spears, and Walla Walla sweet onion rings, and are eagerly anticipated by patrons each year. Ingredients for most of these items are not part of Burgerville's normal food inventory, nor of its distributors' product lines. As such, seasonal ingredients must be sourced and incorporated into the Burgerville supply chain as new items are added to the menu.

Burgerville's mission to support local farms and local businesses has extended to the current day, where local ingredients are needed to supply 39 different locations with standard menu items in addition to these specialty and seasonal items. Burgerville pioneered a unique farmer–distributor system that allows them to maintain relationships with local farmers, as well as introduce those farmers to other potential customers and distribution channels. In this system, Burgerville will find a local farm that produces a specific product that they need for a menu item. Then they will go to one of their two main distributors, Sysco Corporation and Fulton Provisions and arrange for the farmer to supply products to the distributor (Exhibit 11). From this point, Burgerville can simply add the product to the regular orders they receive from that distributor, as well as give other firms that use that distributor access to the products.

Three requirements of a credible certification scheme

Standard: The standard must be clear, unambiguous and publicly available so there is clarity about what compliance with the standard means.

- Certification: All certification against the standard must be carried out by third party, independent organizations following clear, defined procedures. Certification is not usually carried out by the organization which developed the standard, but rather by organizations specializing in certification called certification bodies. Certification bodies must have the systems, procedures and personnel to ensure credible, replicable certification against the standard. To ensure a consistent and high standard of certification, the certification bodies must be approved and monitored through an accreditation program.

Accreditation: This is the process of 'certifying the certifiers' and must be carried out by a competent, independent body capable of ensuring that all certification bodies provide a consistent interpretation of the standard through approved procedures and processes.

Adapted from: Nussbaum, R., Garforth, M., Wenban-Smith, M., and Scrase, H. 2000. An analysis of current FSC accreditation, certification and standard setting procedures identifying elements which create constraints for small forest owners. United Kingdom Department for International Development (DFID) DFID Project R7589 Forestry Research Programme

---

Sourcing the product through a distributor means that the farmers can focus on agriculture instead of distribution. Troy Thomas, head of produce procurement for Sysco Corporation, one of Burgerville's main distributors, says: "This allows us to do what we do best – transport food, while allowing the farmers to do what they do best – grow good food." Burgerville sees the inherent value in this consumer–producer relationship that varies from the more common, consumer–distributor relationship seen in supermarkets around America. The farmer benefits through access to a market that is larger than Burgerville alone, while other customers seeking local products benefit by having access to new products through their normal distribution methods. This farmer–distributor system serves to benefit Burgerville, local farmers, associated distributors, and consumers, all by making local food more widely available.

Third Party Certification

Certifications of consumer products and production processes are used as a signal of the attainment of a set of attributes, or a demonstration of a set of practices that adhere to defined guidelines. The guidelines for these processes and products vary depending on the aim of the individual certification and are created to promote a specific mission, such as an environmental or social focus.

Ultimately, certification is meant to act as a communication medium, transferring specific information about characteristics invisible to the concerned party. In the realm of food and agricultural certifications, examples include: Kosher Certified, USDA Organic, and Rainforest Alliance Certified. With each of these certifications, there is a designated set of guidelines or attributes to which the process must adhere or that the product must attain. For example, in order for a product to receive the USDA Organic certification it must have been produced (or grown) with strict regulations on fertilizers, pesticides, hormones and other "non-natural" additives.[x] The goal of this certification is to provide consumers assurance that the product was produced to the standards of the certification.

There are two essential parts to a certification: establishing a measurable set of characteristics or attributes that comprise and embody the desired certification, and validating the certification. The process begins with an organization that wishes to convey a message about a product or process. Once organizations have drafted a body of attributes, verification processes must be established. This verification can be obtained on a first, second or third-party basis. First-party certification is gained when an organization assesses itself, and determines whether or not it is meeting a set of standards. Second-party certification comes from an outside organization, but that organization has some kind of stake in the company that it is attempting to certify. Third-party certification is gained when an entity totally independent of the firm seeking certification is brought in to assess whether or not the standards in question are being met. Third-party certification is, in that sense, the most objective and unbiased level of certification (Exhibit 12).

There are two major perspectives on third-party certification in the food industry as a mechanism for conveying information to consumers. From one perspective, proper certification is able to convey, in a simple and understandable way, a vast array of codified knowledge to consumers about the product that they consider purchasing. It is a way to encourage producers to meet common regulations beyond those set forth by the FDA. However, another perspective is that certification is a means for producers to hide behind a label 9– to meet a set of minimal standards while ignoring any real and meaningful change to the way that company does business – that third-party certification favors form over substance and lulls consumers into a false sense of security and a state of ignorance of the real impacts of their purchasing habits.

Past sourcing issues

Jack Graves, as a long time Burgerville employee, is well aware of the past supply chain decisions. In various ways, these decisions have built an expectation that, through creative work with suppliers and a willingness to deviate from standard industry practices, Burgerville can indeed maintain its economic vitality while adhering to and promoting its core values. These, and other initiatives Burgerville implemented, have made Burgerville a leader and innovator in sustainability in the quick-serve restaurant industry. Jack is proud of that leadership role.

Country natural beef

Fresh, never frozen, beef has been a vital part of Burgerville's identity since George Propstra grilled the first Burgerville hamburger. In order to meet this requirement, Burgerville must source its beef locally. However, the concerns of procuring beef for Burgerville go beyond geography. While purchasing beef locally met the goal of never serving previously frozen beef, a wide variety of environmental and social issues, including concerns about the health and treatment of the livestock remained important to Burgerville as well. The traditional factory-farming system of beef production is laden with environmental and social concerns; the task of producing the quantities of beef needed to supply an enterprise the size of Burgerville generally leads to farming conglomerates, often contributing to the decline in family farming, farm communities, and the rancher lifestyle. Burgerville was concerned about the treatment of the animals that would eventually be sold as hamburgers to final customers.

In the United States, most conventionally raised cattle are fed a diet of grain, most often corn, in order to ensure a fast and efficient fattening process and a quick turnaround to slaughter. As this lifestyle is not conducive to forming the muscle mass naturally developed in cattle, it is common for industrial beef producers to treat cattle heavily with hormones. This, combined with the tightly packed and unnaturally sedentary lifestyle that this production method encourages, has led to increased social awareness and outcry over treatment of the cattle. Moreover, slaughterhouses have been known for poor sanitation, excessive line speeds, and poorly enforced regulations, all of which contribute to oppressive working conditions, high rates of workplace injuries, and a history of food-borne pathogens.

Country Natural Beef uses a business model that provides a large quantity of dependable production with a stark contrast to conventional factory farming. Due to this more sustainable ranching model they have enjoyed a mutually beneficial relationship with Burgerville.[xi] The Country Natural Beef Cooperative (CNB) consists of nearly 120 family ranches, primarily in the Northwest, all of which come together for the common goal of providing customers with locally raised, humanely treated, and chemical-free natural beef. To ensure that CNB produces consistent, high quality products the ranchers maintain ownership of the cattle throughout the value chain. The only exception is while the cattle are at CNB's partner feedlot, Beef Northwest. At Beef Northwest, the CNB cattle are fed a diet comprised of cooked potato products, sunflowers and dry distillers' grain, in contrast to the factory-farming standard diet of corn.

Once the cattle have reached the appropriate weight, Beef Northwest trucks the cattle to a slaughterhouse owned by AB Foods. AB Foods is a sustainably focused company with ranching roots that focuses on high quality products, animal well-being, and humane slaughter. The cattle are slaughtered two days per week on the first shift of the day to minimize the risk of microbial contamination. AB Foods boxes the beef and sends it to Fulton Provisions, a secondary processor and distributor. Fulton cuts steaks from the boxed beef and packages them for distribution to the end users other than Burgerville. They also grind and form the patties for Burgerville restaurants. Each of these intermediaries abides by Food Alliance certification standards and CNB's additional specifications in regard to treatment of animals, processes for treating sick animals, record keeping, and sanitation.[xii] Importantly, all of these intermediaries are local, which allows ranchers a great deal of control throughout all stages of production (Exhibit 13).

Prior to their relationship with Country Natural Beef, in order to meet the volume requirements of the entire chain of restaurants, Burgerville purchased their beef from conventional sources. Jack Graves saw that, considering Burgerville's values around sourcing, the fit with Country Natural Beef is clear – CNB provides fresh beef, from a local and community oriented source. It has an unwavering focus on sustainability and through a co-op model, has attained the production capacity to meet Burgerville's year round demand.

Liepold Farms berries

As Jack considered the decision for sourcing chickens, he also recalled a decision five years ago, one he was proud of for its social impacts. In that decision he felt that Burgerville had really made a difference that mattered to the local community. He wondered whether this decision could have a similar outcome. He hoped so.

When it comes to sourcing produce for Burgerville, local farmers have always come first, but strawberry farming in the Pacific Northwest is somewhat problematic. Oregon strawberries ripen on the vine more slowly than in other commercial areas such as California and Florida, where the climate is much warmer and drier in the spring months. Because of this slow ripening process during the cooler Pacific Northwest springs, Oregon berries have been shown to be sweeter than others. When the taste and nutritional integrity of six varieties of Oregon strawberries and five varieties of California strawberries were analyzed, five out of the six Oregon varieties were sweeter than all of the California berries tested.[xiii] This sweetness makes them perfect for Burgerville's spring milkshakes.

Unfortunately for Oregon berry producers, however, Oregon-grown strawberries are much more fragile than California strawberries, which can better withstand machine picking as whole berries. When whole berries are desired, Oregon berries must be picked by hand in order to prevent bruising, making it very labor-intensive work. Berry farmers are faced with the task of finding workers willing to do difficult work for low wages for only two months a year.[xiv] Under normal conditions, if wages were to increase in an effort to attract more workers, small Oregon farmers would likely be put out of business. Large-scale corporate farms produce hardy berries from California at a lower price than Oregon farmers can meet. As a result, wages stay low and willing workers stay scarce. In recent years, berries have been rotting on the vine and farmers have lost their crops, not because of a lack of demand, but because the limited number of willing workers cannot pick berries fast enough. Many berry producers have turned to mechanical picking and producing frozen, rather than whole, berries.

Burgerville differentiates itself on its values, and as such tries to live by their values with each purchase they make. When considering the fit between their values and relationships with their berry suppliers they found an opportunity for improvement. Historically, Burgerville purchased the first berries on the market. They were not purchasing consistently and had no embedded relationship with any single berry producer. In 2005, however, they partnered with Liepold Farms, a family farm near a small town not far from Portland, for the majority of their berry needs. In this partnership, Burgerville saw a chance to both obtain local foods and also reinforce its social values. Liepold produced high quality berries, of course, but in addition they also treated their farm workers with uncommon care. Liepold Farms special attention to their workers added costs most farms avoided, meaning that while the farm was socially responsible it was also financially fragile. Graves saw congruence to Burgerville's values with those of Liepold Farms, specifically as they related to the treatment of workers employed on the farm.

Farm workers' rights, always an interest of Burgerville, have also become an important food system issue for consumers.[xv] Burgerville saw, with Liepold, an opportunity to address the issue of farmer workers' rights, and to support a local family farm. Liepold Farms set themselves apart from many of the other local berry farmers by providing good housing for their employees on the farm-site – they house up to 70 employees on their farm during peak season. As an indicator of the worker satisfaction with Liepold, for example, for the past 20 years the same families have returned to work on the farm. Liepold Farms developed relationships with their workers by paying them a fair wage, providing housing, and taking care of additional medical expenses. This is exactly the type of employee treatment that Burgerville looks for when selecting a supplier, reflecting the way that Burgerville treats its own employees. Liepold Farms' values represent the values that embody the Burgerville brand.

Once Burgerville made the decision to partner with Liepold Farms, they helped the farm to become completely integrated in a system of distribution through Sysco Corporation. By bringing Liepold Farms into a larger supply chain, Burgerville now gets regular deliveries of fresh Liepold strawberries and raspberries, making a significant financial difference to the farm. Fresh berries sell at a 100% premium over frozen berries, which is the way most Oregon strawberries must be sold. By having a partnership with Burgerville, Liepold can be confident that they can keep taking care of their workers while still making a profit on the farm. Their products are also now available to all of Sysco's clients, giving Liepold an enormous opportunity for future sales growth. Mr Liepold says "if it wasn't for Burgerville and the fresh market, [we] probably wouldn't be doing what [we] are doing now." If their customers were only buying less expensive frozen berries, Liepold Farms would not exist as it does, and Burgerville would likely not have this kind of partner vendor to provide fresh, local berries.

Portland Roasting Coffee

In recognizing that they might, in order to meet some of the Burgerville values, need to source the chickens from outside the local area, Jack thought about other times Burgerville made intentional, non-local purchases. The most recent example, which Jack thought was well conceived, was sourcing coffee from Portland Roasting Company (PRC).

Coffee presents a special sourcing issue for Burgerville, as there are no local farms in the Pacific Northwest that grow coffee. Coffee can only be grown in tropical and subtropical environments. Coffee is one of the worlds' the most heavily traded agricultural commodities and has considerable social and environmental impact. Throughout coffee's long history, it has traditionally been shade-grown in forested plantations. However, in the last 30 years, coffee plants that are more tolerant to the sun have been developed. Coffee growers have been able to employ growing methods that expose coffee plants to direct sunlight, meaning potential crop yields up to two or three times that of shade-grown methods. This shift in growing methods led to massive deforestation of former coffee-growing regions and a dramatic shift from small farms supporting one or two families to large corporate farms, with a concurrent dramatic reduction in the number of people supported by the farms.

The massive environmental and social disruptions caused by coffee, and the importance of coffee to the developed world, have resulted in the industry becoming a major focus of both the social and environmental sustainability movements. Burgerville, when considering how to create fit between its values and the need to provide coffee to its customers identified a set of options for choosing its supplier. Typically these options include Fair Trade certification, Rain Forest Alliance certification, or no certification and a choice based solely on cost. Fair Trade certification is socially based, with customers such as Burgerville paying more than the base market price to producers in order to help them develop and improve their ability to continue to farm as family farms. The Rainforest Alliance, by contrast, looks at the environmental impact of farming methods, and aims to certify coffee that is grown with techniques that do not diminish or harm the biodiversity of sensitive coffee-growing areas.

In the process of looking for a local coffee vendor for their restaurants, however, Burgerville looked beyond standard third-party certified coffee roasters. The company elected to source their coffee from Portland Roasting Coffee (PRC), due to their "Farm Friendly Direct" program. Farm Friendly Direct is a coffee-sourcing program which aims to support sustainable growth and lifestyle improvement for PRC's coffee growers by paying above-market prices for the coffee, with the stipulation that this premium finances farm and community assistance projects. To date, these projects have included: reforestation initiatives, construction of water treatment facilities and water pumps, community centers, and schools.

Portland Roasting was founded in 1996 with the mission of supporting farmers who had a dedication to stewardship of the land that provided for them. From the outset, Portland Roasting focused on sustainable methods, but struggled to find third-party certifications that aligned with their goals. This eventually led PRC to create a proprietary, first party certification program – Farm Friendly Direct. By focusing on direct and tangible community improvements, as opposed to merely paying an above-market premium, Portland Roasting is able to ensure that their sourcing strategy contributes directly to the betterment of the community of their coffee growers. The fit was clear; while there were no local coffee farmers for Burgerville to support, it could support Portland Roasting, a local roasting company. Further, through this relationship, Burgerville's coffee purchases support direct tangible benefits to farmers and farming communities throughout the developing world, while providing their customers with an award winning, premium product. Jack wondered whether he could learn from the PRC experience to inform his decision about chickens.

Current sourcing issue

American chicken farmers annually raise roughly 35 billion pounds of chicken.[xvi] To generate this level of productivity, farmers have a number of options for raising their animals including conventional methods, pasture-raised methods, and organic methods. By far, the most widespread method of raising chickens for meat is the conventional method. This production method holds the birds in large climate-controlled production houses where they are fed, watered and regularly given antibiotics. These chickens are generally alive for six weeks before slaughter. This method produces the most meat at the cheapest price.

The real cost of this method of chicken production includes social and environmental costs, however. The crowded production houses create conditions highly conducive to disease. To combat this, antibiotics are systematically administered to chickens in their feed, injected into young chicks, and injected into eggs prior to hatching. While antibiotics help to alleviate the problem of disease, they result in additional problems. In 1995, the US Food and Drug Administration (FDA) approved a class of antibiotics, called fluoroquinolones, for use in poultry. Five years later, fluoroquinolones were banned in agriculture, citing evidence that human resistance to the drug had risen since their FDA approval, which could lead to further health problems in humans.[xvii] The use of antibiotics also creates problems downstream of the farm as up to 75% of antibiotics can pass through an animal undigested, enter water reservoirs, and potentially impact humans or other animals.[xviii] The perennial use of antibiotics in commercial production houses develops an environment where resistant bacteria evolve. Over time, chickens come into contact with the more resilient bacteria, which then pass through as processed poultry, and are consumed by humans. If antibiotic resistant bacteria later infect humans or livestock, the primary courses of treatment are unlikely to be effective and potentially lead to health complications.

The most prevalent alternative to production houses is pasture-raised chicken farming, a special case of free-range chicken production. Jack knows that the free-range designation is difficult to interpret as, in the United States, access to the outside is all that is needed to qualify a chicken as being free-range. In many cases, the difference between conventional production and free-range production is that a densely packed production house has an open door at one end. One reason that Burgerville supports certifications such as Food Alliance is that the certification provides more information about the conditions of the animals as they are raised.

Pasture-raised chickens are permitted to roam freely outside, similar to the way cattle are allowed to graze at pasture. This requires a lower animal density and reduces the need for antibiotics. Animals that do get sick while being pasture-raised can be treated with medications, but rarely undergo prophylactic drug therapies to ensure growth. Pasture-raised chickens need more time to grow and gain weight and normally live for eight weeks before slaughter. Since chickens are allowed to roam outside, they are, however, more vulnerable than conventionally raised hens. Production houses are protected from birds of prey, foxes, raccoons, and other predators but chickens venturing out of coops may be susceptible to predators. While farmers keep birds inside during periods of inclement weather, sudden weather changes may catch the birds outside and leave them vulnerable to drowning. Parasitic worms that live in the soil can also infect the birds, another condition uncommon in production houses.

Certified Organic farming further restricts the farm's operations by mandating that all food given to the birds be free of genetically modified feed and organically farmed. Restrictions are also placed on beak-trimming and claw modifications, which are procedures done to prevent hens from eating their own eggs and hurting other chickens. In order to sell poultry as USDA Organic, it must be certified by a USDA approved, third-party certifier.

Burgerville and chicken

Burgerville offers six menu items with fried or grilled chicken and spent over a million dollars on chicken in 2009. Jack Graves wondered if Burgerville should consider changing the source of its chicken to increase its local purchasing quotient. A large regional supplier would be able to supply Burgerville with the quantity of chicken it needs from its processing plants in Washington and Oregon, but these were conventional producers with the social, environmental, and animal treatment problems. Purchasing locally could support smaller local farmers, keeping more of the money within the local communities. The economic impact of this quantity of purchases could have a significant impact on the farms and communities where the purchases are made. An economic impact study of poultry production indicates that every $1 million of sales by a poultry or egg producer generates 20.1 FTE (full-time equivalent) jobs (Exhibit 14). A problem with many of the smaller farms, however, is they lack the ability to supply sufficient numbers of consistently sized portions. Jack recalled an attempt a few years ago to source chicken locally, and the variation in portion sizes caused considerable consumer backlash and excess waste. At this time there is no local farm using non-conventional production processes that can dependably provide the quantity of high-quality chicken that Burgerville needs.

Coleman Natural, a chicken supplier from Colorado is currently under consideration by Jack and his supply chain team. Burgerville has been testing Coleman's product with good results in a few restaurants. Coleman Natural supplies some organic and antibiotic-free chicken and may choose to earn the first Food Alliance certification for at least some of its poultry meat. The chickens themselves will be sourced from the Southern United States, however, as Coleman's processor capable of providing a dependable supply of consistently sized portions is based in Georgia. While this supplier offers some sustainably raised chickens, there is an additional environmental impact that Burgerville would incur for their products, in the form of emissions related to the necessary transportation and storage of chickens to restaurant locations. And of course, purchasing from the South is not really very local. Since Coleman may choose to obtain Food Alliance certification, Jack could see that partnering with Burgerville might provide the impetus to actually make the move to certification. It would be good to see Food Alliance expand its reach into the South, where its impact could be significant.

Jack Graves can see that, regardless of his decision, some of Burgerville's values will be served better than others, and he has a number of alternatives to choose from. Continuing to buy conventionally produced chicken is affordable, but has a long list of negative connotations and misalignments with Burgerville's values. Developing relationships to incentivize individual local farmers to produce sustainable chicken, while appealing on its face, is costly, risky, and slow. Importing chicken from the South violates the desire to buy local, increases food miles, and relies on third parties to monitor the supplier. The task at hand for Jack Graves is to put together a recommendation that best fits as many of Burgerville's core values as possible. In a few days, the supply chain team will meet to make the chicken sourcing decision, and Jack wants to have thought these issues through before the meeting.

EXHIBIT 1
Burgerville organization chart

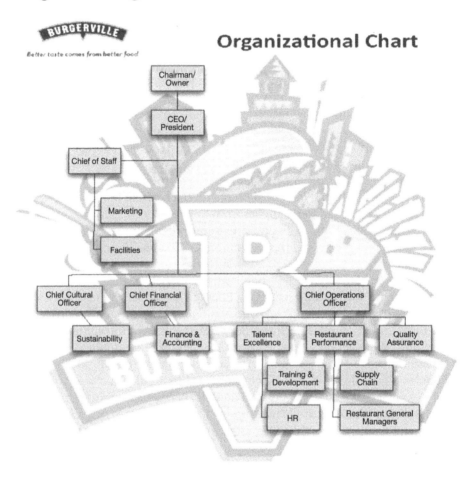

EXHIBIT 2
Food spend

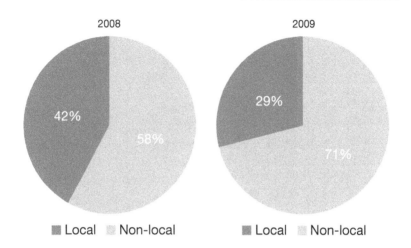

EXHIBIT 3
Burgerville timeline

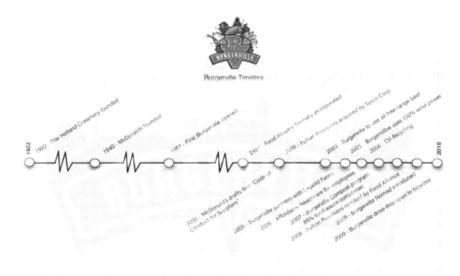

EXHIBIT 4
Map of Burgerville locations

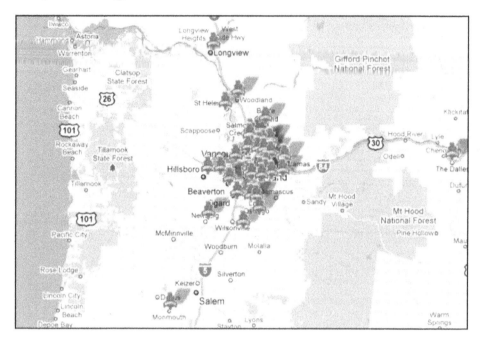

EXHIBIT 5
Burgerville Nomad

EXHIBIT 6
Burgerville menus

Regular menu

Seasonal Items

Entrees and Sandwiches:

- Pickled Pepper Cheeseburger- Toasted Ciabatta bread and topped it with a Country Natural Beef patty, Tillamook Pepper Jack cheese, pickled peppers, spinach and smoky aioli
- Roasted Portobello Focaccia Sandwich- a garlic and olive oil roasted Portobello mushroom with provolone cheese, caramelized red onions, spring greens and garlic aioli on toasted herb focaccia with sundried tomato spread
- Yukon and White Bean Basil Burger-Yukon White Bean patty made for Burgerville by Oregon-based Chez Gourmet, with Basil Aioli, lettuce and tomato on top of a nine grain bun
- Grilled Coho Salmon Sandwich- Wild-caught Alaskan Coho Salmon from fisheries that are certified sustainable by the Marine Stewardship Council, grilled to order and placed atop a bed of fresh frisée with lemon aioli on a toasted Kaiser bun
- Crispy Onion & Spinach Turkey Burger- This delicious creation pairs quality ingredients such as a Diestel turkey burger patty, fresh spinach, onions dusted with Shepherd's Grain flour and fried golden brown, and two types of pestos, all on a French bun
- Grilled Coho Salmon Sandwich – A grilled wild Coho Salmon fillet sprinkled with parsley and served atop frisée on a toasted Kaiser bun slathered in lemon aioli
- Crispy Chicken Sandwich with Pear Chutney- Golden fried chicken breast, Tillamook Swiss cheese, and Oregon D'Anjou pear chutney with lettuce, tomato and mayonnaise on a toasted Kaiser bun
- Ale Battered Albacore and Summer Slaw- Two wild Marine Stewardship Council certified Pacific Albacore Tuna fillets dipped in a Full Sail Amber Ale batter and lightly fried to a golden brown, served with a summer slaw made with dried Oregon cranberries.

Salads, Sides, and Shakes:

- Oregon D'Anjou Pear side salad
- Rosemary Shoestring Potatoes – Crispy, golden shoestring potatoes tossed in rosemary and garlic infused olive oil an dusted with rosemary seasoning
- Golden Fried Asparagus Spears – Lightly battered Yakima valley asparagus gently friend to a golden brown. Served with garlic aioli dipping sauce
- Panko-breaded Portobello wedges
- Sweet Potato fries
- Walla-walla Onion rings
- Fresh strawberry milkshakes, smoothies and lemonade
- Fresh blackberry milkshakes and smoothies
- Fresh Strawberry Shortcake and sundaes

Seasonal items

EXHIBIT 7
Food Alliance Certification

Food Alliance (FA) is a third party nonprofit that certifies farms, ranches, and food handlers according to a holistic standard that takes into consideration working conditions, treatment of animals, environmental stewardship, and social practices (see Food Alliance Standards of Excellence, below). FA also provides independent verification of marketing claims for social and environmental responsibility. By looking at the whole operations of a company, FA reassures food buyers that they are supporting fair working environments, humane animal treatment, and environmental stewardship by their food providers and that supporting their food providers' social initiatives makes a difference.

FA got its start in 1998 with a single apple orchard and has grown to certify over 320 farms and ranches in Canada, Mexico, and in 23 US states. In all, over 5.6 million acres of farmland and ranchland are certified. In addition, FA has certified 6 distribution centers and 18 food-processing facilities. While the certification is voluntary and requires the payment of a nominal fee, businesses that earn the certification see sales increases resulting from positive customer feedback, increased customer loyalty, access to new markets, access to contracts, and price premiums. This is similar to purveyors who opt for organic certifications and otherwise act to differentiate foods that are otherwise viewed as commodities by consumers' eyes.

Nonmonetary benefits are clear as well. According to their website,

> Food Alliance has also documented improved practices on participating farms and ranches leading to better conditions for thousands of workers, more humane treatment of hundreds of thousands of animals, and reduced pesticide use, healthier soils, cleaner water, and enhanced wildlife habitat on millions of acres of range and farmland.

While other certifications focus on the farming process as organic certifications do, or processes, as in ISO certifications, FA aims to certify the sustainable farming of individual crops. As individual crops will have unique needs along these lines, FA has written unique standards for many crops and animals including beef cattle, bison, dairy, pigs, poultry and eggs, apples, barley, beans, citrus, mushrooms, peaches, rhubarb, spinach, and, both, field and sweet corn.

Food Alliance Standards of Excellence
Conserve energy, reduce and recycle waste

Waste streams from food production are minimized while reuse, recycling, and composting of resources is maximized. Businesses invest in innovation and improvement to ensure efficient use and management of natural resources for energy and packaging, transport, and daily operations.

Reduce use of pesticides, and other toxic and hazardous materials

Food businesses avoid use of chemicals that have adverse impacts on the health of ecosystems. Agriculture relies on a biologically based system of Integrated Pest Management. Materials used for sanitation, pest control, waste treatment, and infrastructural maintenance are chosen to reduce overall negative consequences.

Maintain transparent and sustainable "chain of custody"

Farmers and food industry workers have secure and rewarding jobs that provide a sound livelihood. Throughout the entire supply chain, food is produced and handled in accordance with these Principle Values. Transparency is maintained independent standards, third-party audits and clear labeling.

Guarantee product integrity, no genetically engineered or artificial ingredients

Foods are not produced using synthetic preservatives, artificial colors and flavors, genetically modified organisms (GMOs), or products derived from livestock treated with sub-therapeutic antibiotics or growth-promoting hormones.

Support safe and fair working conditions

Employers respect workers' rights and well-being, make safety a priority, maintain a professional workplace, and provide opportunities for training and advancement.

Ensure healthy, humane animal treatment

Animals are treated with care and respect. Living conditions provide access to natural light, fresh air, fresh water, and a healthy diet, shelter from extremes of temperature, and adequate space and the opportunity to engage in natural behaviors and have social contact with other animals Livestock producers minimize animal fear and stress during handling, transportation and slaughter.

Continually improve practices

Food businesses are committed to continually improving management practices. Improvement goals are integrated into company culture, regularly monitored, and acknowledged when achieved. Food buyers are proactively engaged in the food system, and support companies that are transparent about their improvement goals and progress.

EXHIBIT 8
Local farmer map

Burgerville Local Farm Suppliers

Farm/Supplier	Ingredients sourced	Location
Country Natural Beef	Meat	Vale, OR
Odyssey Seafood	Seafood	Seattle, WA
Diestel Farms	Poultry and eggs	Sonora, CA
Stiebrs Farm	Eggs	Yeim, WA
Liepold Farms	Berries	Boring, OR
Lamb Weston	Produce	Quincy, WA
Sunshine Dairy	Dairy	Portland, OR
Tillamook Creamery	Cheese and dairy	Tillamook, OR
LiteHouse Foods	Condiments	Sandpoint, ID
Portland Roasting	Coffee	Portland, OR

EXHIBIT 9
Awards and accolades

Recognition for their commitments to food:

- **Menu Masters Menu Trend Setter Award**

  Recognized by the Menu Masters and the Nation's Restaurant News for their innovative menu that highlights fresh, local, and sustainably produced seasonal indulgences, showing that a chain of restaurants really can support local farmers and suppliers.

- **AOL City's Best**

  Burgerville was selected by AOL users for the "Best Burger" in Portland, Oregon for 2008 for their great taste and use of high quality, local and seasonably ingredients.

- **Foodservice Consultants Society International "Trendsetter Award"**

  Tom Mears was selected as the 2007 winner of the FCSI "Trendsetter Award" for this commitment to purchasing fresh, local and sustainably products, and a commitment to the environment through all of Burgerville's initiatives.

- **Menu innovation recognized in an article in the Nation's Restaurant News:**

  "**VEGETARIAN LOCAVORE**- The 40-unit **Burgerville** chain introduced a **Yukon & White Bean Basil Burger** that consisted of a patty made from locally sourced great northern beans, mushrooms, brown rice, onions, oats, sun-dried tomatoes, molasses, herbs and Yukon gold potatoes. It was topped with basil mayonnaise, tomatoes

Recognition for their commitments to their employees:

- **Oregon Commission for the Blind's Employer of the Year Award**

  Oregon Commission for the Blind (OCB) recognized Burgerville as Employer of the Year for being instrumental in OCB's mission of assisting visually impaired and blind individuals in achieving independence and employment. Four of our managers, specifically, participated in providing visually impaired and blind individuals with work experience which led to employment. This furthers our commitment to developing people throughout our organization.

- **Vancouver Rotary Club's 2009 "Vocational Service Award"**

  Tom Mears was recognized with the Vancouver Rotary Club's 2009 Vocational Service Award for his outstanding commitment to Burgerville since 1966, service on a number of community boards and lasting, positive influence in the vocational area.

- **ComPsych Corporation "Health at Work Award"**

  Burgerville won the Silver Award for the company's commitment to affordable healthcare.

- **YMCA "Spirit of Health Award"**

  Tom Mears received this award for Burgerville's industry-leading employee healthcare benefits and commitment to sustainable business practices. Mears was also honored for his leadership in Clark County-based Community Choices, a nonprofit promoting community health.

- **Association of Washington Business Community Service Award for "Helping People in Need."**

  Burgerville has been awarded the AWB saluted Burgerville for its continuing commitment to helping the community through numerous charitable organizations including: The Special Olympics, The United Way and the American Diabetes Association.

- **Association of Washington Business "Better Workplace Award" for Innovative Benefit/Compensation Programs**

  Burgerville received this award for its continued commitment to health care coverage for its employees.

- **American Psychological Association "Best Practices" Award**

  Burgerville received this award for its implementation of numerous programs that promote employee health and well-being including a comprehensive health care plan.

- **Association of Washington Business "Better Workplace Award" for Job Training**

  Burgerville received this award for its commitment to employee job development and training programs.

- **Association of Washington Business: Better Workplace Award**

  Honoring Burgerville's commitment to affordable employee healthcare and benefits.

- **Clark County Public Health: Corporate Leader Award**

  Honoring Burgerville's commitment to health care and benefits for employees, partnering with Kaiser for healthier food choices, use of trans fat free oils and purchasing fresh, local and sustainable foods.

Recognition for their commitments to their community and the environment:

- **Association of Washington Business Community Service Award for "Helping People in Need."**

  Burgerville has been awarded the AWB saluted Burgerville for its continuing commitment to helping the community through numerous charitable organizations including: The Special Olympics, The United Way and the American Diabetes Association.

- **Association of Oregon Recyclers, Recycler of the Year- Company/Organization**

  Burgerville was selected as a recipient of this year's award.

- **Washington State Restaurant Association: "Restaurant Neighbor Award"**

  Honoring Burgerville's commitment to the community and for its participation in events that serve the American Diabetes Association and The United Way.

- **Oregon State Restaurant Association: "Restaurant Neighbor Award"**

  Honoring Burgerville's commitment to the community and for its participation in events that serve Oregon Special Olympics, the American Diabetes Association and The United Way, among others.

- **Association of Washington Business: Community Service Award**

  Honoring Burgerville's commitment to the community for its participation in events that serve the American Diabetes Association and The United Way.

- **Washington State Recycling Association: Recycler of the Year Award**

  Honoring The Holland Inc./Burgerville for its corporate-wide purchase of wind power.

- **2006 Green Power Leadership Award: U.S. Environmental Protection Agency and U.S. Dept. Of Energy**

  Honoring The Holland Inc./Burgerville for its corporate-wide purchase of wind power.

- **"Wind Farm Opening Hasn't Put a Stop to Local Utility's Green Lights Effort", Columbian, January 1, 2010**

  Even though Oregon has established minimum standards for renewable energy, Burgerville remains committed to offsetting 100 percent of our energy use with renewable power rather than falling back on the basic energy supply. "We see it as a way of contributing to our community in a powerful way, in a leadership role," says [Burgerville's] Chief Cultural Officer Jack Graves.

- **"The Best of 2009" QSR Magazine, December 3, 2009**

  Burgerville created a bike-friendly policy for its 37 drive-thru lanes encouraging patrons to be less reliant on their cars helping to reduce overall air emissions.

EXHIBIT 10
Roasted turkey and cherry chutney wrap

EXHIBIT 11
Burgerville distributor profiles

Fulton Provision

Fulton Provisions Company is an 80-year-old Portland, Oregon based distributor which specializes which company supplies more than 1,000 customers throughout the American West with precision-cut USDA Prime and Choice beef, and high quality ground beef. Fulton was acquired by Sysco in 2000 but has remained an independently run subsidiary that focuses on specialty meat markets. In 2008, Fulton began to focus on and market sustainable business practices by acquiring Food Alliance Certification.

In order to achieve these standards Fulton undertook various sustainability initiatives such as, converting trucks to biodiesel and upgrading old machines with energy efficient models, even going as far as to change their own internal standard processing procedures that verify the integrity of all meat products beyond what the USDA requires.

Sysco

Sysco was founded in 1969 and went public the following year. Over the last 40 years it has grown to become the largest food services distributor in North America. The company services over 400,000 customers, ranging from restaurants to amusement parks, and has yearly revenue of more than 36 billion dollars. In addition to foodstuffs companies also source various non-food items from Sysco, ranging from napkins to kitchen equipment, and cleaning supplies. In addition to its core business Sysco owns a variety of subsidiary companies which focus on specialty markets, with which its main product lines can synergize.

EXHIBIT 12
Comparison of third party certifications

Third-Party Certifications

Logo	Certification	Certifier	Certifies	USDA Organic inputs*	Use of IPM*	Soil Management*	Biodiversity/Conservance*	Watershed Health*	Labor/Social Practice*	Livestock Access to Outdoors*	Prohibits use of Hormones/Antibiotics*	Use of GMOs*
CERTIFIED HUMANE	Certified Humane Raised and Handled Humane	Farm Animal Care PO Box 727, Herndon, VA 20172 703-591-0350, www.certifiedhumane.org	Producers Processors							◆	◆	
(Demeter)	Demeter Biodynamic	Demeter Inc. 25844 Butler Rd., Junction City, OR 97448 541-998-5691, www.demeter-usa.org	Producers	◆		◆	◆	◆		◆	◆	◆
EUREPGAP	EUREPGAP [2]	PrimusLabs 2810 Industrial Pkwy., Santa Maria, CA 93455 www.eurep.org, www.primuslabs.com	Producers	◆	◆	◆	◆	◆	◆			◆
(Food Alliance)	Food Alliance	Food Alliance 1829 NE Alberta St., Ste. 5, Portland, OR 97211 503-493-1066, www.foodalliance.org	Producers Processors	◆	◆	◆	◆[3]	◆	◆	◆	◆	◆
	Free Farmed	American Humane Association 63 Inverness Dr. E, Englewood, CO 80112 303-792-9900 X613, www.americanhumane.org/freefarmed	Producers							◆	◆	
LIVE	LIVE	Low Input Viticulture and Enology Inc. PO Box 102, Veneta, OR 97487 541-935-4333, www.liveinc.org	Wine Producers	◆	◆	◆	◆					
HARVEST	Protected Harvest	Protected Harvest 1211 Brunswick Ct., Arnold, MD 21012 410-757-4234, www.protectedharvest.org	Producers	◆	◆			◆				
SALMON SAFE	Salmon-Safe	Salmon-Safe 805 SE 32nd Ave., Portland, OR 97214 503-232-3750, www.salmonsafe.org	Producers Urban Land Management	◆	◆	◆	◆	◆	◆[1]			
USDA ORGANIC	USDA Organic	National Organic Program, USDA Agricultural Marketing Service 1400 Independence Ave. SW, S Bldg., Rm. 4008 Washington, DC 20250 202-720-3252, www.ams.usda.gov/nop	Producers Processors Manufacturers	◆		◆	◆[4]	◆		◆	◆	◆

* See table key below for more information about these certification criteria. [1] Salmon-Safe monitors the impact of livestock access to pasture on riparian habitat health. [2] EUREPGAP is a food safety certification and also includes standards for sanitation and post-harvest practices. [3] Food Alliance certification verifies that farms also meet criteria for the Federal Conservation Security Program. [4] The National Organic Program approved inclusion of biodiversity criteria in March 2005.

*Auditing Organizations Table Key

USDA Organic Inputs: Organic certifiers must hold producers to the standards established in the USDA National Organic Program materials list. Other certifications may or may not require compliance.

IPM: Some auditors monitor the integrated pest management (IPM) plans kept by farms to ensure minimal use of non-organic pesticides and fertilizers. IPM focuses on use of cover crops, soil amendments and more, but, unlike USDA Organic standards, does not altogether prohibit the use of synthetic pesticides and fertilizers.

Soil Management: Some auditors require growers to have plans or practices in place to improve soil quality, reduce erosion, or otherwise monitor soil health.

Biodiversity/Conservation: Some auditors require growers to take into account local biodiversity or conservation issues in their field planning or land and resource use.

Watershed Quality: Some auditors require growers to ensure their operation improves or does not disturb local watershed health through management of runoff, which may include soil, fertilizer nutrients, or pesticides, which can damage fish habitat and water quality.

Labor/Social Practices: Some auditors require participants to guarantee work conditions, living wages, fair prices, or other "social responsibility" practices that exceed minimum legal requirements.

Livestock Access to Outdoors: Some auditors seek to ensure humane treatment of animals by providing access to the outdoors either for pasture grazing or exercise.

Prohibits Use of Hormones/Antibiotics: Some auditors prohibit the use of growth hormones and preventative antibiotics in livestock production. Some auditors prohibit meat from individual animals treated with therapeutic antibiotics to use the certification label as well.

GMOs: Organic certification prohibits the use of Genetically Modified Organisms (GMOs), yet other auditors may choose not to regulate their use.

EXHIBIT 13
Farmer–distributor–Burgerville network (Sysco model)

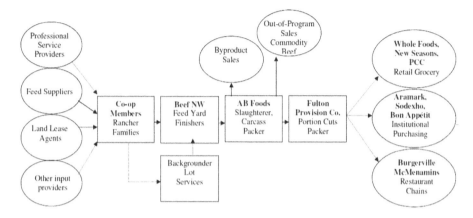

Value Chain	Cow/calf	Background lot	Feedlot	Packer	Retailer
Unit	Ranch	Ranch	Beef NW	AB Foods & Fulton Foods (burger)	Retail Distributor:
CNB	Graze-well Principles & quality guidelines	Rules for In & Out of Program Cattle	Negotiates with Feedlot for financing.	Marketing negotiates with Processor based on CNB cost models. Finance receives final product data and compensation for beef.	Marketing negotiates contract with retail distributors, monitors transparency of credibility attributes
Rancher	Cow/calf timing, ranch management	Negotiates for feed cost and provides CNB criteria	Responsible for feedlot costs	Receives revenues from beef (commodity & placement)	Product demonstrations, interaction with customers
Verification	Food Alliance Cert	Food Alliance Certification	Feed Lot Audit	Food Alliance Cert.	

EXHIBIT 14
Economic Impacts

Input–Output analysis (IO or Inter-Industry analysis) is an economic concept that aims to estimate the economic impact of a known change for any number of downstream factors. The analysis predicts the local changes resulting from purchasing goods from suppliers within a certain geographic area; the model predicts economic impacts upon other industries, both direct impacts and indirect impacts.

The information shown below reflects the impact of $1M of chicken purchases. For more information regarding Input–Output analysis, consult eiolca.net.

Industry	Total additional employment
Poultry and egg producers	14.6
Truck transportation	1.9
Retail trade	1.08
Utilities and government	0.502
Wholesalers	0.352
Veterinary services	0.256
Grain farming	0.131
Agricultural support	0.12
Real estate	0.096
All other	1.063
Total Employment Gain	20.1

Industry	Total economic benefit (million USD)
Poultry and egg production	1.0829
Other animal food manufacturing	0.3855
Wholesale trade	0.0863
Truck transportation	0.0442
Pharmaceutical and medicine manufacturing	0.0312
Rail transportation	0.0226
Power generation and supply	0.0217
Real estate	0.0214
Management of companies and enterprises	0.0168
All other	0.3375

The total economic benefit measures total effect of a $1M increase in sales of chicken.

Adapted from: Carnegie Mellon University Green Design Institute. (2010) Economic Input-Output Life Cycle Assessment (EIO-LCA) US 2002 (428) model. Available from: www.eiolca.net (accessed 25 October, 2010).

Notes

i   Schlosser, E. *Fast Food Nation: The Dark Side of the American Meal.* 2001. Houghton Mifflin Company. Boston.

ii   Hamstra, M. Burger King attacks McD with french-fry launch. *Nation's Restaurant News,* Dec. 22, 1997 accessed online September 1, 2010. Available: www.findarticles.com/p/articles/mi_m3190/is_n51_v31/ai_20105790.

iii   Nieves, E. (March 9, 2005). Accord with Tomato Pickers Ends Boycott of Taco Bell. *Washington Post.* Retrieved from www.washingtonpost.com/wp-dyn/articles/A18187-2005Mar8.html.

iv   www.aboutmcdonalds.com/etc/medialib/csr/docs.Par.96140.File.dat/code_of_conduct_for_suppliers.pdf

v   Martin, A. *Burger King Shifts Policy on Animals.* Available online: www.nytimes.com/2007/03/28/business/28burger.html?ex=1332734400&en=7104231631119310&ei=5124&partner=digg&exprod=digg. Accessed Sept. 7, 2010.

vi   Kulkarni, S. (2009). McDonalds ongoing marketing challenge: social perception in India. *Online Journal of International Case Analysis, 1*(2). Available online: www.ojica.fiu.edu/index.php/ojica_journal/article/viewFile/19/18.

vii   Black, J. (October 2009). Number of Farmers Markets Mushrooms. *The Washington Post.* www.voices.washingtonpost.com/all-we-can-eat/food-politics/number-of-farmers-markets-mush.html?wprss=all-we-can-eat. Accessed September 7, 2010.

viii   Weber, C. L. and Matthews, H. S. (March 2008). *Food-Miles and the Relative Climate Impacts of Food Choices in the United States.* Environmental Science & Technology. Vol. 42, No. 10.

ix   Hill, H. (2008). *Food Miles: Background and Marketing.* ATTRA – National Sustainable Agriculture Information Service. www.attra.ncat.org. Accessed June 14, 2010.

x   United States Department of Agriculture. (2010). *National Organic Program: Accreditation and Certification.* www.ams.usda.gov/AMSv1.0/ams.fetchTemplateData.do?template=TemplateN&navID=NationalOrganicProgram&leftNav=NationalOrganicProgram&page=NOPAccreditationandCertification&description=Accreditation%20and%20Certification&acct=nopgeninfo. Accessed June 14, 2010.

xi   Country Natural Beef: A Maturing Co-op at the Crossroad (CASE STUDY).

xii   Country Natural Beef: A Maturing Co-op at the Crossroad (CASE STUDY).

xiii   Jetti, R.R., E. Yang, A. Kurnianta, C. Finn, and M.C. Qian. Quantification of selected aroma-active compounds in strawberries by headspace solid-phase microextraction gas chromatography and correlation with sensory descriptive analysis. *Journal of Food Science* 72.7 (2007): 487–495.

xiv   Associated Press. (2008, June 7). Oregon strawberry industry tries new spin to spur growth. OregonLive.com. *Oregon Local News, Breaking News, Sports & Weather – OregonLive.com.* Available online: www.oregonlive.com/business/index.ssf/2008/06/oregon_strawberry_industry_tri.html. Accessed June 16, 2010.

xv   Howard, P. (2005). What do people want to know about their food? Measuring Central Coast consumers' interest in food systems issues. UC Santa Cruz: Center for Agroecology and Sustainable Food Systems. Retrieved from: www.escholarship.org/uc/item/75s222dm.

xvi   Poultry and eggs. USDA. Accessed online: www.ers.usda.gov/Briefing/Poultry/Background.htm. Accessed September 27, 2010.

xvii *Antibiotic Resistance: Playing Chicken With Essential Drugs*. USDA. Available online: www.edf.org/documents/619_abr_general_factsheet_rev2.pdf.

xviii *Resistance: Playing Chicken With Essential Drugs*. USDA. Available online: www.edf.org/documents/619_abr_general_factsheet_rev2.pdf.

Portland Roasting Company
Farm Friendly Direct

Madeleine Pullman, Greg Stokes, Gregory Price,
Mark Langston and Brandon Arends

> Coffee is now about not only finding great coffee but showcasing who
> you're buying from. It's about sustainability. What's driving the industry
> is people think of coffee as a commodity that's picked by hand. There's
> a lot of work involved in it. There are people behind this coffee bean and
> that's the cutting edge stuff right now.
>
> *Mark Stell, Managing Partner, Portland Roasting Company*

As Mark Stell waited to board the plane to Bujumbura, the capital city of Burundi in Africa, he contemplated an exciting market opportunity for his coffee roasting company. Within a few short weeks, Portland Roasting Company (PRC) was pitching to Fred Meyer, a major regional grocery retailer, and landing this account could help grow revenues by as much as 25%. Last year, Stell had made significant investments in new roasting and packaging equipment and he knew he had the capacity and infrastructure to supply a large account. PRC would also promote the virtues of the Farm Friendly Direct (FFD) program. From the beginning, PRC had developed trade relationships with individual coffee growers, paid premium prices, and invested additional funds in local projects that directly benefited the lives of coffee farmers and their communities. In 2005, PRC was awarded the prestigious Sustainability Award by the Specialty Coffee Association of America (SCAA). The FFD program is featured on the company website, in marketing materials and on product packaging (Exhibit 1). PRC would have to convince the client that 'Farm Friendly Direct' coffee was superior to conventional third-party certifications such as Fair

Trade, Organic and Rainforest Alliance™ certified coffees offered by competitors. Stell also realized that the FFD program alone would not be sufficient to secure the account. Grocery retailers were also concerned about price, order fulfillment, marketing support, product quality and customer service, in addition to the sustainability attributes of a product. As the last boarding call rang out over the loudspeaker, Stell picked up his laptop bag and headed for the departure gate.

Despite his optimism about the short-term prospects for his business, Stell couldn't help reflecting on the long-term outlook for the coffee industry and the challenges facing coffee growers around the world. The annual conference of the SCAA held in Atlanta two months earlier was very well attended, indicating the vibrancy of the specialty coffee industry despite the recent economic downturn. Although the atmosphere at the conference was upbeat, the research findings on climate change presented during the conference were alarming. With global temperatures continuing to rise, the area of land around the equator capable of growing coffee was shrinking. It was predicted that Ethiopia, the birthplace of coffee, would not be capable of producing coffee by the year 2050. Development of new coffee growing regions such as Burundi and Congo might offset the diminishing supply of land but for how long? Was third-party certification going to drive necessary changes in the industry, or would a direct trade model like FFD ensure a sustainable supply of specialty coffee over the long term? Stell pondered these questions during the long flight.

Company profile

PRC was headquartered in the bustling central eastside industrial district of Portland, Oregon. The 20,000-square-foot facility contained roasting equipment, warehouse space, a coffee-tasting facility and offices for 27 employees. PRC's core business was sourcing, roasting and distributing high-quality coffees to wholesale customers including retail coffee shops, restaurants, businesses, food merchants and institutions. Consumers could purchase PRC coffees directly through the company website. The company sold coffee equipment and associated supplies, including a line of flavored syrups. Coffees were sourced from more than 20 different countries (Exhibit 2) and Farm Friendly Direct relationships existed with farmers and cooperatives in Guatemala, Costa Rica, El Salvador, Ethiopia, India, Papua New Guinea, Sumatra and Tanzania (Exhibit 3). Working with Stell on the management team were Paul Gilles (VP of Operations) and Marie Franklin (National Sales Manager). Gilles' duties were to oversee production, customer service, human resources, risk management, international business development and general administration (Exhibit 4). Franklin led a team of sales, marketing and communications professionals. All PRC employees were encouraged to write blogs about coffee on the company website and most had already visited coffee farms that supplied the company's coffee beans in order to better understand the supply chain and farmer relationships.

Stell had participated in the United Nations Conference on Sustainable Development in 1992 in Rio de Janeiro, and as a member of a student delegation, helped to publish the 'Youth Action Guide on Sustainable Development.' His experience in Brazil exposed Stell to the export side of the industry and inspired him to learn more about the coffee business. After a brief apprenticeship with a local roaster in Portland, Stell opened a retail coffee shop called Abruzzi Coffee Roasters in 1993. Three years later he sold the business and opened PRC with business partner Todd Plummer, choosing to focus exclusively on the wholesale coffee business. Stell described his original vision for the company, 'What we saw was a niche for small quality coffee roasters that had creative marketing, creative design and upscale packaging. We wanted to be synonymous with Portland and we wanted to buy sustainable products, and my involvement with the Earth Summit in '92 was kind of the driving factor to help us steer our direction. We wanted to be as sustainable as possible and that has always been our motivation.'

In the first year of operation PRC sold 40,000 pounds of coffee. Since then PRC achieved an average of 20% annual growth and in 2007 the company sold 600,000 pounds of coffee, yielding approximately $5 million in revenues (Exhibit 5). In 2006, 2007 and 2008, PRC was a finalist for Roast Magazine's Roaster of The Year awards, and since 2005, PRC has made the Portland Business Journal's list of 100 fastest growing local businesses. After learning the pitfalls of having one customer represent 40% of total sales, PRC subsequently diversified across market segments with the largest customer representing no more than 20% of total sales. In anticipation of continued growth through targeting hotels, mass grocers, universities and other institutional accounts, PRC invested in new roasting and packaging equipment in 2008.

Coffee production and trade

Coffee is produced in more than 50 tropical countries generally around 23.5 degrees north or south of the equator, with approximately 63% produced in Latin America, 22% in SE Asia and 14% in Africa.[i] Similar to wine, coffee beans from different regions have distinct characteristics displayed in aroma, body, acidity and nuances of flavor. These variations are dependent not only on the appellation, or geographical location, but also the varietal grown and the manner in which the coffee is produced. The first flowers appear on coffee plants during the third year, but production is only profitable after the fifth year. Coffee cherries typically ripen around 8–10 months after flowering and in most countries there is only one major harvest each year. Shade-grown coffee often results in berries ripening more slowly, producing lower yields but with a higher quality and flavor. Ripened coffee cherries are typically harvested by hand, which is very labor intensive. Some coffee crops are picked all at once, but for better quality coffees only the ripe cherries are picked and for this reason harvesting may be undertaken as many as five times during a season. The ripe berries have higher aromatic oils and lower organic acid content, lending to a more fragrant and smooth flavor. Because of this, the timing of coffee picking is one of the chief determinants of the end product.

After coffee is picked, it must be processed quickly to avoid spoilage. Each coffee cherry usually contains two coffee beans, covered by a silvery skin, a layer of parchment, a pectin layer, a pulp layer and finally the outer skin (Exhibit 6). These outer layers must be removed in one of two processing methods. The dry processing method is used in arid countries where water is scarce and humidity is low. Freshly picked cherries are simply spread out on large surfaces to dry in the sun. In order to prevent the cherries from spoiling, they are raked and turned throughout the day then covered at night. When the moisture content of the cherries drops to 11%, the dried cherries are moved to warehouses where they are stored. In wet processing, the freshly harvested cherries are passed through a pulping machine where the skin and pulp is separated from the bean. The beans are then transported to large, water-filled fermentation tanks for 12–48 hours where naturally occurring enzymes dissolve the pectin layer. The beans are then removed from the tank and dried. Eduardo Ambrocio works for Anacafé, the Guatemalan National Coffee Association, as a master cupper and quality control expert. Anacafé works with Guatemalan farmers to help them establish sustainable farming practices, increase the quality of the coffee and promote Guatemala as a leader in producing the highest quality coffee. Ambrocio explained

> The riskiest process in the industry is the wet milling process, because everything depends on time. You need to control the volume of both the water and the cherries. You need to manage the fermentation process while the cherries are in the tank, and you need to carefully control the drying process. Everything is a chain of different times and events that need to be precisely controlled.

With so many variables involved in the wet milling processes, there is ample opportunity for error, but wet processing can really bring out the brightness and floral acidity of coffees from places like Columbia, Guatemala and Costa Rica.

In order to compete against the larger estates, many small growers[ii] have formed cooperatives to help negotiate better prices and increase access to markets. Most growers dry the coffee themselves and then sell the unprocessed coffee to intermediaries for milling. This involves a mechanical hulling process that removes the parchment layer from wet processed coffee or removes the entire dried husk from dry processed coffee cherries. The coffee beans are then graded and sorted by size and weight. The intermediaries often make a larger profit since small growers may not have direct access to buyers, and are thus forced to accept whatever price the intermediary offers. From the intermediary, the coffee is then sold to exporters or brokers who buy and sell coffee on commission, before passing it onto importers.

Importers then sell the beans to roasters who roast, package and market the coffee to distributors and retailers. Roasting is generally performed in the importing country because coffee freshness diminishes rapidly after roasting. This way the roasted beans reach the consumer as quickly as possible to ensure quality.

Large coffee importers and roasters purchase coffee futures and options traded on the Intercontinental Exchange (ICE). The ICE Futures US Coffee 'C' contract is the benchmark for world coffee prices. The price of coffee has fluctuated dramatically, falling as low as US$0.415/pound in 2001 and having reached as high as $3.148/pound in 1997 (Exhibit 7). These price fluctuations are due to market influences such as natural disasters, supply surplus, transportation costs, political stability in producing countries and investor speculation. For example, a frost in Brazil in 1975 and a drought in 1985 led to a sharp drop in coffee production and significant increases in coffee prices. This price volatility is problematic for both farmers and commercial roasters, directly impacting profit margins and production costs. Just one year of low market prices can potentially put a small farmer out of business. Coffee revenue is also a significant portion of the GDP for many equatorial countries. Burundi, Uganda and Ethiopia earn more than half of their export revenues from coffee alone. The economic disparity between producing and consuming countries, and the determination of a fair price, has long been the subject of active debate within the coffee industry.

The farmers' perspective

Many of the countries with an appropriate climate for producing coffee are in the developing world. This creates a unique set of challenges and opportunities for the coffee industry. Many of the tools, techniques, resources and technologies that farmers in the developed world use are either not affordable or not available to the vast majority of coffee farmers in developing countries. Unfortunately, there is an inverse relationship between the quality of a coffee bean and the volume of coffee that the plant can produce. Plants that produce high-quality coffee generally do not produce high quantities of coffee beans. Generally, the higher the quality of the coffee the more expensive it is to produce. In addition to processing, handling and delivery, specialty coffee requires more resources, time and attention in order to achieve the highest level of quality. The beans mature at different times on the plant and must be hand picked only when they are ripe. Ambrocio noted, 'Coffee is a lot like grapes and many other fruits. We have varieties that probably give you a good yield at times of production, but low quality. As a farmer, you are going to focus on either high quantity or high quality.' Don Jorge, owner of Rancho Carmela, which is located in a region of Guatemala where PRC purchases coffee, has been producing high-quality coffee for decades. Don Jorge said that he spends anywhere from US$0.70–0.85/lb to harvest his specialty coffee depending on the climate, labor rate and other extenuating circumstances. Jorge states that in selling to exporters, 'In a good year I can get almost a dollar per pound for my best beans, but sometimes I have to settle for 80 cents.' Dona Miguelina, owner of El Paternal, one of the oldest coffee farms in Nicaragua, and supplier of specialty coffee for PRC, confessed, 'This has been a very dry year. If we don't get some rain soon we will not have a very good harvest this year. There is a lot that I can do to ensure a quality harvest, but if it doesn't rain, what can I do?' Dona has implemented a number of different water-saving measures, but most coffee farms must rely on rainwater for irrigation, and without it, their yields and their profits suffer.

Unfortunately for many farmers the harvest season is long, averaging two to four months. It then takes time to process the beans, and get the finished product ready to ship. From the first cherry picked to the time the bean arrives at its final destination can take up to six months. For most farmers, this is a long time to wait for payment, particularly when all of their costs for goods sold are incurred up front. This can create a heavy financial burden on coffee farms of all sizes, especially the smaller farms and premium producers who typically have higher costs of production. Historically, this is where the exporters have added value in the supply chain. Exporters will often finance the crop once it is ready to ship, or sometimes before the crop is harvested depending on the needs of the farmer. Arnoldo Leiva, General Manager of The Coffee Source, Inc., and a coffee broker for PRC, said that the role of the exporter has been changing over the last decade. Leiva, who operates out of San Jose, Costa Rica, but works with coffee farmers and purchases coffee from all over the world, stated, 'One of the services we provide for both the producers and the roasters is financing, because we pay the farmer up front and the roaster gets credit upon arrival. In essence, it is a 90-day loan, or port-to-port plus net 30 from arrival.' Such arrangements allow farmers to pay for the labor and processing before the crop has been harvested and for the roasters to purchase coffee beans as they need them versus trying to buy all they need for the season. This helps roasters maintain more stable cash flow, and in some cases eliminates the need for expensive storage and warehousing. Leiva continues by saying, 'We provide a hedging for both the farmer and the roaster. That way, both can fix their price at any given time, but not necessarily at the same time.'

According to Dona Miguelina, the most significant change in the industry for coffee farmers since the time of her grandfather has been the increase in market information. Just over a generation ago, many farmers had no knowledge of the value of coffee in foreign markets, but now it is as easy as looking up current prices on the Internet. Ambrocio stated that access to information is really benefiting the farmer and, 'They now know more about markets, prices, promotion, and perhaps most importantly, the value of consistent quality. Everything is based upon quality and that is the first thing that people need to be convinced of.' Access to information has also led to a growing trend in direct relationships between farmers and roasters. By reducing the number of middlemen, both roaster and grower enjoy higher profits and roasters like PRC can add value to consumers by marketing the additional value they create for farmers. According to Leiva,

The long-term relationships that farmers are developing with buyers, like the one we have with PRC, act as a safety net for them and allows them to forecast their cash flow for more than one year. They know the markets are going to come back since the roasters tend to be more loyal and less price sensitive, since they're more focused on quality.

Jorge and Miguelina agree that mutually beneficial long-term relationships with buyers, especially buyers willing to pay a premium price, is one of the most valuable assets for a coffee farmer.

In addition to fluctuating coffee prices, farmers contend with many other challenges. The rising value of land for real estate development in many Central American countries, as well as competing crops, has pushed thousands of acres out of coffee production. In addition, the average age of coffee farmers is rising and the younger generation is often not interested in following in the footsteps of their predecessors. In Leiva's home country of Costa Rica this problem is growing, 'Coffee has been great for the family and allowed farmers to send their kids to school and even university. But now that they have degrees, they want to go and work for Intel, not in the fields.' Meanwhile, labor rates are also growing at an alarming rate, driving coffee production costs even higher. In Central America, the expansion of the Panama Canal is expected to drive up labor costs throughout the entire continent. It is hard to imagine that this one seemingly unrelated event will likely increase the cost of a cup a coffee for consumers all around the world.

History of the US coffee industry

Ethiopia, where the prized *Arabica* cultivar was first discovered, is considered the birthplace of coffee. One popular legend tells the tale of a shepherd who was bewildered at the sight of his disobedient goats frolicking in an excited state after nibbling on strange bushes high on the hillside. In the days that followed, the goats returned to the same location to repeat the ritual. Locals began experimenting with different methods of brewing tea from the leaves and berries of this mysterious plant and were the first to experience its stimulating and mood enhancing effects. By the 6th century, coffee was being cultivated across the Red Sea on plantations in Yemen then shipped from the famous port city of Mocha. By the 15th century, coffee had spread to the Muslim world via pilgrims traveling to Persia, Egypt, Turkey and across Northern Africa. Traders travelling between Venice and North Africa introduced coffee into Europe. Consumption of coffee in Europe and North America exploded in the late 17th and early 18th centuries, creating unprecedented demand. To meet this demand, cultivation expanded to India, Sri Lanka and the islands of Timor, Sumatra, Java, Celebes and the Dutch East Indies. In 1723, a French naval officer transported a single coffee plant from Paris to the island of Martinique. Plants propagated from this single stock were subsequently transported and cultivated throughout Central America, South America and the Caribbean.

America's demand for coffee grew following the war of 1812, when Britain cut off access to tea imports. By the turn of the 19th century, a small number of entrepreneurial coffee roasting companies achieved multi-state distribution facilitated by innovations in production technology, transportation and mass media. In 1864, the early pioneer John Arbuckle installed the newly patented Jabez Burns roasting machine in his Pittsburgh plant and later added automated packaging equipment. Arbuckle began selling one-pound packages of coffee in thin paper bags, under the brand name *Ariosa*. Sales and distribution on the East Coast soared and in 1913 the Arbuckle family launched the Yuban brand. Other brands gained regional and national prominence during this period including Folgers, Hills Brothers, MJB, Chase & Sanborn and Maxwell House. In 1908, President Theodore Roosevelt famously pronounced Maxwell House as 'good to the last drop.' The larger of these companies were able to distribute nationally, maintaining freshness by shipping their coffee in vacuum-sealed cans. Consumers steadily moved away from purchasing coffee in bulk to buying branded coffee in small packages.

By the 1950s the major companies in the US coffee industry competed aggressively for market share in large US cities and invested heavily in national radio and television advertising. American consumers favored convenience over quality, driving growth in the instant coffee market. Vending machines were installed in office buildings around the country, further driving demand for instant coffee. To defend against increasing competition, growing popularity of instant coffee and rising production costs, roasters began lowering prices and substituting lower quality *Robusta* beans in their coffee blends. Meanwhile, a younger generation of consumers was choosing soft drinks over coffee. These industry forces were the catalyst for significant industry consolidation during the 1960s. The downward spiral of price-cutting and erosion of quality continued for decades and by the late 1970s, the stage was set for a new generation of coffee entrepreneurs.[iii]

The US specialty coffee movement

Alfred Peet, an emigrant from The Netherlands, recognized the lack of quality coffee in the US and opened his first coffee house in Berkley in 1966. Peet's success inspired three college friends, Jerry Baldwin, Gordon Bowker and Zev Siegl, to open a coffee shop in Seattle's Pike Place Market in 1971 to sell whole beans and supplies. They named the store Starbucks. Many more entrepreneurs began to recognize the market opportunity for roasting and selling wholesale specialty coffees to gourmet grocers and serving premium beans and fresh brewed coffee in retail coffee houses. During the 1970s a small yet steadily increasing number of specialty coffee merchants opened businesses in cities along the East and West coasts and began making inroads into supermarket channels. The fledgling SCAA was formed in 1982 by 42 original charter members, at a time when specialty coffee accounted for less than 1% of total US coffee sales.

During a business trip to Milan, Starbucks Director of Marketing, Howard Schulz, observed the popularity of espresso bars and visualized bringing the Italian café experience to America using premium coffee. In 1984, Schulz convinced Starbucks' owners to add an espresso bar inside an existing store and the venture became an instant hit. Schulz left Starbucks the following year to open his own coffee shop, Il Giornale. With the backing of local investors, Il Giornale acquired Starbucks in 1987 and as CEO, Schulz immediately embarked on an aggressive growth strategy driven by new store openings in major US cities. Starbucks went public in 1992 and the initial public offering (IPO) provided capital for rapid expansion both domestically and internationally (Exhibit 8). Other large regional specialty coffee brands including Gloria Jean's, Brothers Gourmet Coffee, The Coffee Connection, Seattle's Best, Caribou Coffee and Coffee People also experienced rapid growth during this time.

Following more than a decade of growth and consolidation among large retail coffee brands, the specialty coffee industry remained fragmented. The number of businesses providing products and services in the specialty coffee industry doubled to more than 26,000 from 2001 to 2009. By then, the SCAA boasted 1,918 member businesses consisting of retailers, roasters, producers, exporters and importers, as well as manufacturers of coffee processing equipment involving more than 40 countries. Amongst members, the SCAA identified at least 369 independent roasters in 2009. The percentage of adults drinking specialty coffee had grown from 3.3% to more than 17% in the past 10 years (Exhibit 9).

New developments in the US coffee industry

The US had grown into the single largest consumer of coffee, buying close to 25% of total global output. Overall, US coffee sales had grown at an average rate of 23% every year since 2003 (adjusted for inflation) with retail coffee sales exceeding $6.5 billion in 2008.[iv] According to the National Coffee Association, 49% of Americans 18-years old or older drank some type of coffee beverage, and roughly three of every four cups of coffee consumed was made at home.[v] Combined, Kraft Foods and Proctor & Gamble commanded greater than 50% share of all roasted coffee sold in the US and marketed numerous coffee brands covering a wide spectrum of price points within various segments. Yet these large companies were still losing share to smaller roasters. Starbucks had grown into the largest specialty coffee company, followed by Peet's Coffee and Caribou Coffee, but was increasingly competing against national fast food retailers interested in gaining market share. Both McDonalds and Dunkin' Donuts began selling their own brands of coffee and espresso drinks (Exhibit 10).

Despite the growth in net sales, consumers were buying less coffee by volume and paying more per pound. In September 2007, the number of Starbucks customers fell in American stores for the first time in the history of the company, and in 2008 the company announced the closure of 600 stores. Consumers were increasingly paying premium prices with expectations of high quality, and given the economic downturn, it was anticipated that more consumers were brewing specialty coffee at home. Meanwhile, foreign markets with consumers who had historically preferred to drink tea, such as in England and much of Asia, represented the largest growing market segment for many US coffee companies.

In conjunction with the industry trend toward higher quality, coffee roasters and retailers were also promoting their coffees on the basis of sustainability. Walmart launched six coffees under the Sam's Choice™ brand as part of an expansion of eco-friendly and ethical products. Whole Foods sold its 365™ brand of coffee, noting fair trade practices and direct relationships with more than 40 growers. Kraft General Foods advertised that 30% of all the coffee beans that went into Yuban coffee were officially certified by the Rainforest Alliance™. Starbucks promoted its Shared Planet™ program with stated goals for ethical sourcing, environmental stewardship and community involvement. Green Mountain Coffee Roasters, long recognized as an industry leader in environmentally friendly and socially responsible business practices, was ranked 11th on the Forbes 100 Fastest Growing Companies list in 2009. In Stell's opinion, 'Most of the growth in the SCAA is around sustainability, so whether it's Fair Trade, Organic, Utz Certified or Rainforest Alliance™, sustainability is what's really moving our industry.'

Certified coffee

There has been significant growth in the number of sustainability related certification and eco-labeling initiatives in response to globalization. An increasing number of corporations operate globally yet environmental, labor and human rights regulations in developing countries often lag behind developed country standards. Scrutiny has perhaps been most intense within the food sector, given concerns over health and safety. Within the coffee industry, the concept of sustainability was initially focused on concerns around the environmental and social impacts of large-scale coffee production. The International Coffee Agreement of 1962 established a quota system that withheld coffee supplies in excess of market demand and also established quality standards in an effort to maintain stable prices and production. However, the initial ICA did nothing to address environmental or social concerns related to coffee production. There have been various renewals of the ICA, with the latest agreements of 2001 and 2007 focused on stabilizing the coffee economy through the promotion of coffee consumption, raising the standard of living for growers by providing economic counseling, expanding research and conducting studies on sustainability.

To address some of the shortcomings of the ICA, a number of worldwide coffee certification initiatives have been established to address what are commonly referred to as the three pillars of sustainability, covering economic, social and environmental development (Exhibit 11). According to Ambrocio, 'Quality and sustainability come first, for the farmer and the consumers. Once that is achieved, farmers can differentiate themselves in a number of different ways to reach a better market, and one way they can compete is using certifications.' Although each certification has unique criteria, they rely on verification by independent third parties to maintain transparency. One of the challenges now facing coffee certifications is balancing the need to maintain reliability and credibility while also keeping certification costs to a minimum so that growers are able to reap economic benefits from the premium or stable prices paid for their coffees. By 2006, certified coffees amounted to more than 220,000 metric tonnes of coffee exports, or close to 4% of the worldwide green coffee market.

Fair Trade

The concept of Fair Trade emerged more than 40 years ago through alternative trade organizations that offered products purchased directly from small producers in developing countries to consumers in developed countries. The first Fair Trade certification initiative began in 1988, triggered by a sharp drop in world coffee prices when the ICA failed to renegotiate price quotas. It was branded 'Max Havelaar,' after a fictional Dutch character who opposed the exploitation of coffee pickers in Dutch colonies. In 1997, the Fair Trade Labeling Organizations International (FLO) united Max Havelaar with its counterparts in other countries and became the international umbrella organization for Fair Trade, representing 17 Fair Trade labeling organizations. Fair Trade's mission is focused on economic and environmental sustainability for farmers and their communities, while guaranteeing a minimum purchase price and social premium to cover costs of production and investments in the community. The base price paid for Fair Trade coffees was US$1.26 in 2009, with an additional $0.15 added for organic coffees. The Fair Trade standards ensure that employees who work for Fair Trade farms are able to work with freedom of association, safe working conditions and fair wages; importers purchase from Fair Trade producer groups as directly as possible, eliminating the middle man and helping farmers to compete in the global market; Fair Trade farmers and farm workers decide how to invest Fair Trade revenues; and farmers and workers invest Fair Trade premiums in social and business development projects such as scholarship programs and healthcare services. However, Stell, as well as others in the sustainable coffee movement, was concerned that a sufficient percentage of the price premiums were not making it past the coops to the farmers. In addition, only cooperatives of small farmers can participate in Fair Trade, excluding both large and small individual farmers who cannot get the certification on their own. In 2008, close to 66,000 metric tonnes of Fair Trade coffee was sold.

Organic

The organic movement began in 1973 as a farming and certification system, solely focused on environmental issues. The International Federation of Organic Agricultural Movements sets international organic standards while the US Department of Agriculture oversees the USDA National Organic Program that also sets guidelines for coffee roasters, who must be certified in order to market organic coffees. Organic certification is focused on regulating agricultural production practices with the aim of eliminating the use of synthetic chemicals that are common in pesticides, herbicides and fungicides. In order for coffee to be certified and labeled as organic in the US, it must be grown on land without synthetic pesticides or other prohibited substances for three years, have a sufficient buffer between the organic coffee and the closest traditional crop, and include a sustainable crop rotation plan to prevent erosion and the depletion of soil nutrients. The initial amount of capital needed to grow an organic coffee crop is less than traditional coffee production since it does not require the purchase of synthetic fertilizers and pesticides, but it typically yields a smaller crop and thus the farms tend to make less money relative to the size of their farm. While there is no set premium for organic coffees, the average price is roughly 20% above non-organic coffees and is closely tied to the quality of the coffee. Many small, family-owned coffee farms are organic by necessity since they can't afford chemical pesticides and fertilizers. However, these small farms also cannot afford to pay for inspections to achieve the certification, and therefore are unable to benefit by selling their beans for higher prices. One common criticism of organic certification is that it focuses solely on environmental criteria while ignoring the social and economic aspects necessary for sustainable business. As Isabela Pascoal, marketing manager with Daterra Coffee explained, 'It is important to have organic coffee, but that doesn't mean that you can be sustainable.' Other certifications focus on sustainability by establishing criteria related to social and economic as well as environmental factors. In 2006, approximately 67,000 metric tonnes of organic coffee was sold throughout the world.

Rainforest Alliance™

The Rainforest Alliance™ is a non-profit, tax-exempt organization whose mission is to conserve biodiversity through the promotion of sustainability in agriculture, forestry, tourism and other businesses. In order to be certified, coffee farms must maintain or restore enough natural forest cover to achieve 40% shade coverage and there must be a minimum of 70 trees per hectare and at least 12 native species. The Rainforest Alliance™ social criteria focus on fair pay, health and safety benefits, and schooling for local communities. If farms do not meet these standards, they can still be certified if they have a plan to meet the goals and are taking active steps to implement the plan. The certification program is managed by the Sustainable Agriculture Network (SAN), a coalition of leading conservation groups in Belize, Brazil, Colombia, Costa Rica, Ecuador, El Salvador, Guatemala, Honduras, Mexico and the US. The first coffee farms were certified through the Rainforest Alliance™ program in Guatemala in 1995. A common criticism of the Rainforest Alliance™ certification is that as little as 30% of the coffee in a container can be grown under Rainforest Alliance™ criteria and the coffee can still carry the certification seal.

According to Leiva, Rainforest Alliance™ has been growing in popularity with many of the farmers that he has been working with, but it does come with a cost.

> Rainforest Alliance™ has a very strict set of standards in regards to the way you manage the farm, the environment, obviously, the forest, how you treat the employees, safety issues with the workers, and it's getting very, very expensive to be certified. And every year, they want more and more and more changes in the farm, to a point that those changes are challenging the volume that the farm produces. If you cannot make significantly more money per pound of certified coffee, then the costs of meeting these standards are not worth the effort to the farmer.

Gaining market acceptance and building perceived value through certification is necessary before consumers will be willing to pay more certified coffee. If the consumer won't pay a price premium, farmers have little incentive to invest the extra effort and money required for certification. In Leiva's opinion, 'If you can see that the prices today are not as good, and the cost of certification is very high, the producers start questioning the real value of this investment.' In 2008, approximately 62,296 metric tonnes of Rainforest Alliance™ certified coffee was sold.

Bird Friendly®

The Bird Friendly® certification was started in late 1996 by staff at the Smithsonian Migratory Bird Center (SMBC). The certification's criteria are based on ornithological research carried out by researchers In several Latin American countries and are focused on biophysical aspects of shade on coffee plantations. The SMBC requires that producers meet the requirements for organic certification first, and then meet additional criteria focused on biophysical aspects of shade in coffee plantations including canopy height, foliage cover (40% shade coverage), diversity of woody species, total floristic diversity, structural diversity, leaf litter, herbs and forbs ground cover, living fences, vegetative buffer zones around waterways and visual characteristics. The Bird Friendly® certification does not address labor conditions. As Robert Rice with the SMBC stated in regards to the Bird Friendly® certification, 'It's a seal that just has a lot of scientific rigor behind it and people can rest assured that they're getting what they think they are paying for.' The biggest challenge to Bird Friendly® certification is related to the difficulty and cost of obtaining organic certification, which can require years of effort and expenses, rather than the habitat requirements. However, the SMBC does certify farms for three years. In 2008, approximately 2,916 metric tonnes of Bird Friendly® coffee was sold.

Common Code for the Coffee Community (4C)

The Common Code for the Coffee Community, also known as 4C, was established by the German Coffee Association (DKV) and the Deutsche Gesellschaft für Technische Zusammenarbeit (GTZ) with the goal of facilitating more sustainable coffee production. Building on best agricultural and management practices, the 4C code of conduct intends to eliminate the most unacceptable practices while encouraging ongoing improvement. 4C distinguishes itself from organic, Fair Trade, Rainforest Alliance™ and Utz certifications by relying on an internal monitoring system incorporated within the initiative's corporate business model, rather than certification of standards compliance by third parties. 4C has no set price premiums, allowing free negotiation between 4C members with price reflecting coffee quality and sustainable production practices and the standards it sets are the absolute minimum in all ecological, social and economic aspects. By December 2007, approximately 360,000 metric tonnes of coffee was 4C verified. However, only about 10% of the available verified 4C coffee was actually purchased by 4C members.

Utz Certified

Utz Certified, originally known as Utz Kapeh which means 'good coffee' in the Mayan language, was founded in 1997 by Guatemalan coffee producers and the Dutch coffee roaster Ahold Coffee Company, and is one of the fastest-growing certification programs in the world. Utz Certified aims to implement a worldwide standard for socially and environmentally appropriate coffee growing practices, and efficient farm management. The program is focused on the mainstream market, and is open to all growers, traders, roasters and retailers across the entire supply chain. Utz Certified has a unique track-and-trace system, showing the buyers of Utz certified coffee exactly where their coffee comes from. As Illana Burk, Business Development Manager with Utz explained, a roaster can print a code on a bag, whereby the customers enter the code in and immediately track their coffee all the way back to the originating farm. The farm's story can be told and transparency ensured. The price for Utz certified coffee is determined in a negotiation process between buyer and seller, which the certification body does not interfere with. Utz certified has been criticized over weak environmental and social standards, the lack of pre-financing standards, and the lack of minimum guaranteed prices. Leiva says, 'Utz was developed for European grocery chains. That's the seal that they developed for their own marketing purpose basically.' Although Utz certification is not recognized worldwide it has slowly been gaining recognition in more countries, particularly in Japan where certification not only yields a premium, but also is necessary to meet the exacting standards of the Japanese consumers. In 2008, 77,478 metric tonnes of Utz Certified coffee was sold.

Direct trade and Farm Friendly Direct (FFD)

Direct trade is a general term for coffees that are imported directly from growers, rather than purchased through brokers at auction. Through a direct trade relationship, individual terms and prices can be negotiated and growers typically receive a higher price since there are no middlemen taking a share of the price. Stell and his team firmly believed in the FFD program that started in 2001 at the La Hilda Estate in Costa Rica. The program evolved to include direct trade arrangements with farmers in Tanzania, El Salvador, Costa Rica, Sumatra (Indonesia), India, Papua New Guinea, Guatemala and Ethiopia. Direct trade with farmers in developing countries is nothing new, but Stell wanted to create a program that embodied his commitment to community and sustainability. The FFD program was based on paying above market prices for premium coffee, then paying an additional premium to finance projects that help improve the lives of farmers and their communities (Exhibit 12). Other direct trade models pay premiums above Fair Trade price to reward quality, but they may not have specifics on how that money is spent by the growers. In creating FFD, Stell strongly believed that direct trade not only resulted in higher quality coffee for customers, but also ensured long-term mutually beneficial business relationships between PRC and their farmers, as well as between the farmers and their community and natural environment. As the quality of coffee improved under direct trade, certain farmers were approached by other buyers, often offering higher prices. Stell and PRC never tied growers into exclusive sourcing contracts, believing that a variety of buyers benefited the growers in the long term. Farmers had the choice of selling to the highest bidders, but tended to stay loyal to PRC trusting that they were making a long-term commitment and paying stable prices over the long term.

Stell would typically sample different coffees from a broker until he found one that had the quality he desired. He would then patiently work on finding the original source of that coffee and begin establishing direct trade relationships with the grower. Each FFD project was then designed and implemented through a collaborative process between PRC employees, farmers and their communities to address some of the most pressing needs. Projects were evaluated by how closely they aligned with the United Nations Millennium Development Goals (Exhibit 13), the potential for improving farmers' lives, overall costs and the visibility of each project with its direct trade relationship. Once a project was undertaken, PRC remained engaged to ensure that the farmers and communities had access to the assistance and materials needed to complete each project. Most FFD projects were short-term in nature and typically completed within a one to two year timeframe before the next project was developed and implemented. FFD projects included building a school, paying teachers' wages, constructing a water treatment facility (Exhibit 14), installing water pumps, implementing a soil and leaf analysis program, supporting a local foundation to fund community needs and planting trees.

There were challenges to the direct trade model. It took time to work through coffee brokers to trace the source of high-quality beans back to the farm, begin a dialogue with those farmers and then begin developing a relationship that could become part of the FFD program. Farmers were often skeptical of foreign companies, and tended to be more comfortable transacting business through local channels and coops. Stell also knew that his team was only able to travel to each farm at most once a year to meet with farmers and monitor ongoing FFD projects. Certain projects required expertise that was outside PRC's core business. In some cases, PRC collaborated with NGOs on FFD projects, relying on their experience, yet this option was not always available or feasible. Stakeholders began asking Stell for specifics on how much PRC invested in FFD projects. There were no internally mandated policies or formulas for determining how much money would be allocated to fund FFD projects. Likewise, PRC had no formal guidelines for selecting and structuring FFD projects nor any metrics defined for measuring the success or effectiveness of FFD projects. Kathleen Finn, a communications and marketing representative at PRC, believed that the FFD program should remain flexible and fluid, argued that

> the program supports sustainability and in order to best do so, the program itself needs to be organic. Sometimes a farmer growing coffee in a developing country like Guatemala or in another part of the world may be doing very well in relation to the rest of their community that supports them, so as a result sometimes the funds from proceeds going to the FFD program are best spent with the community versus the farmer. At other times the farmer needs support to meet quality standards or to help become more environmentally and/or socially sustainable. As a result the program needs to be organic, flexible, transparent, and may need to change from crop-to-crop or farmer-to-farmer in order to meet local needs and be able to bring value to PRC and our clients.

Portland Roasting Coffee Company

Supply Chain

Through the FFD program, PRC worked to minimize the number of middlemen in the coffee supply chain. The broker and importer still played a role by assisting with the necessary functions of transporting, processing, storing, financing or importing. However, PRC negotiated a separate contract with these intermediaries, assuring that the price offered to the growers was not impacted. The containers carrying FFD Central American coffees were shipped into Oakland or Long Beach (California), FFD coffee from Papua New Guinea was shipped into the Port of Tacoma (Washington), and FFD Tanzanian coffees were shipped directly into the Port of Portland (Oregon). PRC coffee that was not part of the FFD program was typically purchased on the spot market through brokers who import coffee into various ports in the US and sell to roasters throughout the US. Since coffee crops ripen at different times throughout the year, roasters must source coffee from different growing regions throughout the year to secure a sufficient quantity of fresh beans to meet annual demand.

PRC works with farmers to ensure their coffee is farmed following the best possible practices, and then takes on the responsibility of trying to maintain this high-quality coffee on its long voyage to Portland to be roasted. Storage and shipping conditions can make a big difference in the overall quality of a cup of coffee. Coffee may leave the processing mill at 12% moisture, but if the coffee isn't shipped right away, problems may result. Humidity is a critical variable, and if coffee absorbs too much moisture, particularly from exposure to humid environments when stored for long periods of time, it may take on a moldy overtone in the cup. The temperature of coffee during shipping can also have an impact on the quality of green coffee, since quick changes in temperature cause condensation and fermentation of the beans. Good circulation is needed to keep humidity and temperature levels constant. PRC might receive Guatemalan coffee from the farm to the loading dock in as little as three weeks, while containers from other sourcing locations might take upwards of three to four months to arrive.

Upon arrival at PRC's facility, unroasted green coffee is stored in a climate controlled warehouse environment. Samples were taken from each lot and inspected for defects to ensure quality. Irregularities in quality can be attributed to the farm, the processing or shipping depending on the nature of the defects found. Having some defects in a lot is quite common and only becomes a concern if abnormally high. Such defective beans are set aside to help the PRC staff learn how to inspect coffee lots for quality. Although green coffee can last significantly longer than roasted coffee, for the same reasons encountered during shipping, it is important for sourced green coffee to be roasted in a reasonable amount of time. Coffee is stored in burlap bags marked with the necessary information about the coffee to keep coffees from being confused. Organic coffees are strictly kept separate from other coffees to conform to certification standards.

The coffee roasting process heats green beans to a specified temperature for a specified length of time. Roasting profiles for each coffee, designating target temperatures throughout the different time intervals in the roasting process, are carefully followed to highlight different flavors in the coffee and ensure consistency in the final product. PRC's roasting equipment is computer monitored so that roast profiles can be highly consistent while maintaining the uniqueness of each roast. However, even with all the metrics the computer records, skilled roasters diligently oversee every stage of the roasting process. As subtle changes such as fluctuations in the ambient temperature or humidity can affect the final product, every roast is slightly different. Most machines maintain a temperature of about 550 degrees Fahrenheit. The beans are kept moving throughout the entire process to keep them from burning as they slowly roast. When the beans reach an internal temperature of about 400 degrees, they turn brown, sugars start to caramelize and the oils locked inside the beans begin to emerge. The hot roasted coffee beans are then quickly spilled out onto a tray where cooling fans return the coffee to room temperature.

Having been returned to a stable temperature, roasted coffee is then ready for bagging and distribution (Exhibit 15). At PRC, whole bean coffee for grocery distribution was packaged in bulk to fill store containers where customers fill their own bags. Whole bean coffee for sale in small bags was simply packaged and stored for distribution. Ground coffee was crushed to a specific size increment depending on customer preferences and their method of making coffee, then bagged and stored. Bagged coffees are contained in a sealed package with a valve to release gases produced by the coffee as it ages. The packaging keeps out air and slows the process wherein coffee ferments or goes stale, but as gases are let off, the coffee also slowly loses its flavor.

Marketing and product differentiation

PRC used a number of different channels to market their coffee and services. They take leading roles in a wide range of industry trade shows, conferences and sampling events. Through these channels PRC showcased their wide range of coffee blends and supporting products and services. PRC also worked with retailers on cooperative marketing efforts including customized labeling, storyboards, decorative packaging and colorful photography that highlighted the FFD program (Exhibit 16). PRC also delivered their message to consumers through their website containing information on company history, products, blogs, their media outreach, the FFED program and PRC's other sustainable initiatives. Marie Franklin, the National Sales and Marketing Director, believed that beyond the overall focus on quality, customer service and a focus on sustainability were two attributes that helped to differentiate PRC from their competition.

Because PRC is a smaller company relative to large-scale roasters, PRC made every effort to provide superior customer service. PRC offered a wide range of training programs for the café staff that prepare coffee beverages, or baristas, along with technical support services for clients using PRC espresso and drip coffee equipment. PRC also offered a range of online training videos available to anyone interested in the art of coffee making. According to Franklin, 'Staying close to your clients is the best way to make sure that you are meeting their needs.' In the PRC tasting room, PRC educated clients on the flavor spectrum of different coffee varietals and provided hands-on experience and training with equipment available for purchase. This ensured that PRC clients were experienced with the technology used to make coffee and equipped to deliver the highest quality product to the end consumer. The training sessions also provided PRC with a valuable opportunity to build personal relationships with café owners. Nick Doughty, general manager for Elephants Delicatessen in NW Portland, emphasized that his business was about good coffee and good people. By doing business with PRC, he was able to bypass the hype of some bigger name competitors, get high-quality coffee and the training and equipment that his business needed, all while working with people he enjoys.

One of the most important differentiators, according to Franklin, was the company focus on social and environmental responsibility. PRC was the first company to create a sustainability-based direct-trade program, even though competitors have introduced direct-trade programs. Paul Tostberg, owner of Coffee Culture in Corvallis, Oregon, stated that sustainability, quality and proximity were at the top of his list of reasons he chose to work with PRC. Paul believed that being a local company working closely with customers, providing thorough customer support services and creating special blends that his customers were looking for, were all qualities that set PRC apart from other coffee roasters. Telling the story of the FFD program, raising customer awareness and being recognized for sustainable practices that exceed the standards of conventional certifications was integral to PRC's marketing strategy.

Distribution channels

Coffee houses

PRC targeted small specialty coffee houses in hopes that they would serve PRC coffee to the increasingly sophisticated palettes of their clients, who are demanding high-quality coffee. However, these coffee houses were not an easy sell. Many of them purchased coffee in low volumes yet had high expectations. Not all coffee house customers choose suppliers for the same reasons. Quality was important to Diana Benting, purchasing manager for Portland Community College, who performed a blind taste test every five years to determine whom they will purchase from. Although she appreciated local businesses promoting sustainable practices, if a new coffee didn't pass her taste test, it would not be considered. Although Benting had her own criteria for selecting companies to purchase coffee from, her students had a whole separate set of motives. According to Benting, many college students don't care so much about the brand or company policy, instead it is all about location. Time is always a premium, especially on campus. If the campus coffee house is the most conveniently located place to purchase a cup of coffee between classes, then that is where students will go, regardless of brand.

Customer service was also important to small coffee houses. Rico from the Coffee Lounge in Portland, purchased coffee from PRC for four years before he decided to switch to another roaster. As with any small business, an entrepreneur's time is money, and there is never enough. The additional support in customer service offered by the new roaster, at a minor cost difference and with similar quality, was enough to lure him away from PRC's business. That is not to say all of PRC's clients feel the same. Most of PRC's clients opt to do business with them because of the additional services they get. Doughty stated that one of his driving motives for selecting PRC was the additional training, sales and technical support the company offered him. As a small company, it was easier for PRC to maintain a personal touch with their clients, reacting quickly to and anticipating customer needs. Cooperative marketing, on-site training, custom labeling and personal attention are all valuable services for small businesses. These services do not come cheap however. One of the disadvantages to being a smaller roasting company is having less capital to work with. Every minute spent with an existing customer, no matter how important, is a minute that could have been spent looking for new customers and building new relationships.

Hotels

While many inexpensive hotel chains did not offer high-quality coffee to guests, there were also plenty of high-end hotels that provided specialty coffee in rooms and restaurants as a way to enhance their visitors' experiences. PRC targeted boutique hotels across the country. These hotels have a value proposition much different than the low-priced chain hotels located along the nation's interstate highways, offering very personalized services with emphasis on everything from their customer service, to food and location. These boutique hotels believe that the quality of the coffee they offer their guests is just one reflection of the quality they place on the rest of their services. Given the plethora of specialty roasters now in the business, and the dispersed nature of these hotels, it is not an easy or inexpensive market to penetrate. Franklin targets several larger boutique chains to reduce the cost of cultivating clients and increase the volume of sales per client, while also seeking one-of-a-kind bed and breakfast establishments.

Institutions

From the beginning, local institutions throughout Oregon were a strategically important market segment for PRC. The company created key relationships with several of the largest universities in Oregon including Portland State University, Portland Community College and Oregon State University. These clients purchased large volumes of coffee from PRC, but also put their products in front of a high-priority market – young and conscientious consumers. In addition, PRC also sold coffee and services to churches, large food distributors such as Food Services of America, casinos and medical centers such as Oregon Health and Science University. These clients were generally consistent, reliable and advertised the PRC brand in highly visible markets, providing exposure and marketing value beyond the direct purchasing of coffee and other products.

Grocers

PRC also sold a high volume of coffee to supermarkets and grocery stores. PRC had created a pilot marketing and sales campaign in partnership with Fred Meyer (a division of Kroger), one of Oregon's largest supermarket chains. This gained PRC an unprecedented amount of floor space to create a unique shopping experience for the coffee consumer (Exhibit 17) and provide consumer education about PRC's coffees and the FFD program. PRC hoped that Fred Meyer would expand this program, along with PRC's shelf space, into hundreds of stores across the Pacific Northwest. PRC also worked with other smaller, gourmet food markets and grocers including Zupan's Market and New Seasons, both of which had great potential for expansion.

Competitors

Wholesale roasters

Although PRC had an innovative business model, they were certainly not the only specialty coffee company to purchase directly from farmers, roast beans to exacting standards and sell to a variety of retailers. Wholesale roasters represented the largest segment of specialty coffee providers in the industry. Unlike PRC, many wholesale roasters also opened retail storefronts which helped to introduce the public to their coffee, build strong brand recognition and provide an otherwise unavailable opportunity to have direct interaction with their consumers. Within Portland, PRC was competing against numerous other roasting companies including Stumptown Coffee Roasters, which also sourced single origin coffees from farmers around the globe and roasted the beans locally.

Retailer roasters

There had been a recent rise in the number of small specialty and boutique coffee roasters. These micro roasters were often purchasing direct coffee either from farmers or coffee importers and then creating specialty roasts to meet the selective and demanding standards of their customers. Mike Ferguson from the SCAA noted, 'This is one way for retailers to differentiate themselves from the competition, by having a wider variety of freshly roasted coffee.' The SCAA estimated that there were well over 2,000 of these small specialty retail roasters, and they estimated that their numbers would continue to grow as consumers became more educated on the wide range of contributing factors that all come together to make a great cup of coffee. With a new generation of coffee-loving students and young professionals joining the aging baby boomers, the market was strong enough to support a wide range of small niche retailers, as well as franchises. Some of the more successful retailer roasters had even been able to branch out their operations locally, regionally and even nationally.

Franchised roasters

Some of the biggest players in the specialty coffee industry have been successful at not only directly sourcing their coffee, but also tapping into both the retail and wholesale markets across the country. Starbucks had been very successful in penetrating the institutional and wholesale markets by creating relationships with hotel chains, airlines and other large franchises like Barnes & Noble. The combination of these markets saw Starbucks capture more than 40% of the specialty coffee market.[vi] Starbucks was not alone in trying to control this franchised market space, and any competitor to Starbucks was a competitor to PRC. Although not a roaster, McDonald's had recently added specialty coffee to their menu, and with thousands of locations across the country, massive economies of scale and a reputation for affordable convenience, McDonald's became a threat to the specialty coffee industry.

Volume roasters

A small number of very large corporations dominated the coffee roasting industry for decades, creating some of the most recognized brands in the US. These large-scale roasters include J.M. Smucker Company (Folgers and Millstone), Nestlé (Nescafe and Taster's Choice), and Kraft Foods (Yuban, Maxwell House, Brim, Gen eral Foods International Coffee, Gevalia, Kenco, Maxim and Sanka). Not nearly as demanding in the quality of the coffee they source, these large roasters often sourced their coffee from very large producers in Mexico, Brazil, Columbia and other countries. Many of these companies also purchased the lower quality portions of a crop from high-end producers. Sales of conventional ground and whole bean coffee have been concentrated amongst these very few brands. Folgers controlled 38% and Maxwell House controlled 33% of ground coffee sales in 2007.[vii] Historically, these volume producers have held the largest share of the market, but their growth had been slowing as consumers moved toward higher quality. Yet these volume producers exerted huge influence on the coffee industry due to their tremendous purchasing power, and were slowly implementing more sustainable practices.

Substitutions

The most obvious substitute for coffee is tea. According to the Tea Association of the United States, in 2007 the wholesale US industry value for tea was $6.85 billion. In other parts of the world, however, tea was not only a larger market but also maintained stronger cultural roots making it very difficult to supplant. Yet specialty coffee began to make some inroads into well-known tea-drinking countries including England, China and Japan. There was also a rapidly growing market in highly caffeinated sodas and energy drinks, often referred to as functional beverages. Many of these brands including Red Bull, Monster and Rock Star were filled with additives and stimulants while packaged in bold colors and designs targeting a younger age group. From 2004–07, sales of energy drinks more than doubled from $1.1 billion to $2.5 billion.[viii] While these drinks were directly competing with coffee for its naturally stimulating effects, they were not part of the coffee café culture that many consumers enjoyed. The coffee industry still had to figure out how best to target new generations.

PRC's commitment to sustainability

Sustainable values played a part in every decision at PRC with regard to its customers, farmers, products and employees, even going beyond the FFD program. Beginning in 2006, an in-house environmental team was tasked with finding environmentally friendly alternatives for all of its operations. As a result, PRC encouraged composting, recycling, using post-consumer office paper and the company-wide use of earth-friendly cleaning products. Employees were encouraged to ride bikes to work and PRC had even contracted with B-Line, a sustainable urban delivery service, to offer bicycle deliveries of coffee beans and supplies to Portland clients (Exhibit 18). One of PRC's two delivery vans ran on biodiesel and the company had declared that all new vehicle purchases would also be powered by biodiesel. The company began working with Trees for the Future with the aim of becoming a carbon neutral company through the purchase and planting of 16,900 trees.

But Stell wanted to have an even larger impact on the environment, and in 2007 began distributing Ecotainer to-go cups. These cups had an inside lining of bio-plastic made from corn, and an outer layer of paper harvested from trees managed in accordance with Sustainable Forestry Initiative guidelines.[ix] All of the bulk coffee the company sold to groceries and all of the consumer bulk bags were 100% compostable. Under the proper conditions, these cups and bags can break down into water, carbon dioxide and organic matter. Finally, in 2009, PRC sponsored a Walk for Water which raised funds to benefit Water for All, a non-profit organization dedicated to bringing clean water to families in sub-Saharan Africa. The inaugural event raised US$28,000 to fund two wells in Yirgacheffe, Ethiopia, a coffee-growing region in Eastern Africa. Such efforts led to the company receiving the 2005 SCAA Sustainability Award and recognition from the City of Portland with the 2007–2009 RecycleWorks Award. PRC signed the Global Compact in 2005 and since then consistently promoted the Millennium Development Goals on cups, product packaging and the company website.

The future of Farm Friendly Direct

As the pilot announced the final approach into Bujumbura, Stell glanced out of the window and down at the city on the shore of Lake Tanganyika. He was joining a trade delegation from the US organized by the US Department of Agriculture and would spend the next two weeks travelling across the country educating farmers to meet the high-quality standards of specialty coffee roasters, which would ultimately enable them to earn higher prices. After years of civil war, officials in Burundi were eager to develop the domestic coffee industry by gaining access to the expertise necessary to improve product quality and ultimately facilitate improvements in trade relations. Coffee was Burundi's main export and economic development from increased coffee revenues would help the country to recover from the turmoil of past years, yet Stell knew the country still faced an array of challenging issues. Environmental protection, labor rights, health and education lagged far behind first world standards and the population was expected to grow exponentially over the next 20 years placing unprecedented demands on infrastructure and resources.

Stell wondered if the next direct trade relationship would be established in Burundi, and he had no doubt that the FFD program could help improve the quality of life for farmers and their surrounding community. However, he was less confident that the FFD program in its current form would provide PRC with the necessary competitive edge needed to secure regional accounts with large retailers in the US. Although Stell believed that the FFD program was unique to the coffee industry and superior to mainstream certification programs in many ways, FFD was not verified by an independent third-party organization and consumer awareness of FFD was relatively low compared with Fair Trade, organic, Rainforest Alliance™ and Bird Friendly® labels. If PRC decided to implement independent verification of the FFD program, what criteria should be used to verify compliance and measure results? What other modifications could be made to FFD to ensure credibility, improve the program and make it stand out against the multitude of established coffee certifications? Should PRC also invest in certification of FFD coffees according to an established standard? If so, which certification should PRC select? From a marketing standpoint, in what other ways could the FFD program be leveraged to build the PRC brand and compel quality conscious coffee consumers to seek out and purchase FFD coffees? Would this be enough to give PRC the edge over major competitors and land the Fred Meyer account? As Stell unbuckled and prepared to exit the small plane, he knew he and his team had some tough decisions to make when he returned to Portland.

EXHIBIT 1
Portland Roasting Company product packaging

EXHIBIT 2
Portland Roasting Company sourcing

Ecotainer   Other Eco-efforts   E-Team   World Water Day

Sustainability Initiatives

Whether it's a commitment to a business partnership with a small, organic coffee farmer or a decision to purchase eco-friendly materials for our office, our company has never veered from its pledge to doing the right thing for the environment and the community — near and far.

You'll see Portland Roasting's employees toting their own ceramic mugs to work and riding their bikes or using public transportation to get to work. But we know the important changes are the ones that not everyone sees – the biodiesel in our vans or the windpower we purchase or our decision to spend more money on an eco-friendly cup. We continually make changes – big and small – to our business operations and are always on the lookout for ways to refine our processes in order to save more energy and resources.

http://www.portlandroasting.com/sustainability/

COSTA RICA

EL SALVADOR

ETHIOPIA

GUATEMALA

INDIA

PAPUA NEW GUINEA

SUMATRA

TANZANIA

The goals of Farm Friendly Direct are two-fold, acquiring quality coffee while adding to the lives of farmers and their communities. Our vested interest in our growers, and their farming methods, secures a healthy future for the farmers' land and livelihood, while producing memorable coffee.

Our efforts are making strides toward the United Nations Millennium Development Goals, a set of attainable and quantifiable benchmarks the organization has laid out to eradicate worldwide poverty by 2015.

EXHIBIT 3
Portland Roasting Company sourcing data

Portland Roasting Coffee Imports in Pounds per Year

Farm Friendly Direct Coffee	2003	2004	2005	2006	2007	2008
Costa Rica FFD	36836	39716	49389	58361	79053	87,207
Ethiopian FFD	28859	35776	42309	57990	74,649	31,407
Guatemala FFD	61173	72753	88746	109023	145,795	171,353
New Guinea Madan Estate FFD	0	0	0	24800	102,051	153,499
Sumatra Organic FFD	8437	15399	24524	25452	24777	31,963
Swiss Water Processed FFD	0	0	0	16,236	60,125	74982

Non Farm Friendly Direct Coffee	2003	2004	2005	2006	2007	2008
Bolivian Organic	39	836	0	0	0	0
Brazil	1902	4039	8127	10061	15128	21,185
Brazil Top Sky	0	0	0	411	1478	621
Colombian	8988	8527	10574	15185	17145	18,711
Colombian Decaf	19831	20320	19453	16026	2905	2509
Costa Rica Organic	281	5146	7073	5333	5798	7893
Costa Rica Decaf	46	0	0	0	0	0
El Salvador	1854	2410	5186	3011	2263	1625
Cup of Excellence – El Salvador	0	0	0	0	0	22

Portland Roasting Coffee Imports in Pounds per Year						
El Salvador Organic	0	0	0	0	0	989
Ethiopian Organic	732	1956	2282	5310	4592	3106
Guatemala Decaf	0	0	0	0	0	111
Guatemala Organic	6805	9233	12660	4802	0	0
India Monsooned Malabar	46	656	29	23	0	0
India Arabica	0	0	0	0	2778	3752
India Robusta	0	0	0	0	0	3154
Indonesian Robusta	4419	697	3774	1424	0	0
Jamaica Blue Mountain	54	86	105	47	15	21
Kauii	237	497	258	179	0	0
Kenyan AA	297	504	616	317	0	33
Kenyan PB	0	0	0	0	0	18
Kona	77	122	163	111	385	396
Mexican Chiapas	8935	9948	1091	0	0	0
Mexican Organic	431	1179	979	132	0	0
New Guinea Amuliba	8197	65	0	0	0	0
New Guinea Kinjibi	16620	27,275	50348	37714	185	0
New Guinea Red Mtn	0	0	0	8268	0	0
New Guinea Organic	3980	11478	12729	13108	9960	11966
New Guinea Peaberry	0	0	0	0	0	1984
Peru Selvanica	1642	8790	2411	5599	0	0
Peru Inkaico	0	0	0	462	241	0

Portland Roasting Coffee Imports in Pounds per Year						
Peru Organic	1601	4314	5453	12982	16,061	19566
Red Sea	344	491	0	0	0	0
Sumatra	68638	76289	53370	59021	66,325	85,566
Sumatra Decaf	12067	15780	18202	15159	1607	2035
Swiss Water Processed Colombian	486	1875	1430	1248	462	0
Swiss Water Processed Espresso Decaf	1280	1470	2478	2105	0	0
Swiss Water Processed Komodo Organic	264	132	0	0	0	0
Swiss Water Processed Mexican Organic	1764	3512	5512	3168	0	0
Swiss Water Processed Peru Organic	1905	1053	0	0	0	0
Swiss Water Processed Sumatra	1683	5335	3728	2376	1703	1,868
Swiss Water Processed Guatemala	0	0	0	0	1010	1870
Swiss Water Processed Ethiopian	0	0	0	702	264	0
Timor Organic	493	2074	228	0	0	132
Ugandan AA	25230	30262	28139	18109	38062	4950
Cascadia Blend Swiss Water Processed	0	240	948	1386	0	0

Portland Roasting Coffee Imports in Pounds per Year						
Celebes Toraja/ Sulawesi	0	126	988	175	1307	1230
Tanzanian	0	0	4983	33831	0	34,063
Tanzanian PB	0	0	0	0	0	1,352
Honduras Organic	0	0	195	0	0	152
Cup of Excellence – Honduras	0	0	0	0	0	13
Salvador Organic	0	0	1560	66	0	0
Nicaragua Organic	0	0	0	15814	21,103	26,619
Cup of Excellence – Nicaragua	0	0	0	0	0	17
Rwanda	0	0	0	0	9867	18,500
Total Green Beans Processed (lbs)	**338,476**	**422,365**	**472,045**	**587,593**	**709,101**	**828,448**
% of total FFD	**40%**	**39%**	**43%**	**50%**	**69%**	**66%**
% of total organic	**8%**	**13%**	**15%**	**15%**	**12%**	**12%**

EXHIBIT 4
Portland Roasting Company organization

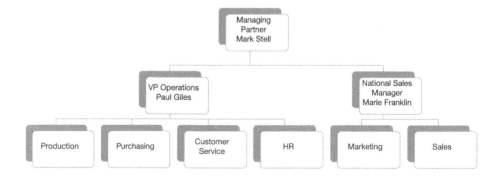

EXHIBIT 5
Portland Roasting Company revenues

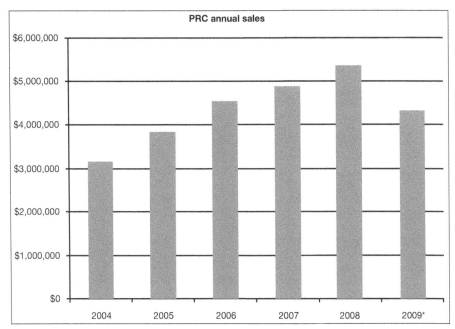

*sales figures as of October 27, 2009

Year	Sales (USD)
2004	$3,160,070.04
2005	$3,842,704.08
2006	$4,548,318.39
2007	$4,910,049.78
2008	$5,368,632.85
2009	$4,333,022.32*

*Sales figures as of October 27, 2009

EXHIBIT 6
Coffee cherry cutout

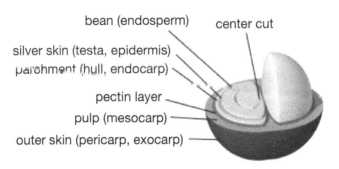

EXHIBIT 7
Coffee 'C' price history

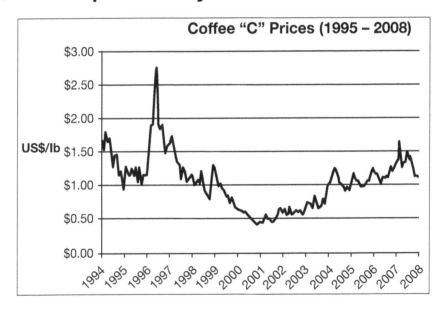

EXHIBIT 8
Growth of Starbucks stores

Year	1995	1996	1997	1998	1999	2000	2001	2002	2003	2004	2005	2006	2007	2008
Total US retail stores	676	1004	1364	1755	2217	2976	3780	4574	5201	6132	7302	8896	10684	11567
Company operated	627	929	1270	1622	2038	2446	2971	3496	3779	4293	4867	5278	6793	7238
Licensed	49	75	94	133	179	530	809	1078	1422	1839	2435	3168	3891	4329
Total international retail stores	1	11	48	131	281	525	929	1312	2024	2437	2939	3544	4327	5113
Company operated	1	9	31	66	97	173	295	384	767	922	1133	1374	1712	1979
Licensed	0	2	17	65	184	352	634	928	1257	1515	1806	2170	2615	3134
Total stores open at fiscal year end	677	1015	1412	1886	2498	3501	4709	5886	7255	8569	10241	12440	15011	16680

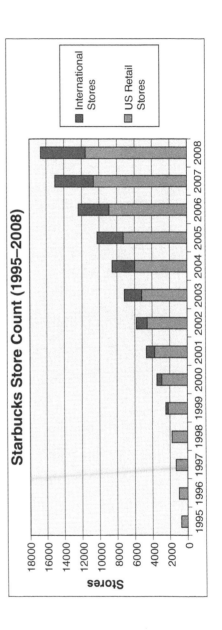

Starbucks Store Count (1995–2008)

EXHIBIT 9
Coffee market historical data (SCAA market data)

Specialty Coffee in the USA
2008

CONSUMPTION
Percentage of adults drinking specialty coffee:

DAILY

1995	1996	1997	1998	1999	2000	2001	2002	2003	2004	2005	2006	2007	2008
2.7%	2.9%	3.0%	3.3%	4.9%	N/A	14%	13%	12%	16%	15%	16%	14%	17%

WEEKLY

2001	2002	2003	2004	2005	2006	2007	2008
30%	28%	27%	36%	35%	36%	37%	34%

OCCASIONALLY

2001	2002	2003	2004	2005	2006	2007	2008
62%	59%	54%	56%	60%	63%	68%	62%

Cups per day, specialty coffee drinkers:

2001	2002	2003	2004	2005	2006	2007	2008
2.45	2.49	2.29	2.27	2.55	2.34	2.49	2.63

Source: *National Coffee Association Annual Drinking Trends Study. Visit www.ncausa.org*

DOLLAR SIZE OF MARKET (in Billions)
Total sales of specialty coffee, beverage, whole bean and ground at retail (YE07)

2001	2002	2003	2004	2005	2006	2007
$8.30	$8.40	$8.96	$9.62	$11.05	$12.27	$13.50

Source: *SCAA, Mintel Group (excludes Walmart)*

ESTIMATED NUMBER OF OPERATING UNITS

1991	1992	1993	1994	1995	1996	1997	1998	1999	2000
1.650	2,250	2,850	3,600	5,000	6,700	8,400	10,000	12,000	12,600

2001	2002	2003	2004	2005	2006	2007
13,800	15,400	17,400	19,200	21,400	23,900	25,700

Source: *SCAA, Mintel Group*

EXHIBIT 10
Competitive advertising from McDonald's and Dunkin' Donuts

EXHIBIT 11

Coffee certification comparisons

Initiative	Fair Trade	Organic	Utz Certification	Rainforest Alliance™	Bird Friendly®	4C
Mission	Ensure equitable trading arrangements for disadvantaged smallholders who are organized into cooperatives.	Create a verified sustainable agriculture system that produces food in harmony with nature, supports biodiversity and enhances soil health.	Set the world standard for socially and environmentally responsible coffee production and sourcing.	Integrate productive agriculture, biodiversity conservation and human development.	Conduct research and education around issues of neo-tropical migratory bird populations, promoting certified shade coffee as a viable supplemental habitat for birds and other organisms.	To achieve global leadership as the baseline initiative that enhances economic, social and environmental production, processing and trading conditions to all who make a living in the coffee sector.
Year established	1970s	1973	1997, 2001 – 1st cert.	1992, 1996 – 1st cert.	1997	2007 1st cert.
History and development	Began as 'Max Havelaar' in The Netherlands in the 1970s. Now there are several national Fair Trade chapters organized by the Fairtrade Labeling Organization (FLO) in Germany. TransFair is the US chapter.	Begun around 1973 as a farming movement and certification system. Developed into internationally recognized system with production throughout the world and annual sales above $20 billion.	Begun in 1997 as initiative from industry and producers in Guatemala, became an independent NGO in 2000. First certified farms in 2001.	Begun in 1992 by Rainforest Alliance™ and a coalition of Latin American NGOs, the Sustainable Agriculture Network (SAN). First coffee farm certification in 1996.	Founded in 1997 with criteria based on scientific fieldwork. Operated out of the SMBC office initially it currently involves 10 organic certification agencies as the eventual managers of the program.	Begun in 2003 by GTZ and DKA. Certified first farms in 2007.

Market focus	All markets	All markets	All markets	All markets	All markets	Mainstream Markets
Scope of program	Economic and environmental sustainability for farmers and their communities. Minimum price and social premium to cover costs of production and investments in the community. Organic premium for organic coffees. Small-producer organization's empowerment.	Organic farming and processing practices.	Sustainability; economics, ethics and environment. Worker safety.	Sustainability; economic, ethics and environment.	Certification aimed at the production of the coffee agro ecosystem.	Sustainability; economic, ethics, and environment.
Code elements for coffee production	Social, economic, environmental, democratic organization of cooperatives.	Environmental, farm production and processing standards.	Social, environmental, and efficient farm management.	Social, environmental, worker safety and efficient farm management.	Biophysical criteria of the shade component, provided that the farm is certified organic.	Social and environmental.

Initiative	Fair Trade	Organic	Utz Certification	Rainforest Alliance™	Bird Friendly®	4C
Scope of the code	Baseline and progress criteria. Continuous improvement required through progress requirements. Applies to democratically organized cooperatives formed by small scale farmers.	Federal standard with practices for producers and handlers applies to all organic product sold in the US.	Baseline criteria with field-tested indicators. Applies to farms and coops of all sizes. All countries possible. Continuous improvement required.	Baseline and advanced criteria with field-tested indicators. Applies to farms and coops of all sizes. Continuous improvement required.	Organic certification as a condition for BF certification. Certification applicable to estate farms and cooperatives. Annual inspections linked to organic inspection.	Baseline criteria; indicators under development. Applies to farms and coops of all sizes. Every country. Continuous improvement expected.
Standard setting body	Fairtrade Labeling Organizations International	International Federation of Organic Agricultural Movements	Utz Certified	Sustainable Agricultural Network	Smithsonian Migratory Bird Center	Common Code for Coffee Community Association
Monitoring body	Autonomous non-profit certifier.	Private certifiers regulated by state and accredited by NGO.	Private third-party certifiers approved by Utz Certified.	Certification by member organizations.	Private certifiers approved by initiative.	Private certifiers approved by initiative.
Inspection frequency and accuracy	Annual inspections by independent and annually trained Fair Trade inspectors.	Annual inspections for certified entities. USDA accreditation required for certifiers of organic product sold in US.	Independent auditors accredited to ISO 65 standard. Annual audits.	At least annual audits by teams of biologists, agronomists, sociologists and other specialists trained, authorized and monitored by the Rainforest Alliance™.	Annual, linked to organic inspection. Inspection/certification arranged/provided by a USDA-accredited organic certification agency.	

Traceability/ chain of custody	Yes, traceability from roaster to producer.	Yes, required by federal statute and historic standards. Organic products traceable from retailer to producer.	Yes, traceability from roaster to producer. Traceable to retailer via internet-based system.	Yes, traceability from roaster to producer.	Yes, traceability from roaster to producer.	
Production strategy	Small farmers	Mostly small farmers, some plantations	Mostly plantations, some small farmers	Mostly plantations, some small farmers	Mostly small farmers, some plantations	
Environmental standards	Standards regarding reduction in agrochemical use, reduction and composting of wastes, promotion of soil fertility, avoidance of GMOs.	Standards that bar the use of synthetic herbicides, fungicides, pesticides, GMOs and chemically treated plants.	Standards for protection of primary and secondary forests.	Standards for ecosystem and wildlife conservation, integrated crop management, and integrated management of wastes.	Requires organic certification. Additional standards for shade cover, canopy structure, secondary plant diversity, stream buffers.	Bans use of pesticides under Stockholm convention, bans destruction of primary forest or other protected areas.
Price differential to farmers	Yes. All purchases must be at or above the floor price.	Yes. Differential set by the market.	Yes. Differential set by the market.	Yes. Differential set by the market.	Yes. Differential set by the market.	

Initiative	Fair Trade	Organic	Utz Certification	Rainforest Alliance™	Bird Friendly®	4C
Price premium associated with code	Price floor of $1.21/lb and social premium of $0.10. Additional $0.20/lb for organic coffee.	US $0.015–0.20/lb	US $0.01–0.12/lb	Estimated at US $0.10–0.20/lb	US $0.05–0.10/lb	None specified. Prices reflect the quality, including the quality of the product and the Common Code quality of sustainable production and processing practices.
Fees to buyers	Licensed roasters pay US $0.05–$0.10/lb. Importers must provide pre-harvest financing when requested by coop.	Vary by certifier from $700–$3,000/year.	US $0.01/lb	None	Importers pay $100/year. Roasters pay US $0.25/lb	Annual membership fee dependent on import levels.
Fees to producers	Cost of auditing and reinspection fee.	Vary by certifier.	Auditing costs.	Auditing costs plus annual fee based on size of farm.	Cost of added days a inspection.	Annual membership fee dependent on production levels.

Source: SCAA.

EXHIBIT 12
Farm Friendly Direct projects

Year	Country	Amount(USD)	
2009	World Water Day Tanzania	$28,000.00	Internship and pump donated
2009	Costa Rica	$4,200.00	Teacher's salary
2009	Papua New Guinea	$8,000.00	Women's literacy and book drive
2008	World Water Day	$16,000.00	Pump sponsor Ethiopia
2008	Costa Rica	$4,200.00	Teacher
2008	Carbon Neutral El Salvador	$2,000.00	Planted trees
2008	Guatemala	$3,000.00	Yield project with Andres
2008	Sumatra(Indonesia)	$500.00	School uniforms
2007	Guatemala	$3,000.00	Yield project Andres
2007	Tanzania	$2,000.00	Agronomy Kit
2007	Costa Rica	$4,200.00	Teacher
2006	Costa Rica	$4,200.00	Teacher
2005	Costa Rica	$1,000.00	Internet setup and computer donated
2005	India	$500.00	School for the blind in Karnataka
2004	Papua New Guinea	$5,000.00	School built
2003	Guatemala	$12,000.00	Built water treatment for farm
	Total	$97,800.00	

EXHIBIT 13
United Nations Millennium Goals

The Millennium development goals are an UN initiative to address eight international development issues with a total of 21 target goals by 2015. They were adopted in 2000 by UN member states in recognition of the need to assist developing world nations in terms social, environmental and economic issues.

Goal 1: Eradicate extreme poverty and hunger

- Halve the proportion of people living on less than $1 a day (ppp).
- Achieve increased employment for women, men and young people.
- Halve the proportion of people who suffer from hunger.

Goal 2: Achieve universal primary education

- Provide primary education for all children by 2015.
- Increase enrollment.
- Increase completion of primary education.
- Increase literacy.

Goal 3: Promote gender equality and empower women

- Eliminate gender disparity in education.
- Equalize men/women rations in education.
- Equalize men/women wage disparity.
- Equalize men/women representation national political assemblies.

Goal 4: Reduce child mortality

- Reduce mortality rates of children under 5 by two-thirds.
- Increase proportion of 1-year-olds immunized against measles.

Goal 5: Improve maternal health

- Reduce maternal mortality ration by three-fourths.
- Increase proportion of births attended by health professionals.
- Achieve universal access to reproductive health.

Goal 6: Combat HIV/AIDS, malaria and other diseases

- Halt and reverse the spread of HIV/AIDS.
- Increase knowledge about HIV/AIDS. Increase condom use for high-risk populations.
- Increase orphan/non-orphan school attendance ratio.
- Achieve by 2010 universal access to treatment for HIV/AIDS.
- Halt and reverse the incidence of malaria and other major diseases.
- Increase preventative care and treatment.
- Decrease malaria and tuberculosis death rates.

Goal 7: Ensure environmental sustainability

- Reverse loss of environmental resources.
- Integrate principles of sustainable development into national policies and programs.
- Reduce biodiversity loss.
- Reduce CO_2 emissions.
- Reduce consumption of ozone depleting substances.
- Reduce percentage of water resources used.
- Reduce number of species endangered. Increase percentage of protected areas.
- Increases percentage of land covered by forest.
- Halve the proportion of people with sustainable access to water and sanitation.
- Achieve a significant improvement in the lives of slum dwellers.
- Decrease percentage of urban populations living in slums.

Goal 8: Develop a global partnership for development

- Further develop an open and fair, rule based and regulated trading and financial system.
- Address the special needs of less developed nations through debt relief development assistance, and financial policies.
- Address the needs of both landlocked and small island developing countries.
- Address the need to deal with the debt problems of developing countries.
- Make debt sustainable through national and international measures.
- Provide access to affordable essential medicine in developing countries.
- Make available access to new technology, especially information and communication technology.

EXHIBIT 14
Farm Friendly Direct in Action

The Clean Water and Balanced Plant Nutrition Project in Guatemala

At the urging of respected plantation owner and grower, Miguelina Villatoro del Merida, PRC invested proceeds from the Farm Family Direct program in a much needed water treatment facility at her Finca El Paternal farm. The fermentation process is important in the development of the flavor of the coffee, due in part to the microbiological processes that take place, but it results in wastewater containing organic matter like pectin, proteins and sugars that result in a decrease in pH. The high acidity of this effluent may deplete the life supporting oxygen of the water as it then flows into streams or other bodies of water, potentially impacting human health and aquatic life if discharged directly into surface waters.

The facility that PRC built for Miguelina sends leftover water from coffee production through a series of filtering tanks that removes much of the organic matter. The water can be reused several times, and then clean water is returned to the river free of contaminants. Other growers throughout the region now tour the state-of-the-art facility in order to learn about the benefits of water treatment and conservation. According to Miguelina the clean water facility has not only saved the farm thousands of gallons of water that they can now reuse for other agriculture, it has also helped them comply with the very rigid standards of the Rainforest Alliance™.

Since completing the wastewater treatment facility, PRC has begun another project to improve plant health and yield at Finca El Paternal, working in collaboration with Karnataka Coffee Estates and Ramaday Micronutrients in India who have used micronutrient applications successfully in many other locations.

EXHIBIT 15
Portland Roasting Company Coffee distribution

Oregon Network

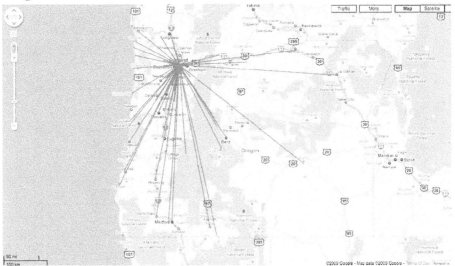

Nationwide Network

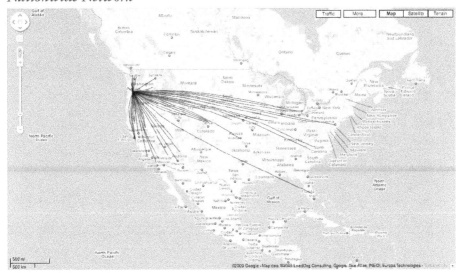

EXHIBIT 16
Farm Friendly Direct marketing images

Farm Friendly Direct

http://www.thehumanbean.com/SectionIndex.asp?SectionID=9

EXHIBIT 17
Portland Roasting Company Coffee display (Fred Meyer)

EXHIBIT 18
Portland Roasting Company local distribution (B-Line sustainable urban delivery)

Notes

i International Coffee Association, Total production of exporting countries, Crop years 2003/04 to 2008/09, www.ico.org/prices/po.htm.

ii Many coffee producers are small, family-owned farms covering two hectares or less, while larger coffee estates may be upwards of several thousand hectares.

iii Pendergrast, Mark. *Uncommon Grounds: The History of Coffee & How it Transformed Our World*. 1999. Mark Pendergrast. Basic Books. New York, NY: Basic Books, 1999. Print.

iv Mintel reports.

v www.msnbc.msn.com/id/8841941.

vi Wikinvest, 2009 www.wikinvest.com/stock/Starbucks_%28SBUX%29.

vii USDA.

viii Mintel's Energy Drinks—U.S., July 2008.

ix www.portlandroasting.com/sustainability/ecotainer.

CASE 11

Chipotle: Mexican Grill, Inc.
Food with integrity[1,2]

Ram Subramanian

On October 18, 2012, Steven Ells, the founder, chairman of the board, and co-chief executive officer (CEO) of the Denver, Colorado-based restaurant chain, Chipotle Mexican Grill (CMG), completed the conference call following the release of the company's third quarter 2012 results. While the reported results were positive, analysts picked on the slowing down of same-stores sales (a key metric for restaurant chains), the competition from Yum Brands' Taco Bell and their recent launch of the Cantina Bell menu and CMG's announcement that food costs were expected to

1 This case has been written on the basis of published sources only. Consequently, the interpretation and perspectives presented in this case are not necessarily those of Chipotle Mexican Grill or any of its employees.
2 Ram Subramanian wrote this case solely to provide material for class discussion. The author does not intend to illustrate either effective or ineffective handling of a managerial situation. The author may have disguised certain names and other identifying information to protect confidentiality.

increase in the near future. Following the announcement of third quarter results, CMG's stock went down by nearly 12 per cent in intra-day trading to finally stabilize at a 4 per cent drop over the previous day's price. At the end of trading on October 18, CMG's stock price was at $285.93, a significant decline from a 52-week high of US$442.40.[i] CMG had been the darling of both Wall Street and its customer base ever since the company's founding in 1993 and its 2006 initial public offering (IPO). Investors were attracted to CMG for its fast growth and sizeable profit margins, while customers responded favourably to its "Food with Integrity" mission of serving good quality food with inputs sourced using sustainable farming practices. Both Ells and his co-CEO, Montgomery F. Moran, had to respond to the challenges confronting the company.

The U.S. restaurant industry[ii]

Profile

For the year 2012, the National Restaurant Association projected total U.S. restaurant sales of $631.8 billion (compared to $379 billion in 2000 and $239.3 in 1990), which represented nearly 4 per cent of the gross domestic product. There were 970,000 restaurant locations, and the industry employed 12.9 million people (10 per cent of the total workforce). The restaurant industry's share of the food dollar was 48 per cent in 2012 compared to 25 per cent in 1955.[iii]

The restaurant industry consisted of a number of segments such as eating places, bars and taverns and lodging place restaurants. The three largest segments were full service, quick service and fast casual. Full service restaurants offered table ordering, and the average check (revenue per customer) was the highest of the three segments. While national chains such as Darden Restaurants (operator of Red Lobster, Olive Garden and Long Horn Steakhouse) and Dine Equity (IHOP and Applebee's) existed in this segment, the majority of operators were individuals, families or limited partnerships. This segment accounted for 31.7 per cent of industry revenues in 2011.

The quick service segment (previously referred to as "fast food") consisted of restaurants that offered fast counter service and meals to eat in or take out. This segment was further broken down into outlets that specialized in selected menu items such as hamburgers, pizza, sandwiches and chicken. Because of this segment's focus on quick service and price (the average check was the lowest of the three segments), large chains tended to dominate. Accounting for about $168.5 billion in revenues in 2011, this segment held a 28 per cent share of the restaurant market.

The fast casual segment was the smallest of the three, accounting for about 4 per cent in market share and $24 billion in 2011 revenues. Operators in this segment offered portable convenient food and focused on fresh healthful ingredients and customizable made-to-order dishes. The average check in this segment ranged between $7 and $10, price points typically lower than the full service segment and higher than the quick service segment. Fast casual was the fastest growing of the three segments, with an 11 per cent growth rate between 2007 and 2011. The NPD Group, an industry research firm, indicated that as this segment was in its growth phase, it faced intense competition from both the quick service and the full service segments. Buoyed by the growth in fast casual restaurants, several full service operators had recently entered this segment. For example, P.F. Chang's opened their Pei Wei locations, and Ruby Tuesday planned to increase the number of its Lime Fresh eateries to 200 locations by the end of 2012. Panera Bread, CMG, Five Guys Burgers and Qduba (owned by Jack-In-the-Box) were the leading fast casual players.

Industry economics

Restaurant running costs varied by segment. In addition, costs were a function of size and location. Upscale formats (typically full service restaurants and some fast casual chains) made higher investments in interior design and also incurred higher input costs. Many chain restaurants typically chose locations with high population density or a large geographic draw. Food and beverage, labour and real estate costs were the three largest expense categories for restaurants. Typically, both food and beverage and labour costs accounted for around 30 per cent each of revenues, while real estate costs were around 5 per cent. Marketing and general administrative overheads were the significant non-operating expense categories. The National Restaurant Association reported that in 2010 the average income before income taxes of a restaurant operator ranged between 3 and 6 per cent of revenues.

To control the cost of inputs, many large national and regional chains negotiated directly with their suppliers (to benefit both company-owned and franchisee-owned restaurants) to ensure competitive prices. Many chains also engaged in forward pricing to ensure stability in input costs. The National Restaurant Association reported that beef prices hit record levels in 2011 and were expected to be even higher when the prices for 2012 were finally tallied. Beef prices rose 53 per cent in 2012 above 2009 levels as the three largest exporters of beef to the United States – Australia, Canada and New Zealand – all reduced their shipments due to a variety of global factors. While the price of various dairy items (milk, butter, cheese) had remained fairly stable over the last few years, the price of grains such as wheat and corn had fluctuated due to changes in supply and demand as well as weather-related factors. The price of a bushel of wheat went up from $6.48 in 2007 to $7.30 in 2011, after falling to $4.87 in 2009. Similarly, while the average price of a bushel of corn was $4.20 in 2007, it rose to $6.20 in 2011 after falling to $3.55 in 2009.[iv]

Key competitors

A former CEO of Taco Bell, the Mexican food chain owned by Yum Brands, captured the competition in the restaurant industry in the following observation: "We are all competing for a share of the customer's stomach."[v]

Players in the restaurant industry competed not only with their segment's players but also with those of other segments. In addition, they competed with meals prepared at home as well as frozen or packaged food items available in supermarkets. While restaurants accounted for about 48 per cent of the dollar amount spent on food in 2012, the economy played a major role in this. In a 2011 National Household Survey reported in Standard & Poor's Industry Surveys, 21 per cent of those surveyed indicated that they would increase their eating out spending in 2012, while 42 per cent would decrease it slightly and 37 per cent would reduce it significantly.

CMG faced two major competitors in the Mexican food category of the restaurant industry. While Taco Bell was a player in the quick service segment, Qdoba competed, like CMG, in the fast casual segment.

Qdoba[vi]

Qdoba was a wholly owned subsidiary of the San Diego, California-based Jack-in-the-Box chain and in 2012 had 600 restaurants in 42 U.S. states and the District of Columbia. Qdoba was founded in Boulder, Colorado, in 1995 and grew nationally by featuring Mission-style burritos (made famous first in San Francisco). After Jack-in-the-Box acquired Qdoba in 2003, it expanded the brand rapidly. Of the 600 restaurants in the chain in 2012, around 350 were franchisee owned and the rest were company owned. A franchisee spoke about his rationale for launching a Qdoba restaurant:

> What attracted us to the chain was quality. What brought us to this is that everything is hand-crafted and made daily. We consider ourselves to be an artisan fast food chain. We come in every morning about three hours prior to opening and start cooking our meals. We start our slow-roasted pork and shredded beef that cooks for 6 to 8 hours. Our chicken is marinated in adobo spices for 24 hours before we serve it. We have an artisan table where we make our pico de gallo salsa, mix our cilantro with rice and prepare our guacamole as customers watch. What makes us stand out is the quality of the ingredients we use and our signature flavors. I believe being fast, friendly and fresh is what makes us successful in business.[vii]

The company reported an average check of $9.74 in fiscal 2011 for company-operated restaurants. The average yearly revenue per restaurant was $961,000 in 2011, an increase of 5.3 per cent over 2010. Jack-in-the-Box had revenues of $2.17 billion and net income of $67.83 million in 2011. The company stated that there was long-term potential to open 1,600 to 2,000 units across the United States.[viii]

Taco Bell

Taco Bell was part of Yum Brands, Inc., which also owned the KFC and Pizza Hut chains. Yum Brands was the world's largest restaurant company in terms of units, with nearly 38,000 restaurants in 120 countries. In fiscal 2011, Yum Brands reported revenues of $12.626 billion and a net income of $1.319 billion. At the end of fiscal 2011, there were 5,670 Taco Bell restaurants in the U.S., of which 27 per cent were company owned. Taco Bell reported a 50 per cent market share in the U.S. Mexican quick service segment. For fiscal 2011, the average annual revenues per restaurant were $1.284 million.[ix]

In March 2012, Taco Bell began testing a new menu called "Cantina Bell" in 75 U.S. restaurants. It worked with a Miami based chef and television personality, Lorena Garcia, to create a new line of upscale menu items including CMG staples such as black beans, cilantro rice and corn salsa. Greg Creed, Taco Bell's president, talked about the motivation behind Cantina Bell:

> Chipotle is an opportunity because what it's done has expanded the trial and usage of Mexican food. It's got people to believe they can pay $8 for a bowl or a burrito. Taco Bell can make food every bit as good as Chipotle and instead charge less than $5.[x]

Taco Bell's target market was an 18- to 24-year-old value-conscious male. Creed saw Cantina Bell as helping Taco Bell appeal to an older and less value-conscious group of customers. The Cantina Bell launch (and subsequent expansion nation-wide in July 2012) was cited as one of the reasons for Taco Bell's same-store sales growth of 7 per cent for third quarter 2012 (compared to the similar period in 2011).[xi] Exhibit 1 presents the summary of a Zagat comparison survey of Cantina Bell and CMG in New York City.

Chipotle Mexican Grill's history and profile

Origin and early growth

In 1990, after graduating from the Culinary Institute of America in New York City, Colorado-born Steven Ells moved to San Francisco to work as a sous chef at a res-taurant. In 1993, he opened a *taqueria* (a Spanish word meaning "taco shop") in Denver, Colorado, using $85,000 as capital obtained from his father. His goal was to reinvent Mexican food. He reflected on the origins of his first restaurant:

> I wanted layers of bold flavors that had nuance and depth, not just hot, not just spicy: cumin, cilantro, cloves, fresh oregano, lemon, and lime. It looked, smelled, and tasted different from traditional fast food. And it didn't take long before there was a line of people waiting to get in. So I thought, maybe I'll open one more. I was always quite rebellious and did things my own way. Friends said Mexican food is cheap – you can't charge $5 for a burrito. But I said this is real food, the highest-quality food. Friends said you can't have an open kitchen, but I wanted the restaurant to be like a dinner party, where everyone's in the kitchen watching what's

> going on. They said people have to order their meal by number. But I said no, you have to go through the line and select your ingredients. And everyone gave me grief over the name: Nobody will be able to pronounce it.[xii]

Ells opened a second restaurant using the profits from the first and a third (all in Denver, Colorado) with a loan from the Small Business Administration. When he had opened 16 restaurants by 1998, McDonald's Corporation (the global leader in fast food in terms of revenue) made an initial investment to help fund the company's growth. The company quickly grew to more than 500 units in 2005 (primarily using McDonald's $360 million capital infusion) and on January 26, 2006, made its initial public offering (IPO). In October 2006, McDonald's fully divested its holdings in CMG for a value of $1.5 billion. Ells talked about CMG and McDonald's: "They funded our growth which allowed us to open 535 restaurants. We learned from each other, but we use different kinds of food, and we aim for a different kind of experience and culture altogether. So we ended up going our separate ways."[xiii]

The push to sustainable sourcing

Ells happened to read an article by Edward Behr that told the story of an Iowa farmer who raised pigs without using antibiotics or confining them. Behr went on to add that the meat tasted much better than the mass-market meat that was served in most restaurants. The Behr article led Ells to learn about concentrated animal feeding operations (CAFOs).[xiv] In many developed countries, the dominant method of raising livestock for commercial purposes was through CAFOs, starting with poultry in the 1950s and extending to cattle and pork by the 1970s. A CAFO enabled raising livestock by using limited space. The U.S. Environmental Protection Agency (EPA) defined a CAFO as "an animal feeding operation that confines animals for more than 45 days during the growing season in an area that does not produce vegetation and meets certain size thresholds."[xv]

CAFO confined large number of animals in a limited space and substituted man-made structures (for feeding, temperature and manure control) for natural ones. A study[xvi] reported that while it took one million farms in 1966 to house 57 million pigs, through CAFO it took only 80,000 farms in 2001 to house the same number of pigs. CAFOs had a negative impact on water and air quality and hence were regulated by the EPA. In addition, many commercial CAFOs established agricultural water treatment plants to control manure, which had a negative impact on the environment.[xvii] After Ells visited several CAFOs, he decided to source from open-range pork suppliers starting in 2000, naturally raised chicken from 2002 and naturally raised beef soon after. The company formalized its sourcing policy in 2001 when it launched its "Food with Integrity" mission statement:

> Food with integrity is our commitment to finding the very best ingredients raised with respect for the animals, the environment and the farmers. It means serving the very best sustainably raised food possible with an eye to great taste, great nutrition and great value.[xviii]

CMG owned and operated 1,316 restaurants in June 2012, of which four were in Canada, three in the United Kingdom, one in France and the rest in the United States. It reported revenues of $2.270 billion and a net income of $215 million in fiscal 2011. It employed 28,370 hourly workers and 2,570 salaried employees. Ells was CMG's CEO till January 1, 2009, when Montgomery F. Moran (who had been the company's chief operating officer since March 2005) was appointed co-CEO along with Ells. Ells, however, retained his title as chairman of the board.[xix]

Business operations

Restaurant operations

All of CMG's restaurants were company owned. They were either end-caps (at the end of a line of retail outlets), in-lines (in a line of retail outlets) or free-standing. A typical restaurant ranged in size between 1,000 and 2,800 square feet depending on the market and cost $850,000 to open. The smaller restaurants were called "A Model" restaurants, the first of which was opened in 2010 to serve less densely trafficked areas. Restaurants served a limited menu of burritos, tacos, burrito bowls (a burrito without the tortilla) and salads, all prepared with fresh ingredients. Customers placed their order (burrito or taco) at the beginning of a line and added ingredients of their choice as they moved along the line. None of the restaurants had freezers, microwave ovens or can openers.[xx]

Given their higher than average food costs, CMG focused on operational efficiency at the restaurant level. The restaurant size was typically smaller than those of its peers, and it economized on labour by keeping their menu options limited and by using an assembly line system for food preparation. Chris Arnold, CMG's communication director, spoke about the company's efficiency focus:

> We are big believers in what author Jim Collins calls "the genius of and."[xxi] You can serve great food made with ingredients from more sustainable sources and do it at a reasonable price. You can have higher food costs than your peers and still have strong margins. It just takes the discipline to figure it out.[xxii]

In 2009, the company entered into a partnership with a company to install solar panels in its restaurants. CMG aimed to be the largest direct producer of solar energy in the restaurant industry in the next five years. Ells talked about this:

> Our effort to change the way people think about and eat fast food began with our commitment to serving food made with ingredients from more sustainable sources, and that same kind of thinking now influences all areas of our business. Today, we're following a similar path in the way we design and build restaurants, looking for more environmentally friendly building materials and systems that make our restaurants more efficient.[xxiii]

CMG's rationale for using solar panels was to reduce the restaurant's traditional energy consumption during the peak period of 11:00 a.m. to 7:00 p.m. Solar panels also reduced the company's carbon footprint. Starting with a restaurant in Illinois, CMG began to obtain LEED certification (Leadership in Energy and Environmental Design, a certification program of different levels) by using on-site wind turbines and cisterns for rainwater harvesting. It was the first restaurant to obtain the highest level (platinum) of LEED certification.[xxiv] By 2012, three of its restaurants were LEED certified.

Supply chain

CMG's supply chain was closely tied to the company's "Food with Integrity" mission. The company's 22 independently owned and operated distribution centres served restaurants in a specific geographic area. These centres sourced inputs from suppliers who were evaluated on quality and understanding of the company's mission. Key ingredients included various meats; vegetables, such as lettuce, cilantro and tomatoes; and dairy items, such as sour cream and cheese.

In 2008, the company embarked on a program to increase local (grown within 350 miles of the restaurant) sourcing to 35 per cent of at least one bulk produce item. The seasonal produce program was meant to cut down on fossil fuels used to transport produce, give local family farms a boost and improve the taste of the food served to customers by using ingredients during their peak season. CMG created a network of 25 local farms to supply some of its romaine lettuce, green bell peppers, jalapeno peppers, red onions and oregano to area restaurants.[xxv] The local sourcing program resulted in five million pounds of produce in 2009 and 10 million pounds by 2012.[xxvi]

In 2012, 100 per cent of CMG's pork, 80 per cent of its chicken and 50 per cent of its beef were classified as "naturally raised" meat – defined as open-range, antibiotic free and fed with a vegetarian diet. Forty per cent of CMG's beans were organically grown, while all of its sour cream and cheese were made from milk that came from cows that were not given rBGH (recombinant bovine growth hormone). In addition, a substantial percentage of the milk for sour cream and cheese was sourced from dairies that provided pasture access for their cows.[xxvii]

Organic agriculture[xxviii] was still in its infancy in the U.S. in 2012. Less than 1 per cent of the total agricultural area was managed organically. Of that, the percentage was highest for produce, followed by livestock and then poultry. Starting in the 1990s, the demand for organic food drove the conversion of traditional farms to organic at a rapid rate (for example, 14 per cent in 2007–08). The U.S. Department of Agriculture (USDA) reported that the average annual profitability of organic farms in 2011 was $45,697 versus $25,448 for traditional farms. However, the downturn in the economy that started in 2008 slowed down the conversion to organic farming to 6 per cent between 2009 and 2011.[xxix] Retail chains such as Whole Foods and Trader Joe's competed with full service restaurants and other restaurant chains for organic inputs, often driving up the prices well above those for conventional inputs. Ells commented on the pricing challenges and continuing availability of organic inputs: "The supply chain has yet to catch up, organic ingredients are still pricey, and supply is limited. What we are doing is an 'incremental revolution.' If we went all-organic and natural now, a burrito would be like $17 or $18."[xxx]

Marketing

CMG's marketing budget was $32 million in 2011 versus $26 million in 2010 and $21 million in 2009. The company had reduced its advertising spending for more than three years from $7.9 million in 2009 to $7.5 million in 2010 and $5.8 million in 2011.[xxxi] It stated its policy on advertising in its annual report: "Our marketing has always been based on the belief that the best and most recognizable brands aren't built through advertising or promotional campaigns alone, but rather through all of the ways people experience the brand. Our main method of promotion is word-of-mouth publicity."[xxxii]

When CMG hired Mark Crumpacker as its first chief marketing officer in 2009, the first decision that he made was to bring the company's advertising in-house rather than use the services of an outside agency. He also made the decision not to advertise in traditional media such as TV and instead rely on various loyalty programs. He gave his rationale for it:

> The alternative is to switch to the type of marketing that every other fast-food company uses with these new menu items and big ad campaigns to promote them. I think once you get on that model, I think it's very, very hard to get off. I want to try to do this [loyalty programs] as long as I can.[xxxiii]

One loyalty program was called "Farm Team." This was an invitation-only online program that quizzed users on sustainability, organic farming and humane food sourcing, and rewarded them when they shared the knowledge with others via social media. Arnold talked about the program: "This is a passion program. Through Farm Team, we are looking to identify our most loyal and passionate customers, and giving them tools to share their passion for Chipotle. It's much more about building evangelism than it is about rewarding frequency."[xxxiv]

In August 2011, CMG released an online commercial titled "Back to the Start," that featured Willie Nelson singing a reworded version of Coldplay's "The Scientist." The commercial told the story (in animated form) of a farmer who moved from inhumane industrial farming that used confined spaces to a more humane sustainable farming method. The popularity of this commercial led to CMG releasing it first in 5,700 movie theatres in September 2011 and running it once on television during the 2012 Grammy Awards show.[xxxv]

A one-day festival called "Cultivate" held in Chicago in October 2011 brought together farmers, chefs and music bands. The goal of the festival was to promote sustainable family farms. Other promotional items included iPhone games and local print advertising to accompany store openings.[xxxvi] A marketing expert assessed CMG's non-traditional marketing strategy:

> Chipotle has found a "sweet spot" with millennials by solidifying its reputation for freshness and offering a healthier fare than its competitors. The brand also gains reputation by shying away from traditional media, because younger audiences feel like it's more authentic, down-to-earth and easy to connect with. Millennials view the lack of TV as more authentic. Millennials are likely to dismiss a lot of claims. They are responding to everything the brand does and says.[xxxvii]

Finances

Exhibit 2 gives a cost comparison of key expenses for CMG and its competitors, Exhibit 3 presents CMG's financial statements, while Exhibit 4 gives a list of the company's stock on specific dates. Third quarter 2012 results showed a revenue increase of 18.4 per cent over the same period in 2011 and a net income increase of 19.6 per cent. Same-store sales increased by 4.8 per cent in the quarter compared to 11.3 per cent in third quarter 2011. Revenue growth was attributed to both new restaurant openings and menu price increases. The company launched a system-wide menu price increase in 2011 whose implementation was completed in third quarter 2012.[xxxviii]

The "Einhorn effect"

On October 2, 2012, Jeff Einhorn, who headed a hedge fund, made a presentation at the Value Investors Conference in New York City. In his presentation, Einhorn said that CMG was an attractive stock for short sellers because the company faced significant competition, principally from Taco Bell's Cantina Bell menu, and increased food costs, both due to its sustainable sourcing practices and a global increase in food commodity prices. He said that a survey conducted by his firm found that 75 per cent of self-identified Chipotle customers also frequented Taco Bell and that Taco Bell came out on top on both price and convenience. Einhorn stated:

> 23 per cent of Chipotle customers had already tried Taco Bell's Cantina Bell menu – which features burritos and burrito bowls made with fresh ingredients – and two-thirds of those customers indicated they would return. What's more, the customers most likely to return to Taco Bell were also those most likely to eat at Chipotle, a dynamic that indicates to me that Chipotle is most at risk of losing its frequent customers.[xxxix]

Within hours of Einhorn's presentation, CMG's stock began to fall. It fell by more than 4 per cent by the end of the day, and stock analysts stated that CMG had been "Einhorned."[xl]

CMG's challenges

In his conference call with analysts on October 18, 2012, Ells indirectly compared Cantina Bell with CMG (without actually naming his competitor):

> The way Chipotle does its business is not an easy thing to copy, and though a competitor could offer a similar item, it's probably only on the surface. Take a company that sells grilled chicken, for instance. Yet that company does not have a grill, nor do they have knives or cutting boards. So how do they make real chicken and cut it up? And in the end the customers realize the difference. Be careful of those who have a lower cost opportunity. The customer's not easily fooled. Our interactive format – the burrito assembly line that every customer runs through – is an important part of what Chipotle does.[xli]

He also indicated that CMG would consider raising its menu prices in 2013 to make up for expected higher food costs. As he conferred with co-CEO Moran following the call, both men listened in on Chief Financial Officer Jack Hartung talking to a reporter:

> The company will be patient with its pricing decisions, so as not to deter customers. We could move quickly, but we're going to choose not to be in too much of a hurry. We don't want to be the first ones out of the box with price increases. We'd rather see what happens with the economy, see what happens with consumer spending, see what other competitors do and how consumers respond.[xlii]

CMG faced a host of challenges. While the depressed economy favoured quick service and fast casual restaurants over full service restaurants because of lower check prices, consumer sentiment indicated that the majority of them would either curtail their spending on eating or at best maintain it at current levels. In addition, Taco Bell was proving to be a formidable competitor with its 5,670 U.S. restaurants pushing the higher margin Cantina Bell menu through aggressive and large-scale advertising. Finally, the expected increase in food costs was bound to affect CMG both in its margins and in its quest to increase its usage of sustainable inputs. Both men recalled a statement made by Arnold to an interviewer a few years ago:

> Chipotle is a good example of what can happen when you buck conventional wisdom. We've built a chain of fast food restaurants shirking many of the things the industry was built on – we spend more on food, not less; we own our restaurants rather than franchising; and we don't market using lots of price promotions and other gimmicks. Going that route, we've built one of the most successful restaurant companies in years.[xliii]

Were sustainability and the "Food with Integrity" campaign luxuries that CMG could ill afford in these difficult economic times? Could CMG continue to use quality and sustainably sourced inputs as differentiators to justify a higher priced menu?

EXHIBIT 1
Zagat comparison of Cantina Bell And CMG in New York City

	PRICE	
ITEM	CANTINA BELL	CMG
Burrito bowl with chicken	$5.99	$9.88
Steak burrito	$5.99	$10.34

Overall assessment: For practically half the price, the Cantina Bell menu is a definite value, but you get what you pay for, and the overall quality and taste of Chipotle still has an edge over Taco Bell.

Source: www.blog.zagat.com/2012/07/taco-bell-vs-chipotle-taste-testing.html., accessed October 19, 2012

EXHIBIT 2
Selected cost comparison — key competitors (costs as percentage of revenues)

	2011	2010	2009
YUM BRANDS[1]			
Food & packaging	30.57	29.09	28.62
Labour	30.40	29.63	29.99
Occupancy & other restaurant operating costs	26.97	27.06	27.50
Qdoba			
Food & packaging	29.00	28.30	29.80
Labour	28.00	27.70	28.30
Occupancy & other restaurant operating costs	29.40	30.00	28.90
CMG			
Food & packaging	32.55	30.56	30.69
Labour	23.93	24.71	25.36
Occupancy & other restaurant operating costs	17.56	18.10	19.20

[1] YUM Brands does not break down data for each of its three chains (KFC, Pizza Hut, and Taco Bell).

Source: Company 10-K's.

EXHIBIT 3
CMG consolidated statement of income (for year ending December 31 in $ thousands)

	2011	2010	2009
Revenue	2,269,548	1,835,922	1,518,417
Restaurant operating costs			
Food, beverage and packaging	738,720	561,107	466,027
Labour	543,119	453,573	385,072
Occupancy	147,274	128,933	114,218
Other operating costs (marketing, credit card, etc.)	251,208	202,904	174,581
General and administrative expenses	149,426	118,590	99,149
Depreciation and amortization	74,938	68,921	61,308
Pre-opening costs	8,495	7,767	8,401
Loss on disposal of assets	5,806	6,296	5,956
Income from operations	**350,562**	**287,831**	**203,705**
Net income (after interest and taxes)	**214, 945**	**178,981**	**126,845**

Consolidated balance sheet (condensed for December 31 in $ thousands)

	2011	2010
Assets:		
Current assets:		
Cash and cash equivalents	401,243	224,838
Accounts receivable (net)	8,389	5,658
Inventory	8,913	7,098
Current deferred tax asset	6,238	4,317
Prepaid expenses and other current assets	21,404	16,016
Income tax receivable		23,528
Investments	55,005	124,766
Leasehold improvements, property and equipment, net	751,951	676,881
Long-term investments	128,241	
Other assets	21,985	16,564
Goodwill	21,939	21,939
Total assets	**1,425,308**	**1,121,605**

Liabilities and shareholders' equity		
Current liabilities:		
Accounts payable	46,382	33,705
Accrued payroll and benefits	60,241	50,336
Accrued liabilities	46,456	38,892
Current portion of deemed landlord financing	133	121
Income tax payable	4,241	
Deferred rent	143,284	123,667
Deemed landlord financing	3,529	3,661
Deferred income tax liability	64,381	50,525
Other liabilities	12,435	9,825
Total liabilities	**381,082**	**310,732**
Total shareholders' equity	**1,044,226**	**810,873**
Total liabilities and shareholders' equity	**1,425,308**	**1,121,605**

Summary consolidated statement of cash flows[1] (for year ended December 31, in $ thousands)

	2011	2010	2009
Net cash provided by operating activities	411,096	289,191	260,673
Net cash used in investing activities	(210,208)	(189,881)	(67,208)
Net cash used in financing activities	(24,268)	(94,522)	(61,943)

[1] *The company made an adjustment for exchange rates to reconcile opening and closing cash balances.*
Source: *Chipotle Mexican Grill, Inc. 2011 10-K.*

EXHIBIT 4
CMG selected stock price data (in $ at close of day)

Date	Stock price
January 26, 2006 (IPO)	45.00
January 3, 2007	59.42
January 2, 2008	120.38
January 2, 2009	47.76
January 4, 2010	96.46
January 3, 2011	218.92
January 3, 2012	367.29
April 2, 2012	414.15
April 13, 2012	442.40
May 1, 2012	413.07
June 1, 2012	379.95
July 2, 2012	292.33
August 1, 2012	288.64
October 1, 2012	316.33
October 2, 2012 (**Einhorn**)	302.96

Source: Compiled from Yahoo Finance, www.finance.yahoo.com/echarts?s=CMG+Interactive#symbol=cmg; range=5y;compare=;indicator=volume;charttype=area;crosshair=on;ohlcvalues=0;logscale=off;sourc e=undefined;, accessed October 19, 2012.

Notes

i   Yahoo Finance, accessed October 18, 2012.
ii Unless otherwise indicated, the information in this section is based on Standard & Poor's Industry Surveys: Restaurants, June 7, 2012.
iii National Restaurant Association, "Restaurants by the Numbers," www.restaurant.org, accessed October 10, 2012.
iv John T. Barone, "Commodity Outlook 2012," National Restaurant Association, www .restaurant.org, accessed October 10, 2012.
v   Thomas O. Jones and W. Earl Sasser, Jr., "Why Satisfied Customers Defect," *Harvard Business Review*, November—December 1995, pp. 88—99.
vi Jack-in-the-Box, 2011 10-K.
vii Paul Sebert, "Good Eats: San Francisco Style Hits Huntington with Qdoba," www .herald-dispatch.com/entertainment/x1543286410/San-Francisco-style-hits-Huntington-with-Qdoba?i=0, accessed October 11, 2012.
viii Jack-in-the-Box, 2011 10-K.

ix Yum Brands, Inc. 2011 10-K.

x "Taco Bell Takes on Chipotle with New Menu," www.brandchannel.com/home/post/2012/01/24/Taco-Bell-vs-Chipotle-012412.aspx, accessed October 11, 2012.

xi Yum Brands, Inc. Press Release., October 9, 2012.

xii Margaret Heffernan, "Dreamers: Chipotle Founder Steve Ells," www.rd.com/advice/work-career/dreamers-chipotle-founder-steve-ells, accessed October 12, 2012.

xiii Ibid.

xiv Chipotle website, "About Us," www.chipotle.com/en-us/company/about_us.aspx, accessed October 11, 2012.

xv www.epa.gov/region7/water/cafo, accessed October 11, 2012.

xvi Polly Walker, Pamela Rhubart-Berg, Shawn McKenzie, Kristin Kelling, and Robert S. Lawrence, "Public Health Implications of Meat Production and Consumption," Public Health Nutrition, 8(4): 348-356, 2005, www.jhsph.edu/sebin/y/h/PHN_meat_consumption.pdf, accessed October 11, 2012.

xvii Ibid.

xviii Chipotle 2011 10-K

xix Chipotle 2011 10-K.

xx Thomson Reuters, Chipotle Mexican Grill, Inc. Stock Report, https://research.scottrade.com/qnr/Stocks/GetPDF?docKey=1581-AB585-6CJHB2E4R1H0C6R0PI1L9MO8A6, accessed October 9, 2012.

xxi Jim Collins was the author of two popular business books: *Good to Great* (Harper Business, New York, 2001) and *Great by Choice.* (Harper Business, New York, 2011). In the former book, Collins introduced the notion that most companies are ruled by the tyranny of "or" where they choose between options rather than attempting to do both, the "and."

xxii "Chipotle's Unique Take on Sustainable Sourcing," www.cokesolutions.com/Business Solutions/Pages/Site%20Pages/DetailedPage.aspx?ArticleURL=/BusinessSolutions/Pages/Articles/ChipotlesUniqueTakeonSustainableSourcing.aspx&smallImage=yes&LeftNav=Customer+Spotlight+, accessed October 12, 2012.

xxiii "Chipotle Plans Major Solar Power Initiative," *Business Wire*, October 20, 2009, www.thefreelibrary.com/Chipotle+Plans+Major+Solar+Power+Initiative.-a0210101557, accessed October 12, 2012.

xxiv Ibid.

xv "Chipotle Expands Locally Grown Produce Program," *Food Business Week*, June 4, 2007.

xvi Chipotle Press Release, July 30, 2012.

xvii Chipotle, 2012 Third Quarter 10-Q.

xviii While the terms "organic" and "sustainable" are used interchangeably, the two are different. Organic products can be unsustainably produced on large industrial farms, and farms that are not certified organic can produce food using methods that can sustain the farm's productivity for a long time. The term "organic" is used to mean products produced or grown at a facility that is certified as such, while sustainable is more a philosophy or way of life. Since organic farming generally falls within the accepted definition of sustainable agriculture and since data is collected on organic rather than sustainable agriculture, most observers believed that organic was a good proxy for sustainable.

xxix United States Department of Agriculture, Alternative Farming Systems Information Center, www.afsic.nal.usda.gov/organic-production, accessed October 19, 2012.

xxx Sarah Rose, "A Fast Organic Nation?" *Plenty*, October/November 2005, pp. 70–75.

xxxi   Jim Edwards, "How Chipotle's Business Model Depends on Never Running TV Ads," *Business Insider*, March 16, 2012, www.articles.businessinsider.com/2012-03-16/news/31199897_1_chipotle-advertising-marketing, accessed October 19, 2012.

xxxii   Chipotle 2011 10-K.

xxxiii   Edwards, "How Chipotle's Business Model Depends on Never Running TV Ads."

xxxiv   "Building Evangelism: Chipotle's Farm Team," www.reasonedpr.com/blog/building-evangelism-chipotles-farm-team, accessed October 20, 2012.

xxxv   Chipotle Press Release, February 10, 2012.

xxxvi   "Chipotle's Bold New Marketing Plan," www.monkeydish.com/ideas/articles/chipotle%L2%00%00s-bold-new-marketing-plan, accessed October 20, 2012.

xxxvii   Edwards, "How Chipotle's Business Model Depends on Never Running TV Ads."

xxxviii   Chipotle Press Release, October 18, 2012.

xxxix   Chris Barth, "Hold the Guacamole, Einhorn's Shorting Chipotle," Forbes, www.forbes.com/sites/chrisbarth/2012/10/02/hold-the-guacamole-einhorns-shorting-chipotle/?partner=yahootix, accessed October 19, 2012.

xl   Kate Kelly, "GM, Chipotle Get "Einhorned" by Comments," www.finance.yahoo.com/news/gm-chipotle-einhorned-comments-201207168.html, accessed October 19, 2012.

xli   Kim Bhasin, "Chipotle CEO Shreds Unnamed Competitor for Not Having Grills, Knives or Cutting Boards," *Business Insider*, www.businessinsider.com/chipotle-ceo-taco-bell-2012-10, accessed October 20, 2012.

xlii   Annie Gasparro, "Chipotle Shares Sink on Outlook," www.online.wsj.com/article/SB10000872396390443684104578066484037301320.html, accessed October 21, 2012.

xliii   "Chipotle's Unique Take on Sustainable Sourcing," www.cokesolutions.com/BusinessSolutions/Pages/Site%20Pages/DetailedPage.aspx?ArticleURL=/BusinessSolutions/Pages/Articles/ChipotlesUniqueTakeonSustainableSourcing.aspx&smallImage=yes&LeftNav=Customer+Spotlight+, accessed October 21, 2012.

About the oikos Case Writing Competition

Concept

The annual oikos Case Writing Competition promotes the development of new, high-quality teaching case studies reflecting on sustainability within the fields of management, entrepreneurship and finance. Consequently, the competition hosts three different tracks, namely on 'Corporate Sustainability', 'Social Entrepreneurship' and 'Sustainable Finance'.

The competition welcomes entries from scholars from all continents to any of the three tracks. The case studies should be suitable for use in management education and should be related to managerial issues faced by organizations and individuals. Applicants may be teachers, research assistants or students of business administration (or related areas) at a registered university. Case entries may have more than one author, and each applicant may submit one case per track only. The case studies and associated materials should concentrate on corporate sustainability, social entrepreneurship or sustainable finance, be presented in English, be based on real cases, be focused on a recent situation or development (not older than two years before the launch of the call for cases for each edition) and be released by management of the subject organization/company for use by other business schools. A completed case submission form and a comprehensive teaching note must accompany each case.

Accepted submissions are subject to a two-step double blind review process. For all of the three competition tracks the judging committee pays particular attention to:

- Concept and content: the integration of the different sustainability dimensions (economic, social and environmental), the topic relevance and its ability to create a learning experience.

- Teaching note: a comprehensive teaching note must accompany each sub-mission and include a thorough analysis of questions suggested as well as strategies and teaching approaches recommended in the class room.

- Form: the style of writing, quality of presentation and clarity of data.

In each track the top three cases are awarded with prize money. The annual first prize is 5000 Swiss Francs (CHF), second place is 2000 CHF and third 1000 CHF.

Copyright ownership remains with the author(s) and/or their employer(s). Inspection copies (without teaching notes) are published in the oikos online case collection.

List of the Award Committee Members

Since the inception of the competition in 2003, oikos has been fortunate to have leading international faculty members join the jury of the oikos Case Writing Competition. This volume is based on a selection among the best cases that took part in the Corporate Sustainability Track between the editions of the competition of 2010 and 2013. Within this period the following list of scholars actively partici-pated as reviewers and members of the award committee of the oikos Case Writing Competition.

- Prof. Dr. Daniel Arenas, ESADE Business School, Spain

- Prof. Dr. Frank-Martin Belz, Technical University of Munich, Germany

- Prof. Dr. Oana Branzei, Ivey, Canada

- Prof. Dr. Magali Delmas, University of California, Los Angeles, USA

- Prof. Dr. Thomas Dyllick, University of St. Gallen, Switzerland

- Prof. Dr. Andrew J. Hoffman, University of Michigan, USA.

- Prof. Dr. P.D. Jose, Indian Institute of Management Bangalore, India

- Prof. Dr. Stephen Kobrin, University of Pennsylvania, USA

- Prof. Dr. Bala Krishnamoorthy, NMIMS University, India.

- Prof. Dr. Michael Lenox, University of Virginia, USA

- Prof. Dr. Renato Orsato, Getúlio Vargas Foundation, Brazil.

- Prof. Dr. Esben R. Pedersen, Copenhagen Business School, Denmark.

- Prof. Dr. Stefano Pogutz, Bocconi University, Italy.

- Prof. Dr. Forest Reinhardt, Harvard Business School, USA.

- Prof. Dr. Carlos Romero Uscanga, EGADE, Mexico.

- Prof. Dr. Michael V. Russo, University of Oregon, USA.

- Prof. Dr. Stefan Schaltegger, Leuphana University in Lüneburg, Germany.

- Prof. Dr. Christian Seelos, Stanford University, USA

- Prof. Dr. Paul Shrivastava, Concordia University, Canada.

- Prof. Dr. Claude Siegenthaler, Hosei University, Japan.

- Prof. Dr. Terence Tsai, CEIBS, China.

- Prof. Dr. Michael Yaziji, IMD, Switzerland.

- Prof. Dr. Friedrich M. Zimmermann, University of Graz, Austria.

Short Biographies of the Award Committee Members

Prof. Dr. Daniel Arenas
ESADE Business School, Spain

Daniel Arenas is Associate Professor and Director of the Department of Social Sciences at ESADE Business School, where he is also the Head of Research of the Institute for Social Innovation. He holds a Ph.D. and a M.A. from the Committee on Social Thought at the University of Chicago, a Degree in Philosophy from the University of Barcelona and a Diploma from the Program of Executive Development at ESADE. He teaches courses on sociology, business ethics and corporate social responsibility. His research interests focus in the area of stakeholder theory, NGO-business relations, and social shareholder engagement. He has been a professor at ESADE since 2002.

Prof. Dr. Frank-Martin Belz
Technical University of Munich, Germany

Professor Belz conducts both international and interdisciplinary research on sustainability innovation and sustainability marketing, including the invention, incubation, introduction and diffusion of sustainable products such as electric cars and energy plus homes. His work has taken him to Gothenburg, Sweden (1997), Boston, USA (2001) and Toronto, Canada (2009). Dr. Belz studied business administration at the Universities of Giessen and Mannheim. He earned his Ph.D. in 1995 and acquired his postdoctoral teaching qualification (habilitation) in 2001 from the University of St. Gallen where he served as staff president and assistant professor until his appointment at TUM in 2003.

Prof. Dr. Oana Branzei
Richard Ivey School of Business, Canada

Oana Branzei is the David G. Burgoyne Faculty Fellow, the Building Sustainable Value Research Fellow, and Associate Professor of Strategy at the Ivey Business School. Oana is also the convener and Ivey faculty for the Ph.D. Sustainability Academy, a global event of the Alliance for Research on Corporate Sustainability. As an academic, teacher and consultant, Oana enables executives and students to successfully transform local and global tensions among economic, social and environmental issues into future sources of competitiveness. Oana explores the origins of competitive advantage with an emphasis on how social interactions and/or socio-emotional resources pattern the creation, capture, conversion and distribution of value. Her current initiatives explain how social innovation can help organizations attain and sustain competitive advantage at the intersection of markets and social movements.

Prof. Dr. Magali Delmas
University of California, Los Angeles, USA

Magali Delmas is a Professor of Management at the UCLA Institute of the Environment and UCLA Anderson School of Management. She is a UCLA Luskin Scholar and the Director of the UCLA Center for Corporate Environmental Performance. Magali Delmas has written more than 50 articles, book chapters and case studies on business and the natural environment. Standing at the crossroads of policy and management, her research focuses on interactions between environmental policy and business strategy at the national and international level. She seeks to understand how environmental policies influences the strategy and performance of firms and in turn how firms help shape environmental policy. Professor Delmas' current work includes analysis of the effectiveness of firms' voluntary actions to mitigate climate change. Her latest book *Governance for the Environment: New Perspectives*, co-edited with Professor Oran Young, is published by Cambridge University Press.

Prof. Dr. Thomas Dyllick
University of St. Gallen, Switzerland

Thomas Dyllick is Professor of Sustainability Management at the University of St. Gallen (Switzerland), managing director of the Institute for Economy and the Environment and university delegate for responsibility and sustainability. He served as university Vice-President for Teaching and Quality Development (2003–11) and as Dean of the Management Department (2001–03). Professor Dyllick is member of different editorial boards including the Environmental Management Forum (UWF); Gaia, Ecological Perspectives in Science, Humanities, and Economics; and the *Journal of Environmental Law and Policy* (ZfU). His research interests cover the area of corporate sustainability with emphasis in its competitive aspects. Additionally, he is also interested in topics related to responsible management education as well as quality management at universities. Professor Dyllick is member of the Foundation Council of the Oikos Foundation and member of the Advisory Board of the Oikos Student Initiative at the University of St. Gallen.

Prof. Dr. Andrew J. Hoffman
University of Michigan, USA

Andy Hoffman is the Holcim (US) Professor of Sustainable Enterprise at the University of Michigan; a position that holds joint appointments at the Stephen M. Ross School of Business and the School of Natural Resources and Environment. Within this role, Andy also serves as Director of the Frederick A. and Barbara M. Erb Institute for Global Sustainable Enterprise. Professor Hoffman's research uses a sociological perspective to understand the cultural and institutional aspects of environmental issues for organizations. He has written extensively about: the evolving nature of field level pressures related to environmental issues; the corporate responses that have emerged as a result of those pressures, particularly around the issue of climate change; the interconnected networks among non-governmental organizations and corporations and how those networks influence change processes within cultural and institutional systems; the social and psychological barriers to these change processes; and the underlying cultural values that are engaged when these barriers are overcome.

Prof. Dr. P.D. Jose
Indian Institute of Management Bangalore, India

Dr. P. D. Jose is Associate Professor in the Corporate Strategy and Policy area at IIMB. He is a Fellow of the Indian Institute of Management, Ahmedabad. He has a Post-graduate Diploma in Forestry Management from the Indian Institute of Forest Management, Bhopal, and a Bachelors in Physics from the Institute of Science, Bombay. Prior to joining IIMB, he was a member of the faculty at the Administrative Staff College of India, Hyderabad. He was also a Fulbright Fellow at the Massachusetts Institute of Technology, Boston and Kenan Flagler Business School, North Carolina, during 1999–2000. His research interests include strategy formulation and implementation, crisis management and organizational renewal, competitive implications of environmental regulations, and business and society linkages. Jose has several publications in both international and national journals. Jose is also an advisor to the Network of Indian Environment Professionals, and a member of the environmental education sub-committee of India's Ministry of Environment and Forests.

Prof. Dr. Stephen J. Kobrin
University of Pennsylvania, USA

Stephen J. Kobrin is William H. Wurster Professor of Multinational Management and Publisher of Wharton Digital Press at the Wharton School of the University of Pennsylvania. His interests include globalization, global governance, and the politics of international business. He has a Ph.D. from the University of Michigan, an MBA from Wharton, and a B.Mgt.Eng. from Rensselaer Polytechnic Institute. Recent articles and book chapters include: "The transnational transition and the multinational firm" (2011); "Private political authority and public responsibility: transnational politics, transnational firms and human rights (2009); and Globalization, transnational corporations and the future of global governance" (2008). He was President of the Academy of International Business and Chair of the International Division of the Academy of Management and served on the editorial boards of *The Academy of Management Review, International Organization* and *The Journal of International Business Studies*. Professor Kobrin was a Fellow of the World Economic Forum from 1994–2007.

Prof. Dr. Bala Krishnamoorthy
NMIMS University, India

Dr. Bala Krishnamoorthy is Associate Dean and Professor at the School of Business Management, NMIMS. She teaches and trains in the areas of general management, strategy, environmental management and corporate social responsibility. Dr. Bala holds at Post-graduate Degree from the University of Madras. She did her Post-graduate Diploma in Planning at the School of Planning, Centre for Environmental Planning and Technology, CEPT, Ahmadabad. She holds a Doctorate in Management from JBIMS, University of Mumbai. Dr. Bala takes up consultancy assignments for developing sustainability reports, writing case studies for companies, designs, conducts modular training programs, and conducts training programs for industry participants. She has written several articles in leading journals and presented research papers in conferences. Her book on *Environmental Management Text and Cases* was published by Prentice Hall of India (2008). Richard Ivey Publishing and the case centre (ECCH) has published her case studies.

Prof. Dr. Michael Lenox
University of Virginia, USA

Professor Lenox is the Samuel L. Slover Professor of Business at the University of Virginia's Darden School of Business where he coordinates and teaches the core MBA strategy course. He also serves as Associate Dean and Executive Director of Darden's Batten Institute for Entrepreneurship and Innovation and as the Faculty Director for the multiple-university Alliance for Research on Corporate Sustainability. Prior to joining Darden in 2008, Professor Lenox was a professor at Duke University's Fuqua School of Business where he served as the area coordinator for Fuqua's Strategy Area and the faculty director and founder of Duke's Corporate Sustainability Initiative. At Duke, he coordinated and taught the core MBA strategy course and was runner-up for the Chrysler faculty teaching award on multiple occasions. He received his Ph.D. in Technology Management and Policy from the Massachusetts Institute of Technology in 1999 and the degrees of Bachelor and Master of Science in Systems Engineering from the University of Virginia. Professor Lenox has served as an assistant professor at New York University's Stern School of Business and as a visiting professor at Harvard University, Oxford University, and IMD.

Prof. Dr. Renato J. Orsato
Getúlio Vargas Foundation (FGV), Brazil

Renato J. Orsato is Professor at São Paulo School of Management (EAESP) and academic director of the Centre for Sustainability Studies at the Getúlio Vargas Foundation (FGV), São Paulo, Brazil, as well as Visiting Scholar at INSEAD, Fontainebleau, France. He is the author of "Sustainability Strategies: when does it pay to be green?", finalist of the Academy of Management 2010 ONE Book Award and translated into Chinese, Arabic and Portuguese. Professor Orsato has also written several book chapters and teaching cases, and published in academic journals such as Energy Policy, California Management Review, Organisation Studies, Journal of Cleaner production and Journal of Industrial Ecology.

Prof. Dr. Esben R. Pedersen
Copenhagen Business School, Denmark

Esben Rahbek Gjerdrum Pedersen is associate professor at the CBS Center for Corporate Social Responsibility, Copenhagen Business School, and does research within the areas of corporate social responsibility (CSR), environmental management, and non-financial performance measurement. The results from his research has been published in a wide range of international journals, including the *Journal of Business Ethics, Management Decision, Supply Chain Management, International Journal of Operations and Production Management, Business Ethics: A European Review, Business and Society Review, Business Strategy and the Environment, Corporate Social Responsibility and Environmental Management,* and *Journal of Corporate Citizenship.* The research has been recognized internationally and been awarded with, for example, the 2010 Social Impact Award and the 2009 Emerald Literati Award. Esben has international working experience from projects within the field of entrepreneurship education, SME development, environmental management/labelling, private sector development, and NGO capacity building.

Prof. Dr. Stefano Pogutz
Bocconi University, Italy

Stefano Pogutz is a Tenured Researcher and Assistant Professor of Management in the Department of Management and Technology at Università Bocconi, Milan, Italy. He is chair of the Faculty Group Business and the Environment of the CEMS (The Global Alliance in Management Education) Master in International Management. He has been the Director of Bocconi's master program in Green Management, Energy and CSR and he is a Senior Researcher at the Center for Research on Sustainability and Value (CReSV). His expertise and research are in the fields of sustainability and innovation, green technologies, environmental management, and corporate social responsibility. He has published several books in Italian and in English. His academic work has appeared in national and international refereed journals.

Prof. Dr. Forest Reinhardt
Harvard Business School, USA

Forest L. Reinhardt is the John D. Black Professor of Business Administration at Harvard Business School. Reinhardt recently served as course head for the required MBA course, Strategy, which covers topics in industry analysis, competitive advantage, and corporate strategy. Reinhardt currently serves as the faculty chair of Harvard Business School's Asia-Pacific Research Center and the chair of the HBS Executive Education Asia-Pacific Region. He is the author of *Down to Earth: Applying Business Principles to Environmental Management,* published by Harvard Business School Press. Like that book, many of his articles and papers analyse problems of environmental and natural resource management. He has written numerous classroom cases on these and related topics, used at Harvard and many other schools in MBA curricula and in executive programs. Reinhardt received his Ph.D. in Business Economics from Harvard University in 1990.

Prof. Dr. Carlos Romero Uscanga

EGADE, Mexico

Prof. Romero is director of International Alumni Relations at Tec de Monterrey and professor at the Tec de Monterrey and EGADE Business School. At EGADE he served as Director of the Master in International Business and Postgraduate. He has also been visiting professor at EMI (Bolivia), University of San Diego, University of Texas at Austin, University of North Carolina, ESSCA in France and Harvard Business School. Romero Uscanga, Ph.D. is a member of the Executive Board of CEMS (Community of European Business Schools) and advisor to the doctoral programme at St. Gallen University in Switzerland.

Prof. Dr. Michael V. Russo

University of Oregon, USA

Michael V. Russo is the Lundquist Professor of Sustainable Management at the University of Oregon's Lundquist College of Business. Mike's current research projects include a study of the impact of social and environmental issues on global supply chains, and analyses of geographic clustering of mission-driven companies and of wind and solar energy firms. His articles have appeared in the *Academy of Management Journal, Administrative Science Quarterly, Management Science, Organization Science, Production and Operations Management,* and *Strategic Management Journal,* and he serves on the editorial boards of the *Academy of Management Journal* and *Strategic Management Journal.* Mike has won a number of research and teaching awards, including the Moskowitz Prize in Social Investing, the oikos Sustainability Case Writing Competition Grand Prize, and most recently a Silver Nautilus Book Award for his 2010 book, *Companies on a Mission: Entrepreneurial Strategies for Growing Sustainably, Responsibly, and Profitably.* In 2005, he completed his term as Chair of the Organizations and Natural Environment Interest Group of the Academy of Management.

Prof. Dr. Stefan Schaltegger

Leuphana University in Lüneburg, Germany

Stefan Schaltegger is full professor of sustainability management at the Leuphana University in Lüneburg (Germany) and head of the MBA Sustainability Management (www.sustainament.de). He is the head of the Centre for Sustainability Management (CSM), an academic competence centre focused on corporate sustainability management. Stefan is founding member of the Sustainability Leadership Forum (SLF), has published extensively on various topics of sustainability management and is a member of the editorial boards of various international academic journals, including *Business Strategy and the Environment, Corporate Social Responsibility and Environmental Management, International Journal of Business Environment, Sustainability Accounting, Management and Policy Journal, Accounting, Auditing & Accountability Journal, Meditari Accountancy Research, Journal of Corporate Citizenship,* and *Journal of Cleaner Production.*

Prof. Dr. Christian Seelos

Stanford University, USA

Christian Seelos is a visiting scholar at the Stanford Center on Philanthropy and Civil Society. Most recently he served as the Director of the IESE Platform for Strategy and Sustainability and a Senior Lecturer in the Strategic Management Department at IESE Business School. He teaches MBA and executive courses in international business, global strategic management, social entrepreneurship and strategy and sustainability. Christian researches the interface between organizational strategy and global sustainability including social innovation, new business models for poverty alleviation, climate change and water stress. The Strategic Management Society recognized his recent research on innovative corporate strategies in emerging markets with the Best Paper Award for Practice Implications and also the Gold Price of the highly contested IFC-FT essay competition on private sector development. He has published more than 60 papers in peer-review journals in the natural and social sciences, held managerial positions in the private industry, served as Senior Adviser to the Chairman at the United Nations Special Commission on Iraq (UNSCOM) and led inspection and disarmament efforts on biological weapons in Iraq.

Prof. Dr. Paul Shrivastava
Concordia University, Canada

Dr. Paul Shrivastava is the David O'Brien Distinguished Professor of Sustainable Enterprise at the John Molson School of Business, Concordia University, Montreal. He served as Senior Advisor on sustainability at Bucknell University and the Indian Institute of Management-Shillong, India, and is on the Board of Trustees of DeSales University, Allentown, Pennsylvania. Dr. Shrivastava received his Ph.D. from the University of Pittsburgh. He was tenured Associate Professor of Management at the Stern School of Business, New York University. He has published 17 books and over 100 articles in professional and scholarly journals. He served on the editorial boards of leading management education journals including the *Academy of Management Review,* the *Strategic Management Journal, Organization, Risk Management,* and *Business Strategy and the Environment.* He won a Fulbright Senior Scholar Award and studied Japanese environmental management while based at Kyoto University. He founded the Organization and Natural Environment Division of the Academy of Management. His work has been featured in the *Los Angeles Times,* the *Philadelphia Inquirer,* the *Christian Science Monitor,* and on the McNeil-Lehrer News Hour.

Prof. Dr. Claude Siegenthaler
Hosei University, Japan

Prof. Dr. Claude Siegenthaler is a lecturer at the Department of Management, Technology, and Economics of ETH Zurich and holds a tenured position as full professor for Corporate Sustainability and Environmental Accounting at Hosei University in Tokyo. Claude Siegenthaler graduated from St. Gallen University with a diploma in economics in 1993, where he also worked as a research assistant with the Institute for Economics and the Environment (IWOE-HSG). From 1993 to 2004 he co-founded and served as the CEO of Sinum Inc. EcoPerformance Systems, a software and consulting company focused on Life Cycle Assessment and Environmental Performance Evaluation. His portfolio of projects comprised mandates a.o. for Canon Europe, CocaCola Beverages, Komatsu, Samsung, Swisscom, SwissRe and Environmental Ministries in Switzerland, Austria and Japan. In 2005 he received a PhD in economics from St.Gallen University, where he is a member of the MBA faculty and lectures in Corporate Ecology and Sustainability. Among others, he received a scholarship from the oikos foundation and the Japan Science and Technology Agency, the Switzerland Technology Award 2000 and the Peter Werhahn Prize from the University of St. Gallen.

Prof. Dr. Terence Tsai
China Europe International Business School, China

Terence Tsai is Associate Professor of Management at China Europe International Business School in China and Visiting Professor of Management at Chang Gung University and Sun Yat-Sen University in Taiwan. Prior to joining CEIBS, he served as Acting Associate Dean (Graduate Studies), Director of Centre for Case Teaching and Research and Acting Director and Associate Director of MBA Programmes at The Chinese University of Hong Kong. Dr. Tsai's research interests include multinational corporations, sustainability strategy, environmental management, organisational theory (environmental adaptive theories), and Chinese management. His scholarly work has appeared in the *Journal of General Management, International Studies of Management and Organisation, Journal of Management Studies, Organisation Studies, Business Strategy and the Environment, Asia Case Research Journal, Case Journal of Dalian University of Science and Technology*, the *Globe and Mail, Financial Times, Harvard China Review*, and the *Sun Yat-sen Management Review.*

Prof. Dr. Michael Yaziji
IMD, Switzerland

Michael Yaziji (Ph.D. Strategy and Management; Ph.D. Analytic Philosophy) is Professor of Strategy and Organizations at IMD. He teaches in the areas of strategy, nonmarket strategy, stakeholder management, ethics and change management, and governance. He is currently or has recently directed programs for Metso, PepsiCo, Shell, Wartsila, Ruukki, Cargotec, and Ericsson. He is widely recognized for his research focus on the relationships among corporations, NGOs, and government. His most recent publications include an article on capitalism in *Harvard Business Review* (2008) as well as the book *NGOs and Corporations*, published by Cambridge University Press (2009). He is also especially interested in the challenges and opportunities in the environmental space. He believes there are tremendous strategic opportunities (and imperatives) within industrial ecology. Professor Yaziji drove the initiative to make IMD the first and only top tier business school in the world to be carbon neutral. He was the founding director of the Business and Society Forum while at INSEAD.

Prof. Dr. Friedrich M. Zimmermann
University of Graz, Austria

Friedrich M. Zimmermann is Professor and Chair of the Department of Geography and Regional Science at the University of Graz, Austria. He is director of the RCE Graz-Styria (UN-certified Regional Center of Expertise: Education for Sustainable Development). Former Vice-Rector for Research and Knowledge Transfer (2000–07) he is now the Sustainability Commissioner of the University of Graz. Former President of the COPERNICUS Alliance, the European Network on Higher Education for Sustainable Development. He also holds international affiliations at the University of Munich, at Universities in Pennsylvania and Oregon, US, as well as Croatia and Serbia. Zimmermann worked with interdisciplinary and transdisciplinary research teams in more than 50 national, European and international projects. His research interests concern sustainable urban and regional transformation processes; sustainable tourism planning and prognosis and sustainability processes, and knowledge transfer.

About oikos

oikos is an international student-driven organization for sustainable economics and management. Founded in 1987 in Switzerland, we today empower future leaders to drive change towards sustainability worldwide.

Our programs embed environmental and social perspectives in faculties for economics and management. They comprise conferences, seminars, speeches, simulation games and other initiatives to transform teaching and research. They promote the integration of sustainability in curricula. And they provide platforms for learning, creating and sharing solutions.

The heart of our organization is our student members who turn ideas into action in currently close to 40 oikos chapters around the world. They are supported by a global community of oikos alumni, advisors, faculty and partners, as well as an international team based in Switzerland.

For more information about our programmes please refer to our website (www .oikos-international.org) or contact us at via mail or e-mail at the address below.

oikos
Tigerbergstrasse, 2
9000 St. Gallen
Switzerland

Telephone: +41 71 224 25 90
Email: info@oikos-international.org

About the editor

Jordi Vives is an oikos PhD fellow pursuing his PhD studies at the University of St. Gallen (Switzerland) where he is also associate researcher at the Institute for Business Ethics. He regularly collaborates with the social science department at ESADE Business School as visiting lecturer. Jordi received a M.Sc. in Research in Political Science by Pompeu Fabra University, a master in Business Administration and a BBA from ESADE Business School. At oikos, Jordi is responsible for the oikos Cases Programme, which involves the management of the oikos Case Writing Competition as well as the edition of the *oikos Case Quarterly*. In his PhD research, Jordi focuses on the responsibilities businesses face in connection with human rights. More specifically, he attempts to analyse these responsibilities from the perspective of global democracy theories. Jordi has published his work at the *Journal of Business Ethics* as well as in several practitioner-oriented publications. Prior to entering academia, Jordi worked for Hewlett-Packard and Deloitte.